MW00633214

Uriah
SMITH

ADVENTIST PIONEER SERIES

George R. Knight, Consulting Editor

Published volumes:
James White: Innovator and Overcomer,
by Gerald Wheeler

Joseph Bates: The Real Founder of Seventh-day Adventism,
by George R. Knight

W. W. Prescott: Forgotten Giant of Adventism's Second Generation,
by Gilbert M. Valentine

John Harvey Kellogg, M.D.: Pioneering Health Reformer,
by Richard W. Schwarz

E. J. Waggoner: From the Physician of Good News to the Agent of Division,
by Woodrow W. Whidden II

Lewis C. Sheafe: Apostle to Black America,
by Douglas Morgan

A. T. Jones: Point Man on Adventism's Charismatic Frontier
by George R. Knight

J. N. Loughborough: The Last of the Adventist Pioneers,
by Brian E. Strayer

To order, call **1-800-765-6955.**
Visit us at **www.reviewandherald.com**
for information on other Review and Herald® products.

Uriah
SMITH

Apologist and Biblical Commentator

GARY LAND

REVIEW AND HERALD® PUBLISHING ASSOCIATION
Since 1861 | www.reviewandherald.com

Copyright © 2014 by Review and Herald® Publishing Association.

Published by Review and Herald® Publishing Association, Hagerstown, MD 21741-1119.

All rights reserved. No portion of this book may be reproduced, stored in a retrieval system, or transmitted in any form or by any means (electronic, mechanical, photocopy, recording, scanning, or other), except for brief quotations in critical reviews or articles, without the prior written permission of the publisher.

Review and Herald® titles may be purchased in bulk for educational, business, fund-raising, or promotional use. For information, e-mail SpecialMarkets@reviewandherald.com.

The Review and Herald® Publishing Association publishes biblically based materials for spiritual, physical, and mental growth and Christian discipleship.

This book was
Edited by Gerald Wheeler
Copyedited by Ted Hessel and James Cavil
Designed by Derek Knecht/Review and Herald® Design Center
Photos compiled by Kevin Burton
PRINTED IN U.S.A.

18 17 16 15 14   5 4 3 2 1

Library of Congress Cataloging-in-Publication Data

Land, Gary, 1944-2014.
  Uriah Smith : apologist and biblical commentator / Gary Land.
      pages cm — (Adventist pioneer series)
  Includes index.
  ISBN 978-0-8280-2779-3
1. Smith, Uriah, 1832-1903. 2. Seventh-Day Adventists—Clergy—Biography. 3. Clergy—United States—Biography. I. Title.
  BX6193.S63L36 2014
  286.7092—dc23
  [B]
                                    2014008186

ISBN 978-0-8280-2779-3

CONTENTS

INTRODUCTION

Uriah Smith! The name was in the early Adventist air. His presence was everywhere. Aside from Smith and J. N. Andrews, the only names more well known in early Adventism were those of the three founders of the church—Joseph Bates and James and Ellen White.

Beginning in the early 1850s, Smith and Andrews were the premier protégés of James White as he sought to move the budding Adventist movement from a rather amorphous, shapeless collection of like-minded believers into an organized movement equipped to accomplish its mission effectively. While White utilized the intellectual abilities of Andrews to clarify many of the theological issues facing Sabbatarian Adventism, he found in Smith not only a man with writing and editing skills but also one with workhorse energies who could assume many of the heavy responsibilities in Adventist publishing that James himself had carried during the earliest years of the movement.

As such, Uriah Smith became the editor of the influential *Review and Herald* for most of the next 50 years. From that position his editorials and articles did much to shape the thinking of nineteenth-century Adventists. But that task was merely one aspect of his contribution to the denomination. Among other things, Smith functioned for more than two decades as secretary of the General Conference, and he became Adventism's foremost authority on the prophecies of Daniel and Revelation. His book on that topic became an Adventist classic and remains so to this day. His many other books helped form the denomination's ideas on such topics as spiritualism, the state of the dead, the law of God and the Sabbath, and end-time events.

Gary Land's *Uriah Smith: Apologist and Biblical Commentator* is a major step forward in our understanding of a key individual in Adventism's formative period. Yet Land's biography is not the first scholarly book on the man. Eugene F. Durand published *Yours in the Blessed Hope, Uriah Smith* in 1980. Based largely on his Ph.D. dissertation at George Washington

University, Durand's volume did much to help us grasp the life of Smith. But in the past 35 years Adventist historians have come to a much better understanding of the denomination's history and the contextual forces that shaped it. Beyond that, many more documents have become available to the researcher. All of those factors call for a fresh treatment of this Adventist pioneer.

Land's volume takes a very different approach from that of Durand's. He asks different questions of the historical data and arrives at new perspectives regarding a crucial player in Adventist history. It should also be noted that this new biography provides a chronological view of the major events in Smith's life, whereas Durand's tended to be topical. That new format provides fresh insights as its subject is seen more fully in his historical context.

One of the fascinating contributions of this new biography is its portrayal of Smith's relationship to Ellen White. It helps us who live at a century's distance from her death to realize that it is one thing to look back endearingly at a long-dead prophet and quite another to deal with a live one in the daily flow of life.

As series editor I am especially pleased to see the publication of Land's biography. For many months its completion hung in the balance as Gary struggled with life-threatening cancer. The good news is that Gary came back from the edge to finish not only his biography of Smith but also the editing of *Ellen Harmon White: American Prophet* (Oxford, 2014) and the second edition (forthcoming) of *Historical Dictionary of the Seventh-day Adventists* (Scarecrow Press, 2005). The sad news is that he passed to his rest a few days after the completion of the last of those works. It is almost as if his historical work kept him going and that when it was completed he was free to let go.

Gary's death is a major loss to the community of Adventist historians. His contributions in the field are both many and insightful. All of us are indebted to him. I will miss him personally. Our lives have been intertwined for a half century, beginning with our student days at Pacific Union College, up through three decades working together as historians at Andrews University, and on into shared retirement projects—including the present biography.

Uriah Smith is the ninth volume in an unprecedented series on Adventist biography. Thus far the series has seen treatments of James White, Joseph Bates, W. W. Prescott, John Harvey Kellogg, E. J. Waggoner, Lewis C. Sheafe, A. T. Jones, and J. N. Loughborough. Upcoming volumes already scheduled for publication include Arthur G. Daniells (2016), S. N. Haskell (2017), Ellen G. White (2017), W. C. White (2018), J. N. Andrews (2019), G. I. Butler (2020), and Dudley Canright (2021). And those contributions are merely the beginning of the titles projected for the Adventist Pioneer Series, which will eventually include more than 30 volumes. Each book will focus on the individual's major contributions to the church and will be written by a person well versed in his or her topic.

Meanwhile, we are indebted to Gary Land for enabling us to understand better the story of Uriah Smith and the church he dedicated his life to. I trust that reading this book will be a fascinating and profitable journey.

George R. Knight
Series Editor
Rogue River, Oregon

FOREWORD

When asked to contribute a volume to the series of biographies of Adventist pioneers, I chose Uriah Smith, because I thought it would be interesting to trace the growth of his thought. I soon discovered, however, little development, for once he staked out a position he virtually never changed his mind, a characteristic that led to several theological and administrative conflicts. Although Uriah did not alter his overall theological outlook, he had to apply it to a constantly altering world. Thus it is the application, rather than the development, of his ideas that is interesting, as the American nation as well as Europe went through religious, economic, and demographic shifts that provided opportunity for new applications of Adventist prophetic understanding.

Smith's previous biographer, Eugene F. Durand, approached the man topically. I have also used a similar approach but have placed themes within the framework of chapters that succeed one another chronologically, although there are a few overlaps, particularly the sixth and seventh chapters. Hopefully, such a chronological arrangement will give a sense of the thrust of Smith's life through time. Although it is not historically significant (except for its impact on his health), his European/Middle Eastern trip in 1894 has been given an entire chapter, for it is the most fully documented part of his personal life. The letters of both Smith and his son Wilton (who accompanied him), Wilton's diaries, and Smith's almost weekly reports to the *Review* offer glimpses of his personality seldom seen in other material. In an effort to let Uriah and others speak for themselves, especially during his conflicts with the Whites and other church leaders, I have quoted extensively from the primary documents, keeping my commentary to a minimum. Similarly, because Smith was such a good wordsmith, I frequently use direct quotations, rather than paraphrases, from his editorials and books. Hopefully, the approach will give the reader a more direct understanding of the man.

A serious illness interrupted work on this project for more than a year.

George R. Knight, editor of the series, and the Review and Herald Publishing Association kindly extended my deadline by several months. Although unable to complete some minor lines of research, I trust that the biography gives a full picture of Uriah Smith as editor, writer, churchman, and husband and father.

ACKNOWLEDGMENTS

A project such as this requires the help of many people. I am grateful for the assistance of Merlin Burt, director, and the staff of the Center for Adventist Research (CAR) in the James White Library of Andrews University. The preservation and organization of the Smith/Bovee papers was indispensable, as well as the microfilm copies of correspondence of Ellen White, George I. Butler, A. T. Jones, and others located in CAR . Also, Bert Haloviak helped lead me to sources at the General Conference Office of Archives and Statistics that proved to be extremely valuable, particularly in relationship to the 1888 controversy over righteousness by faith.

In addition to proofreading the manuscript, Brian Strayer of the Andrews University Department of History and Political Science lent me some necessary books since my copies were inaccessible, having been packed away after a broken pipe flooded our basement, where I had stored my books and papers after retirement.

Finally, I am grateful to the physicians and staff of Memorial Hospital in South Bend, Indiana, Michiana Health and Rehabilitation, Michiana Hematology/Oncology, P.C., and the East-West Center for Natural Medicine, for helping me regain my health sufficiently to finish this project. I am also thankful for the visits, concern, and prayers of family members, friends, and colleagues during this difficult period. And, ultimately, I am thankful to God, who worked through these people to provide the care and support I needed.

As always for an author, I am responsible for any errors of fact or interpretation in this biography.

SOURCES AND ABBREVIATIONS

Most of the documents cited in the footnotes may be found in the Center for Adventist Research, which includes the Smith/Bovee collection as well as letters of James White, Ellen G. White, George I. Butler, A. T. Jones, A. G. Daniells, and others. The letters of Dan T. Jones are part of the Seventh-day Adventist General Conference Archives.

For space reasons, in the footnotes I have abbreviated the names of frequently cited authors and publications. Those abbreviations are listed below.

AGD	Arthur G. Daniells	GWA	George W. Amadon
AH	*Adventist Heritage*	HS	Harriet Smith
AS	Annie Smith, daughter of Uriah and Harriet Smith	JB	John Byington
		JNL	John N. Loughborough
ATJ	Alonzo T. Jones	JW	James White
DMC	Dudley M. Canright	MRH	Milton Raymond Hook
DTJ	Dan T. Jones	OAO	O. A. Olsen
EFD	Eugene F. Durand	PS	Parker Smith
EGW	Ellen G. White	*RH*	*Review and Herald*
GC	General Conference of Seventh-day Adventists	SNH	Stephen N. Haskell
		US	Uriah Smith
GIB	George I. Butler	WCW	William C. White
GMV	Gilbert M. Valentine	WS	Wilton Smith
GRK	George R. Knight	WWW	Woodrow W. Whidden
GW	Gerald Wheeler		

The FINAL BOOK

In 1853 the *Advent Review and Sabbath Herald* published a 35,000-word poem entitled "The Warning Voice of Time and Prophecy." Its author was a young, brilliant, new believer whose biography you currently hold in your hands. As this volume will attest, Uriah Smith was present almost at the inception of Adventist publishing, lending his gifts to the fledgling paper that would one day birth the Review and Herald Publishing Association. Perhaps it is fitting, then, that *Uriah Smith: Apologist and Biblical Commentator* be the final book to roll off the presses of the Review and Herald Publishing Association located at 55 West Oak Ridge Drive in Hagerstown, Maryland. This volume pays homage to the hundreds of men and women who faithfully served the publishing ministry in Hagerstown, and who look forward with great anticipation to the day God shall reveal the harvest of a job well done.

Dwain Neilson Esmond
Vice President for Editorial Services
Review and Herald Publishing Association
Hagerstown, Maryland

Uriah Smith

CHAPTER I
CHILD OF NEW HAMPSHIRE, 1832-1853

Nestled in the hills of southern New Hampshire, the village of Wilton and what we might call its "suburb," West Wilton, had a population of a little more than 1,000 when Uriah Smith was born in 1832. King James I had granted a loosely defined territory to a Captain John Mason in the 1620s, with the first settlers moving into the area in 1739. In 1748 a company known as the "Masonian Proprietors," mainly wealthy residents of Portsmouth, purchased charters from the Mason family and began selling townships the following year. Township "Number Two," the area that became Wilton, incorporated in 1762 and again in 1765.[1]

WILTON, NEW HAMPSHIRE

By the time of Smith's birth the village had become a small industrial center, serving the surrounding agricultural area. By its centennial celebration in 1839, Wilton had eight sawmills, five gristmills, three tanneries, two fulling mills (which cleaned woolen cloth), a bobbin factory, a potato starch factory, and a cotton factory. In addition, the town boasted four blacksmiths, 10 shoemakers, two cabinetmakers, one hatter, three stores, and two taverns.[2]

Smith's family had contributed to its industrial growth. Coming from Massachusetts, his grandfather Uriah (c. 1744/45-1829) purchased about 20 acres of land from his brother-in-law, Simon Keyes, in Wilton, where he established the town's first tannery. After selling the tannery, Uriah built a gristmill and later a clothing mill, both of which burned in 1791 or 1792, after which he constructed another gristmill. Uriah's son, Samuel Smith (1787-1852), carried on the family tradition of enterprise. He established mills in West Wilton prior to 1824, operated a knob shop, and established a tavern or inn that he and his family occupied. Beginning in 1825 he primarily focused on road building for the remainder of his life. A contemporary source described him "as a man of much common sense, firm, and of equable disposition, and it is not believed that any of his many employees was ever treated in any other way than was just and right." In 1823 he married Rebekah Spalding (1794-1875) of Belgrade, Maine, with whom he had five children: John Spalding (1825-1903), an unnamed daughter who lived for only one day (1826), Annie Rebekah (1828-1855), Samuel Wood (1830-1905), and Uriah (1832-1903).[3]

In addition to its business enterprises, Wilton also had a few cultural institutions. During its early years the only church was the Congregational church, whose building also served as the location of the town meetings, but its increasingly liberal views prompted the organization in 1823 of a second Congregational church that embraced a more traditional Trinitarian theology, and in 1830 the congregation dedicated its own church structure. Meanwhile, the Universalists had established a church in 1813 and the Baptists in 1817. About 1815 or 1816 some of the citizens of Wilton also organized a Literary and Moral Society, and in 1834 the Wilton Temperance Society formed, attaining more than 300 members by 1839. Also, by 1839 Wilton had nine school districts with 10 schoolhouses.[4]

URIAH SMITH'S CHILDHOOD

Uriah Smith, son of Samuel and Rebekah Smith, thus grew up in a small but prosperous village in which his family played a prominent economic role. Although we know little about Uriah's childhood, two events do stand out that influenced him throughout his life. The first was the loss of his leg, amputated by Dr. Amos Twitchell of the nearby town of Keene, who frequently provided medical services to the citizens of Wilton. When the operation occurred has been the object of some disagreement, for Uriah himself left contradictory evidence. In a brief biographical sketch written for the New Hampshire State Library, Smith stated that he had lost his "leg, by fever sore, in 1836," at which time he would have been 4 years old. However, writing in 1893 to a correspondent who had inquired about faith healing, Smith stated that "I had a fever-sore on my leg when 4 years of age. At 12, I found myself with a shriveled, drawn-up leg, and a stiff knee, and the sore breaking out again. It was evident to anyone that the leg must be taken off, or I lose my life." The much greater detail in the latter statement lends credence to the conclusion that he lost his leg at age 12. According to family tradition, the operation took place on the kitchen table and lasted 20 minutes, during which his mother held his hand. Because anesthesia was not available at the time, Uriah probably endured the procedure with a towel or similar object placed in his mouth to bite down on, as was the common practice. One can only imagine the pain he endured. His mother and his sister Annie provided care afterwards. The loss of his limb, as Smith put it, "caused his attention to be turned to literary pursuits."[5]

The second event to shape his young life was his conversion to Millerism. The movement grew from the biblical interpretations of William Miller, a New York farmer. After studying the 2300-day prophecy of Daniel 8:14, Miller concluded by 1818 that the second coming of Jesus would occur about the year 1843. After he began to proclaim his views publicly in 1831, he gradually gained prominence as a revivalist in New York, Maine, and Vermont. In 1840, however, Joshua V. Himes, a Christian Connexion minister, adopted his interpretations and began publishing a paper, the *Signs of the Times*. From that point on a distinctive Millerite movement emerged, attracting some 50,000 followers in the Northeast. Pressed for more specificity regarding the time of Christ's coming, Miller in January 1843 wrote that, based on his analysis of the Jewish calendar, Christ would return sometime between March 21, 1843, and March 21, 1844. When the Advent did not occur as expected, the movement experienced confusion until in August of that year Samuel S. Snow advanced a new interpretation that Jesus would appear on October 22, 1844, the Jewish Day of Atonement. It swept through the movement like wildfire, giving it new life.[6]

Although we have no explicit evidence regarding the Smith family's original religious affiliation, Rebekah's statement that Annie was baptized into the Baptist Church at age 10 suggests that they were Baptists. We do not know when the family encountered William Miller's teaching, but Rebekah appears to have become an enthusiastic exponent of the doctrine, with both Annie and Uriah accepting the teaching in 1844. Writing shortly before his death, Uriah recalled that he was baptized by an Adventist elder early in the summer of 1844 (which would have been before Snow's views caught hold of the movement), and that because of what Millerites considered as the signs of the end—the Dark Day (May 19, 1780) and the falling of the stars (November 13, 1833)—he raised "from the doorsteps of his home in West Wilton, N.H., the cry, 'The Lord is coming,' as far as the voice was able to reach relatives and friends in the neighborhood."[7]

The Millerite experience ended eventfully for Smith. On October 21, 1844, the day before the expected return of Jesus, Smith, his mother, and an older brother, who had apparently accepted Snow's teaching, attended an Adventist meeting in the "dooryard" of a Brother Tolman, in Fitchburg, Massachusetts. Ruffians attacked the meeting with apples, cut the tent down, and pushed a hog into the collapsed tent. "And there we were—women, children, and the hog—in darkness under the cover of the tent—not a very pleasant companion, and not a very agreeable situation." Tolman then opened his house to the women and children, but soon the mob attacked the house. Uriah and his brother took refuge in the barn. By the next day the mob had left them alone, but Jesus had not appeared in the skies. Greatly disappointed, the people went home. "And false reports followed them," Smith wrote. "For instance, it was said that the writer took cold by exposure at that meeting, and lost a leg in consequence. We received no harm from that meeting. No report could be more false than that. We have no charge of that kind to make against Adventism."[8]

EDUCATION

We do not know how Uriah responded to the Great Disappointment, as it became known, although he later stated that "on that doctrine [the Second Coming] he has never had a misgiving from that day to this." In contrast, his sister Annie experienced doubt and pursued a career as a teacher, working in seven district schools by 1850 and attending several terms in other schools, including the Ladies' Female Seminary in Charlestown, Massachusetts, where she prepared to teach oil painting and French. Meanwhile, Uriah went to school in Hancock, New Hampshire, during the autumns of 1845 and 1846 and then entered Phillips Exeter Academy, located in Exeter, New Hampshire, in August 1848.[9] At the time the academy had an enrollment of about 70 students. Under the leadership of Gideon Lane Soule, who had become principal in 1838, students went through long searching drills in Latin and Greek. Whether Soule's obvious conservatism shaped Uriah's outlook is not known, but throughout his life Smith preferred to stick to old paths once he had chosen a position. Although a dormitory opened in 1849, we do not know whether he lived there or lodged with a local family, as he would necessarily have done the previous year. Prior to 1854 the students were not organized into classes, but rather remained at the school "until they were fitted for some college class, without special reference to the time of entering or leaving the Academy."

Uriah attended the academy with the intention of preparing to enter the sophomore class at Harvard College. In 1849 tuition at Phillips Exeter was $14 annually, and room and board, if one lived in the dormitory, $1 to $2 a week, costs presumably paid by Samuel Smith. That Uriah's academic and literary attainments received recognition we see from his membership in the elite Golden Branch Literary Society, organized in 1818,[10] and for which he presented anniversary poems in 1850 and 1851. Following the classical poetic model taught him, in 1851 Smith challenged his fellow students:

"Then let us from the high resolve
　　To make our lives sublime,
And mark a clear and noble track
　　Upon the sands of time,
And bring fresh honors to the list
　　Of men and heroes all,
Whose power is felt from pole to pole—
　　The sons of Phillips Hall."[11]

About the time that Uriah completed his work at Phillips Exeter, his father became ill, dying in 1852, which interrupted his plans to attend Harvard. Forced to rely on his own resources during the year after his graduation, Smith taught school and worked for a business that failed. Meanwhile, his mother, who had maintained her connection with former Millerites, by 1851 had aligned herself with the Sabbatarian Adventists, one of several small groups that had emerged after the Great Disappointment. Led by Joseph Bates, a former sea captain, and James and Ellen White, he a minor Millerite preacher and she a visionary, the Sabbatarians had adopted the seventh-day Sabbath and believed that the mistake with regard to October 22, 1844, did not involve the date but the identity of the event that was to take place. Instead of the cleansing of the sanctuary referred to in Daniel 8:14 as meaning Christ's return to earth, as Miller had understood, the Sabbatarians believed it meant that on October 22, 1844, Jesus had moved from the holy to the Most Holy Place of the heavenly sanctuary described in Hebrews 9, to begin his final work of judgment. James White, encouraged by his wife to publicize the new views, began publishing a periodical named *Present Truth* in 1849 and then *The Advent Review* in 1850, combining them as *The Advent Review and Sabbath Herald* shortly thereafter, around which the small Sabbatarian movement coalesced.[12]

CONVERSION TO SABBATARIAN ADVENTISM

In 1850 Annie began to suffer eye problems that prevented her from teaching. Before she returned home, however, Rebekah requested that she visit a Sister Temple in Boston and attend a Sabbatarian Adventist meeting conducted by Joseph Bates. According to John N. Loughborough, both Bates and Annie had dreamed of meeting each other at the gathering, and when events turned out as dreamed, she became convinced that God was leading her into truth. About three weeks later Annie accepted the Sabbath doctrine. A poet, she had published four poems in *The Ladies' Wreath*, a New York literary annual. Shortly after her conversion she sent a poem to the *Advent Review and Sabbath Herald*. The editor, James White, then invited her to become part of the journal's staff, at the time located in Saratoga Springs, New York. Annie joined the Whites in early 1852 and a few months later moved with them to Rochester. Although most of her work involved copy editing, she edited the *Review* when James was away on speaking trips and contributed 45 items to the *Review* and the *Youth's Instructor*, James's magazine for young people, during her three and a half years as his employee. In 1852 she seems to have recruited her brother, not at the time an adherent to Sabbatarian Adventist doctrines, to provide three wood engravings illustrating the law of God for the March 23 issue of the *Review and Herald*. The engravings, two of which also appeared in the *Youth's Instructor*, were the only illustrations in the first volumes of the paper. As J. Paul Stauffer writes: "The drawing is naïve, without grace or refinement. Its intent is simply and clearly utilitarian, to help readers understand and remember the observations made in the text. The work betrays on the draughtsman's part no least thought of giving visual pleasure to readers of the *Review*." In November 1852 Annie returned home because of her father's illness.[13] Upon his death she penned lines that expressed her Advent hope:

"Hope, pointing upward, disperses its gloom,
    Soon will the King in his glory descend,
    Triumph o'er Death, and the grave's fetters rend;
    Kindred and friends shall we meet as they rise,
    Bright and immortal, ascending the skies."[14]

While at home, Annie and her mother convinced Uriah to attend a Sabbatarian conference in Washington, New Hampshire, that took place in the fall of 1852. Although he had paid little attention to the Millerite experience and the prophecies during all the "scattering and dividing" that had occurred since 1844, he was impressed by what he heard. As he later reported to readers of the *Review*, he subsequently studied the Sabbatarian Adventist arguments and "fully decided . . . to go with the remnant, who keep the commandments of God, and the faith of Jesus." He observed that "the more I look into our position, the clearer, more beautiful, and harmonious it seems." His decision ultimately had its roots in his mother's influence on him since his childhood, for as Smith stated at the time of her death in 1875, "the earliest recollections we have of mother were her efforts to interest her children . . . in the Bible as the word of God."[15]

"THE WARNING VOICE OF TIME AND PROPHECY"
It appears that Uriah, almost immediately upon his conversion, began composing an epic poem entitled "The Warning Voice of Time and Prophecy." When Annie returned to the *Review* office, she seems to have taken a portion of the poem with her to give to James White, for on February 17, 1853, White wrote that "Annie has arrived," going on to say that Uriah's poem was "excellent. I have no disposition to flatter any mortal. I speak the real sentiment of my heart. It is a valuable production thus far. May God help you to complete it to His glory. . . . Its style is sweet, rich, and impressive. It will attract attention, and do good." James stated that he planned to publish the poem in the *Review* and later issue it as a pamphlet.[16]

The 3,000-line blank verse "The Warning Voice" first appeared in the *Review* on March 17, 1853, continuing to August 11, 1853. When it was reprinted as a small book, Smith explained that its purpose was "to give a general outline of the foundation, rise, and progress of the Advent movement up to the present time, showing that it was the work of God, also, its connection with prophecy, and the prophetic fulfillment upon which it is based." The first of its two parts covered the emergence of the Advent message through the Great Disappointment. The second part described the effects of the Disappointment, explained the sanctuary doctrine, and portrayed the last days of earth before the coming of Jesus. John Waller, an English professor who studied the poem, stated that the young poet was "almost equal to the artistic challenge of capturing this overwhelming feeling [that Sabbatarian Adventists were "God-directed protagonists in the central epic of the universe"] in words and lines and soaring poetic periods. It is a poem composed for the voice . . . a poem to be declaimed, intoned, to reach and move the believing heart by way of the listening ear."[17]

In his analysis of the poem as poetry Waller found that Smith's compositional unit was the sentence or paragraph, not the single line. Uriah had learned from John Milton's *Paradise Lost*, which he undoubtedly studied at Phillips Exeter, how "to avoid the worst pitfalls of blank verse monotony—specifically, how to vary the pauses within his lines, and how to sweep his thought past the death-trap of excessive end-stopping. The reader is left free to concentrate upon Smith's thought and feeling, not overly conscious of his lines." Beyond simply recounting the Adventist experience, Smith was also summoning those who had lost courage and abandoned their faith. In what Waller identified as probably his "most eloquent passage," Smith called out to his readers:

> "Ho! all ye scattered ones, who ever once
>   Stood on the side of God and fought for truth,
>   Into whatever lone and dreary path,
>   The cloudy day and dark has seen you stray,
>   Return around the standard of your King!"[18]

White was so pleased with Uriah's poem that in 1853 he offered him a job setting type and doing engraving. Probably he had more in mind as well, for he told Smith that he was "fast getting at your command the arguments, or theory of our position." However, James said that he could not pay "suitable recompense for your labor. And now I can only say, come and share with us toil, care, perplexity, and food and raiment." Shortly before receiving White's request, Uriah and Annie had both been contacted about heading a school in Mount Vernon, New Hampshire, with a salary of $1,000 annually (double or triple what many earned at the time). Although they must have been tempted to accept such a lucrative position, both declined, instead choosing to work for James White without any salary.[19]

[1] Abiel Abbot Livermore and Sewall Putnam, *History of the Town of Wilton, Hillsborough County, New Hampshire With Genealogical Register* (Lowell, Mass.: Marden and Rowell, 1888), pp. 2-26, 231.

[2] *Ibid.*, pp. 162-173.

[3] *Ibid.*, pp. 499-502; "Genealogical Record of Uriah Smith, the Third." Although the main text of Livermore and Putnam's *History* dates the burning of the mills as 1781 or 1782 (p. 162), the genealogical section of their book, apparently prepared by family members, places the events 10 years later, 1791 or 1792 (p. 499).

[4] Livermore and Putnam, pp. 46, 118, 129-137, 143, 190.

[5] US to Arthur H. Chase, Dec. 11, 1899; US to J. F. Barbaret, Nov. 29, 1893; US, "Sketch of Uriah Smith, by Himself"; US to W. W. Church, June 18, 1890; Livermore and Putnam, p. 153. Lolita (?) to Mark Bovee, Jan. 7, 1986, refers to a book, no title given, that tells of Dr. Amos Twitchell, who performed the amputation on Uriah Smith. He is described as a "skilled surgeon." Barbara Hoare [granddaughter], "Notes on the Life of Uriah Smith"; EFD, *Yours in the Blessed Hope, Uriah Smith* (Washington, D.C.: Review and Herald Pub. Assn., 1980), p. 20.

[6] For the history of the Millerite movement, see GRK, *William Miller and the Rise of Adventism* (Nampa, Idaho: Pacific Press Pub. Assn., 2010).

[7] Rebekah Smith, *Poems: With a Sketch of the Life and Experience of Annie R. Smith* (Manchester, N.H.: John B. Clarke, Printer, 1871), p. 97; *RH*, Jan. 6, 1903, pp. 4, 5. Andrew E. Rothovius states that Uriah's father did not accept Millerism. See "Pegleg Prophet: Uriah Smith of Wilton," *The Olden Time Historical Newsletter,* June 1951.

[8] *RH*, Jan. 13, 1903, pp. 3, 4.

[9] *RH*, Jan. 6, 1903, p. 4; R. Smith, p. 97; US, "Sketch."

[10] Laurence M. Crosbie, *The Phillips Exeter Academy: A History* (Norwood, Mass.: Plimpton Press, 1924), pp. 94-98, 201, 207.

[11] US, "Ode," Anniversary of the Golden Branch Society of Phillips Exeter Academy, June 28, 1851.

[12] EFD, p. 22; GRK, *Joseph Bates: The Real Founder of Seventh-day Adventism* (Hagerstown, Md.: Review and Herald Pub. Assn., 2004), p. 178.

[13] R. Smith, pp. 98, 99; GRK, p. 178; Ron Graybill, "The Life and Loves of Annie Smith," *AH*, Summer 1975, pp. 14-17; J. Paul Stauffer, "Uriah Smith: Wood Engraver," *AH*, Summer 1976, p. 17.

[14] Annie R. Smith, "Lines Occasioned by the Death of My Father, Samuel Smith, of Wilton, N.H., who died Dec. 1st, 1852, aged 65 years."

[15] US to *Review*, *RH*, June 9, 1853, p. 16; Mar. 4, 1875, p. 79.

[16] JW to US, Feb. 17, 1853.

[17] *RH*, Mar. 17, 1853–Aug. 11, 1853; John O. Waller, "Uriah Smith's Small Epic: The Warning Voice of Time and Prophecy," *AH*, Summer 1978, pp. 53-55.

[18] Waller, pp. 56, 59. Waller quotes many more lines to illustrate this "eloquent passage."

[19] JW to US, Feb. 17, 1853; R. Smith, pp. 99, 100.

CH,APTER II
EARLY DAYS AT THE *REVIEW,* 1853–1855

In April 1852 the Whites had rented a house on Mount Hope Avenue at the edge of the Rochester city limits. With little income, they lived frugally, furnishing the house with secondhand, often broken furniture, and eating mainly porridge, beans, and turnips. According to William C. White, writing 80 years later and not citing any contemporary source, Uriah Smith "remarked to a comrade, that though he had no objection to eating beans 365 times in succession, yet when it came to making them a regular diet, he should protest." Originally James planned to house a printing press as well as his own family and assistants in the building, but soon the place became too crowded, and he had to rent a third-floor office downtown on South St. Paul Street, where he placed the handpress that he acquired in May 1852.[1]

THE *REVIEW* OFFICE

Meanwhile, several individuals arrived to serve the burgeoning publishing house, including Luman Masten, who served as foreman of the printing crew; George W. Amadon and Oswald Stowell, printers; and Warren Bacheller and Fletcher Byington, apprentices. Ellen White's brother-in-law Stephen Belden oversaw business matters, and his wife Sarah took care of housekeeping. James's brother Nathaniel and his sister Anna also joined the extended family, while John Nevins Andrews and John N. Loughborough, who did not live at the house, assisted in various ways. Also, Clarissa Bonfoey served as a kind of nanny during the Whites' absences. It was this group of about a dozen people that first

Annie Smith and then her brother Uriah connected with in the early months of 1853.[2]

Smith, speaking to the General Conference session in 1889, described the effort put into their early tracts and papers: "The instruments we had to use were a brad-awl, a straight-edge, and a pen-knife. Brother Loughborough, with the awl, would perforate the backs for stitching; the sisters would stitch them; and then I with the straight-edge and pen-knife would trim the rough edges on the top, front, and bottom. We blistered our hands in the operation, and often the tracts in form were not half so true and square as the doctrines they taught."[3]

Loughborough later similarly recalled the effort to produce their first tract. After printing sheets on the handpress, "a number of believers in the Rochester company united with the office workers in folding, stitching, covering, and trimming these books. The office had no folding machine, no stabbing machine, no stitching machine, no paper cutter. The sisters folded and gathered the signatures, the writer stabbed the books with a shoemaker's pegging awl. After they were stitched with needle and thread, Sister Mary Patten . . . pasted on the covers, and Brother Uriah Smith trimmed the edges with his pocket-knife, while Brother and Sister James White wrapped and directed advance copies to our people in other places."[4]

Unfortunately, with the cramped living quarters, poor nutrition, and long hours of work, infectious disease took its toll. A cholera epidemic sickened both Edson White, the White's 3-year-old son, and Masten, but both eventually recovered. More significant, when Nathaniel and Anna White arrived, they probably had already contracted tuberculosis, for Nathaniel died on May 6, 1853, and Anna about a year and a half later on November 30, 1854. Meanwhile, Luman Masten also died in 1854, and Annie Smith began showing symptoms in November of that year. The 10-month-old son of Stephen and Sarah Belden died in 1855.[5]

After becoming ill, Annie returned to her home in West Wilton, New Hampshire, on November 7. She received hydrotherapy treatments, perhaps in nearby New Ipswich, coming back home in February 1855. The treatments proved unsuccessful, and, knowing that she was going to die soon, Annie sought to complete a long poem, "Home Here and Home in Heaven," and then have her poems compiled into a small book. She finished her poem on May 28, 1855, and Uriah arrived the next day to arrange for publication of the book. During the next few weeks, Annie prepared the final manuscript, which Uriah took with him when he left for Rochester on July 17. A little more than a week later Annie, age 27, died at 4:00 a.m. on July 26.[6]

EARLY *REVIEW* CONTRIBUTIONS

In addition to helping physically produce the *Review* and other publications, Uriah Smith contributed several articles to the journal while in Rochester from 1853 to 1855. They touched on themes that would dominate his writing throughout his life. Not surprisingly, since prophecy had been the subject of his first publication, it remained a primary interest. Because the Millerites had been wrong only about expecting Jesus to return in 1844, he argued, he saw no need to change the Adventist interpretation of the prophetic periods. "If the 2300 days have ended," he asserted, "the cleansing of the sanctuary is going on." He expected the end of time to arrive soon: "There is yet left a brief hour of probation, while the work of the sanctuary is closing." Although the fulfillment of the prophetic promise was near at hand, believers walked by faith, not sight, and must wait patiently.[7]

Smith also argued for the perpetuity of God's law, including the seventh-day Sabbath, calling for biblical evidence from those who believed otherwise. "We want no inferences, assumptions or assertions; if God has annulled His law or any portion of His law, surely the record of such an event can be found." In October 1853 the *Review* began publishing another ambitious Smith project, a long poem entitled "A Word for the Sabbath, or False Theories Exposed." Although not nearly as lengthy as "The Warning Voice," his new poem consisted of six chapters, beginning with "Truth and Error" and continuing through "The Sabbath Instituted at Creation," "The Sabbath a Memorial," "The Sabbath Not Abolished," "Apostolic Example," and "Vain Philosophy." Interestingly, only the last installment carried Smith's name as author. As the chapter titles suggest, Smith's main argument was that the Sabbath is a perpetual requirement. Some representative lines from chapter 4 illustrate his approach:

"Still Thy requirements hold, that we must rest
  Upon the seventh day, which God has blest,

His fixed decrees He ne'er will disarrange,
For God can never lie, and never change."

In a later edition of the poem Smith stated that "we have thrown it [the Sabbath doctrine] into the form of rhyme and meter, with the idea that it might thus secure a perusal from some who would otherwise give no attention to this important subject." He admitted that because the content was primarily argumentative, it was "not particularly adapted to the flights and fancies of poetry, it claims no particular merits in that direction. The effort has been chiefly to guard against introducing an unnecessary amount of verbiage, and sacrificing perspicuity for the sake of the rhyme."[8]

Beneath his particular doctrinal and interpretive positions he held a clear conception of the nature of truth, which reflected the "common sense" philosophy that pervaded nineteenth-century American thought. Drawn from the Scottish philosophers Francis Hutchenson (1694-1746), Thomas Reid (1710-1796), Adam Smith (1723-1790), and Dugald Stewart (1753-1828), it held three major tenets. In epistemology, the study of the nature of knowledge, it followed a Baconian inductive science that emphasized the collection of facts. Regarding ethics, it believed that one could find God's intentions for humanity through commonsense moral reasoning, and, in conclusion, it applied the term *self-evident* to both epistemology and ethics. American religious historian Mark Noll writes that "Protestant commitment to theistic common sense became deeply ingrained because it seemed so intuitive, so instinctive, so much a part of second nature. As a result, many Protestants denied that they had a philosophy or deferred to an intellectual authority; they were merely following common sense." Adventist historian George Knight further comments that for Millerites, "commonsense philosophy avoided complicated rational explanations and focused on the facts (including biblical facts) as they appeared to the person on the street."[9]

Although we have no evidence that Smith had read the Scottish philosophers, it is likely that the commonsense philosophy underlay the teaching at Phillips Exeter Academy in addition to influencing him through its general expression in American culture, and more specifically the Millerite thought to which he had been exposed. Consequently, throughout his life he held to a highly rational approach to the Bible and Christianity that emphasized biblical proof texts and the facts of history in support of a truth clearly distinguished from error. In October 1853, not quite a year since his own conversion to Sabbatarian Adventism, he wrote that "I do most confidently assert that we have the truth—I know of no class of people who have any truth that we have not. I know of no class of people who have all the truth that we have." A week later he asserted that "we have settled upon our present belief not without reason, the Word of God, and the history of the past to sustain us; nor is it wholly with us a matter of belief; for what we see that we do know." His last phrase referred to fulfilled prophecy. Furthermore, the following year he stated that "truth is a unit, and cannot be divided. It is a firm pillar and will not bend to the crooked theories of those who are limping along in the shackles of error. It is a shining light and has no union with the shades of darkness. It has but one voice and cannot speak with a diversity of tongues. It has but one path, and those who walk thereon will not be groping their way through the devious mazes of blindness and error."[10]

The idea that truth was unified appeared occasionally in his discussion of specific doctrinal issues. In an article on the Sabbath, for instance, he argued that in the "third angel's message," a phrase that Sabbatarian Adventists used to describe their teachings, the sanctuary and the Sabbath were "inseparably connected." Further noting that the Sabbath was grounded in the Creation account, he reiterated the harmonious doctrinal system that he believed Adventism provided: "Such is the connection, relation and dependence of one great truth upon another, that every additional evidence upon one, proportionably, strengthens all the rest." Similarly, in his prophetic interpretation, he said that the fact that the 70 weeks were part of the 2300 days was confirmed by several lines of evidence, particularly the way that the years added up: 457 B.C. to A.D. 27 was 483 years, A.D. 27 to A.D. 31 was a half week, 457 plus the 490 years ended in A.D. 34, and A.D. 34 plus 1810 years led to 1844.[11]

Although the Adventists had found truth, Smith believed, they did not necessarily yet have all truth. What they held to was a "further development" of Millerite belief that had an "immovable foundation on the Word of God." Just as a progressive understanding of truth had occurred during their immediate past, one would expect that they would continue to advance into increased enlightenment. "It will not do for the people of God at anytime to imagine that they have truth enough," he commented in 1855, "and so calmly settle down on that and look for no further light." He never envisioned, however, that the future unfolding of progressive truth would in any way conflict with that already found.[12]

With such a view of truth combined with his apocalyptic expectations, Smith not surprisingly took a strong stand against the mainstream Christianity of his day. Sunday observance he called the "offspring of Paganism." He declared that popular theology spiritualized the literal nature of the Christian hope in a new Jerusalem, a new earth, and a new body. Adventists were not about to conform to the "so-called Christian world" that did not observe the Sabbath. "We are not willing to poison our belief with a multiplicity of errors for the sake of being in the world's eye liberal, or noble-minded." Christians were compromising with evil at the very time that it was increasing. "That the world is ripening for destruction needs no proof," he asserted. In addition to pointing to the Russo-Turkish war, he drew attention to the "Know-Nothing" or American Party that had recently emerged in response to immigration, the treatment of Native Americans, and the antislavery riots in the United States. With regard to slavery he noted the contradiction at the heart of the American experiment: "We sometimes . . . wonder why such a diabolical abomination as slavery should ever have been permitted to take such deep root in the very bosom of this country, and how a nation can act so signally contrary to its own profession; but we must remember, that, to fulfill the prophecy, the two-horned beast *must* speak as a dragon."[13]

What is interesting and significant about the views Smith expressed during his first two to three years with the *Review*, during which time he was only an occasional contributor, is that he staked out positions that he continued to put forward with virtually no deviation for the rest of his life. It seems that once Smith adopted something, he stuck with it.

MOVE TO BATTLE CREEK, MICHIGAN

Meanwhile, James White struggled to keep his publications alive, working up to 18 hours a day on the *Review*, the *Youth's Instructor*, and tracts and books, as well as continually seeking money on which to operate.

In addition to such pressures, his decision in 1850 not to publish his wife's writings in the *Review* aroused considerable criticism. In November 1854 J. N. Andrews, R. F. Cottrell, and Uriah Smith issued a statement, saying, "We do not deny the gifts of the Holy Spirit, but we regard them as designed only to lead men to the Word of God. This has ever been our position, the malice of our enemies to the contrary notwithstanding." By early 1855 James was expressing his desire to reduce his responsibilities, perhaps even to the extent of leaving the publishing house. Later that same year, as criticism mounted regarding his refusal to print his wife's writings, he exclaimed: "What has the *Review* to do with Mrs. W.'s views? The sentiments published in its columns are all drawn from the Holy Scriptures. No writer of the *Review* has ever referred to them as authority on any point. The *Review* for five years has not published one of them. Its motto has been 'The Bible, and the Bible alone, the only rule of faith and duty.' "[14]

Meanwhile, money continued to be an issue. Although the small publishing house was essentially James's private enterprise, he had appointed a publishing committee of Joseph Bates, J. N. Andrews, and Joseph Baker to give him guidance. At a meeting held June 23 to 26, 1854, the committee decided to charge a $1 annual subscription fee for the *Review*, and a new committee of Uriah Smith, J. N. Andrews, and R. F. Cottrell was appointed so that it "might be nearer the office." Because various members of the Adventist community questioned White's handling of finances, the publishing committee found it necessary in November 1854 to defend his actions. The committee then published an article in December explaining the financing of the *Review* and stating that it had power to supervise and remove the editor. Three weeks later the committee appealed for $500 in aid, saying, "You are aware, dear brethren, that we are engaged in the publication of unpopular truth, and that we cannot hope for favor from the men of the world, or from the popular churches, and that steady opposition must be expected, and that we can only continue in this work by committing toil and sacrifice."[15]

While these organizational changes were taking place, James had apparently expressed interest in moving the *Review* office out of Rochester, for in March 1855 Vermont Adventists sent him a check for $492, suggesting that he relocate to their state. A short time later believers in Michigan proposed that he transfer to Battle Creek. In response James observed that "the brethren in Battle Creek and vicinity are generally awake to the wants of the cause and are anxious to establish the *Review* office in that place. They are able and willing to do so, and manifest much anxiety to relieve us of those cares and responsibilities which we have too long borne. The climate, water, prices of rent, fuel, provisions, etc., seem favorable to the location." Not yet ready to make a decision, however, he visited Vermont the following summer, but by the end of August he had decided on Battle Creek, probably because the believers there had collected $1,200 to buy a lot and put up a building.[16]

Expressing a desire for relief from some of his responsibilities, White recommended the establishment of a financial committee composed of three Battle Creek believers, and that Uriah Smith become the resident editor, while R. F. Cottrell, J. N. Andrews, J. H. Waggoner, Stephen Pierce, and himself would serve as corresponding editors. Writing about their functions, James stated that "no one man confined to the office can know the wants of the cause as well as if he were in the field. Let Brother Smith as resident editor, attend to office matters, prepare matter for the press, read proof, etc. Let it be the duty of each of the corresponding editors, to furnish something for each paper over their initials, if possible, considering their other duties." Following up on White's recommendation, a September meeting in Battle Creek decided to shift the publishing house office to Battle Creek and created a publishing committee composed of Daniel R. Palmer, Henry Lyon, and Cyrenius Smith. Another meeting in December chose Uriah Smith to be the resident editor.[17]

In the same issue that announced his appointment, Smith wrote to the *Review* readers stating that he expected "the aid and cooperation of all my brethren." He went on to say that "I do not enter upon this position for ease, or comfort, or worldly profit; for I have seen by my connection with the *Review* thus far that neither of these were to be found here. But there are burdens to be borne, there are sacrifices to be made, and it becomes us each in the light of present truth, willingly and cheerfully to do what we can in the cause of God."

Noting that the "world is swiftly rushing down the broad road to destruction," he declared that the purpose of the journal was to "aid God's peculiar people in the all-important work of preparing for that

glorious translation which we soon expect." Despite his expectation
that time was short, Smith was entering a new and very long chapter
of his life.[18]

---

[1] GW, *James White: Innovator and Overcomer* (Hagerstown, Md.: Review and Herald Pub. Assn., 2003), pp. 71, 72; *RH*, June 13, 1935, p. 10.

[2] GW, p. 73.

[3] *General Conference Daily Bulletin*, Oct. 29, 1889, p. 105.

[4] *RH*, Apr. 7, 1903, p. 8.

[5] GW, pp. 76-78; MRH, *Flames Over Battle Creek* (Washington, D.C.: Review and Herald Pub. Assn., 1977), p. 17.

[6] R. Smith, *Poems,* pp. 100-106; R. Graybill, "Annie Smith," *AH,* pp. 20, 21; *RH,* Aug. 21, 1855, p. 31.

[7] *RH*, Sept. 18, 1855, p. 44; Oct. 2, 1855, pp. 52-54; May 29, 1855, p. 236.

[8] *RH*, Oct. 18, 1853-Dec. 20, 1853; US, *A Word for the Sabbath or False Theories Exposed* (Rochester, N.Y.: Advent Review Office, 1855), p. 21; US, *A Word for the Sabbath or False Theories Exposed*, 3rd ed., revised and enlarged (Battle Creek, Mich.: Steam Press of the Seventh-day Adventist Pub. Assn., 1875), p. 3. Through the course of his career Smith also published several shorter poems and hymns. See EFD, *Yours*, pp. 191-194; Ron Graybill, "Uriah Smith Upon the Swanee River," *Journal of Adventist Education* (October/November 1994), pp. 30-32.

[9] Mark Noll, *America's God* (New York: Oxford Univ. Press, 2002), p. 113; GRK, *Millennial Fever and the End of the World* (Boise, Idaho: Pacific Press Pub. Assn., 1993), p. 37.

[10] *RH*, Oct. 4, 1853, p. 100; Oct. 11, 1853, p. 108; Feb. 28, 1854, p. 44.

[11] *RH*, July 25, 1854, p. 196; Mar. 21, 1854, pp. 69, 70.

[12] *RH*, Feb. 14, 1854, p. 29; Oct. 16, 1855, p. 62.

[13] *RH*, Oct. 24, 1854, p. 87; May 9, 1854, p. 124; June 20, 1854, p. 164; Feb. 7, 1854, p. 20.

[14] *RH*, Nov. 7, 1854, p. 101; GW, p. 81; Ronald L. Numbers, *Prophetess of Health: A Study of Ellen G. White*, 3rd ed. (Grand Rapids: William B. Eerdmans, 2008), p. 73.

[15] *RH*, July 4, 1854, p. 173; Nov. 21, 1854, p. 116; Dec. 5, 1854, pp. 124, 125; Dec. 26, 1854, pp. 149, 150.

[16] GW, pp. 81, 82; *RH*, Aug. 7, 1855, p. 20; JW to A. A. Dodge, Aug. 30, 1855.

[17] JW to A. A. Dodge, Aug. 20, 1855; *RH*, Dec. 4, 1855, p. 73. This issue was the first to list Smith as "Resident Editor."

[18] *RH*, Dec. 4, 1855, p. 76.

CHAPTER III
BATTLE CREEK, 1855-1860

Joseph Bates had brought Sabbatarian Adventism to Jackson, Michigan, in 1849 and nearby Battle Creek in 1852, baptizing David Hewitt, M. E. Cornell, and J. P. Kellogg, among others. Kellogg and three of Bates's Jackson converts—Dan Palmer, Henry Lyon, and Cyrenius Smith—provided the money for the publishing house to move to Battle Creek. According to George Amadon, 10 Sabbathkeeping families lived in Battle Creek at the time, and the five members of the James White family together with their helpers Clarissa Bonfoey and Jennie Fraser, Warren Bacheller and his mother and sister, Stephen and Sarah Belden, Uriah Smith, and G. W. Amadon now joined them. They formed the Battle Creek church in 1855 with 24 charter members and some 50 persons in the Sabbath school. During the fall and winter of 1855-1856 the congregation constructed an 18' by 24' building on the west side of Cass Street near Champion Street. In 1857 the growing congregation sold their building and constructed a larger one, 28' by 42', on Van Buren Street.[1]

The Whites and their helpers initially lived in a rented house on Van Buren Street, while the Belden and Bacheller families found other housing. George Amadon and Uriah Smith, the bachelors, lodged with a local family. Smith, however, did not remain single long. Harriet Newall Stevens, who had grown up in Paris, Maine, but had recently moved with her family to Iowa, had joined the *Review* office in 1854, where she probably first met Smith, but appears to have returned to Paris about the time of the transfer to Battle Creek. At some point she arrived in Battle Creek, where

Elder J. B. Frisbie married her and Uriah on July 7, 1857. The newlyweds
took up residence in a house on Kalamazoo Street.[2]

   At the time the Adventists arrived, Battle Creek was a small village located at the confluence of the Battle Creek and Kalamazoo rivers in south
Michigan's Calhoun County. The first settler had arrived in 1831, and
by 1850 the village had a population of 1,083. Originally called Milton
Township, in 1849 the residents renamed their community Battle Creek,
which they incorporated one year later. With the arrival of the Michigan
Central Railroad in 1845, several businesses developed during the 1840s
and 1850s, many of them serving the needs of farmers in the area. The
first gristmill had been built in 1837. By 1855 the town had at least three
flour mills, two woolen mills, several sawmills, and one planing mill. The
Battle Creek Iron Foundry, established in 1845, manufactured plows and
other agricultural implements, and became best known for its "Merrill's
Separator," introduced in 1851. Two more manufacturers of agricultural
equipment, the Peter H. Jewel Iron Works and the Nichols and Shephard
Company, which made the "Vibrator Threshing Machine," made their appearance in 1848. By that same year the village also had a wagonmaking
shop and a blacksmith shop. And 1850 saw the first of several lard oil
factories, the oil produced for lighting and heating rather than for food.[3]

   The emerging economic diversity of the community became apparent in
the 1850 census, which listed 312 men working in 57 occupations. They
included 16 merchants, nine lawyers, six physicians, 37 carpenters, and
10 masons. Construction became an important element of the growing
community, with the number of houses increasing from 200 in 1850 to
760 in 1860. To build them and other structures the quantity of carpenters
and masons grew correspondingly, increasing to 137 by 1860. About half
of the population in 1850 originally came from New York State. By 1860,
when Battle Creek numbered nearly 3,500 residents, the percentage of
New Yorkers had dropped to 47 percent, as people came from elsewhere
in Michigan and surrounding states. The village also had 363 foreign-born
residents, mostly from Canada, the British Isles, and Germany. The number of African Americans had risen from 34 in 1850 to 121 a decade later.[4]

   Although located far from the amenities of the large cities, the population
had access to a wide variety of products that simplified and beautified their
lives. When Mumford's General Store went bankrupt in 1852, the legally

required inventory offered a glimpse of the variety of items available to the villagers. The store had 832 different ones, including hardware products, such as carpenter tools, knives, and fishhooks. Among the available foods were tea and spices. The stock contained manufactured clothing, such as hats, caps, boots, and shoes, while needles and thread served the needs of those who made garments at home. Other items ranged from perfumes to schoolbooks. Clearly the people of Battle Creek had available to them some of the comforts of the growing American market economy.[5]

The community also began developing several civic and cultural institutions. After several destructive fires, residents organized the Protection Company No. 1 in 1846. A brass band formed in 1848 and became well known in the area, while a singing school developed in 1850. A Union School organized in 1850, followed by separate elementary schools in 1857 and 1861. The Battle Creek *Journal*, the village's oldest continuous newspaper, appeared in 1851. In addition to the typical churches found in the American west, particularly the Baptist and Methodist denominations, by the mid-1850s Battle Creek had attracted several unorthodox religious groups, including Swedenborgians, spiritualists, Universalists, and Quakers. One of the Quakers, Erastus Hussey, provided a "station" on the Underground Railroad that aided escaped slaves from the South. In 1857 Sojourner Truth, an African American abolitionist leader, moved to Harmonia, a spiritualist and Quaker community located near Battle Creek. Ten years later she transferred into the growing village.[6]

The Adventists arrived just as Battle Creek was developing a thriving economy, a diverse population, and an environment tolerant of new religions. The village's businesses and residences were located near the railroad, leaving what became known as the "West End" largely undeveloped and therefore inexpensive. As a result Adventists found the area a convenient place to settle and make their own contribution to the growing community. When James White and his associates arrived in 1855, several Adventist businessmen had already established themselves in the "West End," thereby paving the way for their small but ambitious denomination to come to Battle Creek. Among them were David Hewitt, a "peddler" who also became an agent for the *Review and Herald* in 1853; Merritt Cornell and Henry Lyon, builders and contractors; Jonah Lewis, a shoemaker; Henry Dodge, a clockmaker and repairer; and John P. Kellogg, who managed a small store and broom factory. Working from this base, the Adventists were to make their own contribution to the development of Battle Creek.[7]

THE STEAM PRESS

Meanwhile, Smith established himself as editor of the *Review*. In January 1856 he announced that the journal had acquired 130 new subscribers and, seeking to expand the subscription base further, said the publishing house would send the *Review* to inquirers on a three-month trial basis, but if the recipient did not subscribe by the end of that period of time, the issues would cease. In 1857 he called for people to write for the journal, requesting articles that presented "clear and earnest arguments, great bulwarks of the truth, we trust will be duly furnished by all who are so disposed." About a year later he again called for contributions, this time emphasizing the need for diversity. "There is need of variety, and different gifts should be called in to make a paper lively and interesting." Perhaps in an effort to avoid discouraging potential contributors, he said that the paper would publish a range of perspectives. "Let all views, we say, be freely submitted to the crucible of investigation. The gold will surely remain, and come forth seven times purified."[8]

From his post at the editor's desk, Smith was quite pleased with the state of the young church. In January 1856 he wrote that "our correspondence has of late been quite cheering. There seems to be a desire among the remnant in all parts, to rise in spirituality, to be more consecrated to God, and manifest more zeal and energy in His service. May this work go on till God shall indeed have upon this earth a peculiar people, zealous of good works."[9]

As the number of subscriptions grew and the house planned additional tracts and books, it became obvious that the handpress brought from Rochester was inadequate. Consequently the publishing committee investigated the possibility of purchasing a power press. Noting that it took three days to produce the *Review* on the handpress, James White in March 1857 called for funds to buy the new equipment. The following month the *Review* announced an official vote to obtain a power press and stated that people had already pledged $1,600 of the $2,500 needed. At the end of July White reported that "this no. of the *Review* is printed on the power press. Up to this time everything connected with this enterprise has gone off most pleasantly and prosperously." After two months of operating the press by hand, in October the three-horsepower steam engine had arrived, enabling the October 8 issue of the *Review* to roll off the press by power. It must have been an exciting time.[10]

But the paper still demanded a tremendous amount of work. Paid about $7.00 a week, Smith acted not only as editor but also as secretary, maintaining the subscriber list and overseeing the hand wrapping of the paper for mailing. John N. Loughborough later recalled that Uriah continued his secretarial work until 1862, when the publishing house bought a hand mailing machine. Smith then used the device for several years to mail the weekly paper.[11]

LEGALISM AND THE SABBATH

Now that he was editor, Smith was responsible for writing up to three editorials each week. His editorials as well as other articles offer insight into his major concerns. From the very beginning he sought clearly to establish the perpetuity of God's law and the necessity of obeying it. He distinguished between the ceremonial laws of the Old Testament that applied to a specific time and place and the moral law, "which all must admit God has instituted to govern mankind, in all places, under all circumstances, and in all times. These are generally conceded to be the Ten Commandments as written by God's own finger upon tables of stone." Repeatedly he emphasized that the Bible contained no statement indicating that the moral law had changed. Commenting on Romans 7, he denied that Paul was teaching that the Ten Commandments had been done away with. Furthermore, the law was lodged in heaven, where no human being could alter it.[12]

Obedience to the law was a requirement for salvation, according to Smith. "If we keep the commandments of God and the faith of Jesus, we *shall* have right to the tree of life, we *shall* enter in through the gates into the city," he wrote in early 1856. A short time later he stated that "the condition of eternal life in the kingdom of God is the keeping of the commandments." Obedience was absolutely necessary, "but obedience is no obedience which does not extend to every requirement which God has given to regulate our conduct, and yield to them each implicit service."

About a year and a half later he defined a Christian as "one who unites with the faith of Jesus the love of God and obedience to his commandments." But perhaps his strongest statement was an editorial "Note," published in 1856: "The truth must be obeyed at all hazards," he wrote, for it does not matter what family and friends think. "The moment a person enlists under the banner of pure and living religion, that moment he declares war with the world, the flesh, and the devil; and from them he can expect no more peace, unless by compromise or treachery he unites with them again.

"Break every tie. Burst every such fetter asunder; nor be afraid to let the world know that you, as an independent and accountable being, are seeking eternal life."[13]

Such positions, of course, opened Smith and his fellow Adventists to the charge that they were legalists, something that Uriah always denied. He was willing to concede that not all individuals recognized the full light of truth. Such people, he believed, were accountable only to the degree of truth available to them. "But when further light comes," he said, "it becomes his duty then to follow that light. If it is rejected, then comes sin and condemnation." Furthermore, Christ had fulfilled the claims of the law through His death, and sinners appropriate His righteousness through their faith in Him. Nonetheless, the current dispensation was one that had a mixture of law and gospel. "Having inherited a carnal heart, a fallen nature, we must look to him for grace to enable us to keep the law in the future." Thus, for Smith, fulfilling the requirements of the law remained a condition of eternal life, but we do that through the grace of Jesus rather than earning salvation through our own efforts.[14]

Perhaps his fullest statement regarding the relationship of the law and gospel he made at this stage of his career appeared in an 1859 editorial. "Thus the law and the gospel are inseparably connected in the great scheme of our redemption. We can do nothing without Christ; and yet the righteousness of the law must be fulfilled in us. . . . Thus the commandments of God and the faith of Jesus are set before a guilty world as the way and passport to eternal life; and we can understand the expressions of the apostle, that by the deeds of the law shall no flesh be justified; and yet that the doers of the law (and they only) shall be justified."[15]

The Ten Commandments, of course, included the Sabbath, which Adventists explicitly identified as the seventh day of the week. The Exodus recording of the commandments states that we are to observe the day in remembrance of the Creator. Smith took pains to demonstrate that the Sabbath was not a "type or shadow" or associated with the ceremonial Sabbaths that ceased with Christ's coming. Furthermore, because it is necessary to both humanity's physical and moral needs, the gospel could not have abolished it. Finally, "wherever the sacred writers would point out the true God in distinction from false gods of every description, an appeal is made to the fourth commandment."[16]

Repeatedly Uriah denied that anything in the Bible supported the idea that the Sabbath had changed. "*We* are not the *innovators*—introducers of a new and novel institution," he argued, "as some would fain have us believe, . . . to have supplanted by any means an institution more ancient. . . . The burden of proof then is 'transferred to where it belongs.' The advocates of the more modern institution of Sundaykeeping are bound to show us its lease on life." He blamed the shift of the Sabbath from Saturday to Sunday on the Papacy and identified Sundaykeeping with the "mark of the beast." Protestants simply followed the Papacy in justifying Sunday sacredness. "Most of the arguments which Protestants so nimbly wield in defense of Sundaykeeping," he stated, "are the inventions of the Papacy. The daughter has sat for instruction at the feet of her mother." Eventually, he believed, society will "resolve itself into two classes: Sabbathkeepers and Sundaykeepers."[17]

For all these reasons, true Christians should observe the seventh-day Sabbath. "The secret of our zeal on the Sabbath question . . . is this: We know that all acceptable worship must be performed in spirit and in truth. . . . It must not only be done in spirit, but it must be in *accordance with the truth*. Hence, if it be a fact that the original Sabbath is still binding on the world; if the command which enforces it is still a *living* oracle, as vital as any other precept which enters into the constitution of God's government, woe unto those persons who, with the statute-book in their hands, are found living in its constant and determined violation!"[18]

TRUTH AND THE CHURCHES

As noted previously, with his commonsense understanding of truth, Smith brooked no room for ambiguities or uncertainties. In early 1857 he asserted that when two people interpret Scripture in different ways, one of them must be wrong. He believed that the Christian church had departed from the truth because it did not love the truth.

"Had that Spirit of Truth, which Christ promised His followers, ever been cherished in the bosom of the church and no departure made from the plain, literal teachings of Christ and the inspired writers no divisions nor heresies would ever have entered the church. . . . Such a church we believe is coming forth—a church free from every denominational creed, planting itself upon the broad bases of the Bible, keeping the commandments of God and the faith of Jesus."[19]

We should note several significant things about his statement. First, he emphasized that we must understand Bible teachings as literally true. Second, if people had followed this principle, there would have been no disagreement. Facts were facts, and commonsense dictated that all honest minds would understand them in the same way. Finally, he believed that his own Sabbatarian Adventist movement followed those principles and was, therefore, different from all other churches. Although he did not say it here, Sabbatarian Adventism's only creed was the Bible, which he believed needed only to be read plainly rather than interpreted.

Whenever anyone suggested that some specific aspect of Sabbatarian Adventist belief needed changing, Smith responded by saying that all of its elements were interconnected. "The bearings of all its portions upon each other are like clockwork; but break out one cog, and the work is stopped; break one link, and the chain is broken; let down one stitch, and we may unravel the whole." He also spoke frequently of the "chains of prophecy" all terminating in one place. Although his conservatism, which became increasingly apparent as time passed, was probably rooted in his personality, it also grew out of his intellectual understanding of the unity of truth, and therefore in his mind any proposed shift threatened the whole.[20]

To Uriah such a position was rational. "But to produce conviction, a view must draw plain credentials from both reason and revelation," he wrote. "There must exist not only reasons for believing it, but reasons which prohibit its being otherwise." When some people in 1857 regarded a comet as foretelling the end of the world, Smith said, "It is none of our work to raise any excitement on such a foundation as this." Nonetheless, as he had stated previously, truth is also progressive in the sense that new light will be added to existing understanding. Christians have the responsibility to continue their investigation of truth—they must "maintain an inquiring frame of mind," looking to the Sprit of truth to "set it home."[21]

Believing as he did that the Sabbatarian Adventists had the truth, Uriah was highly critical of the other Protestant churches. He claimed that they had "rejected as plain a message as need be given to the world," and asserted that they were "apostatizing from the Bible." Furthermore, he argued that those who took the Bible seriously would find themselves "differing more and more widely from those around them."[22] Attempting to conform to the customs of surrounding society had ever been the bane of the church, which rather should hold up a high standard. In 1858 he strongly stated his view of the popular churches by using nautical metaphors: "The worldly churches have taken to the huge raft of popularity and worldly honor, which Satan has towed along by its side, to lure the mariner from the only ark of safety, by promising him a better or an easier passage to his desired haven. Floods of Jehovah's wrath will swamp and swallow up all those ere long. But to the bark of truth will safely anchor in the harbor of eternal safety."[23]

With such a view of the mainstream churches, it is not surprising that he advised his Adventist readers to avoid "any friendship with the world, or fellowship with its votaries." For him, separation from the surrounding society was a necessity if Adventism was to maintain its purity.[24]

He further explained his position in an 1859 editorial: "If, as we claim, the Sabbath is an essential part of our rule of duty, a vital portion of the law of God, then to violate it, and zealously and incessantly fight against it as they do, does involve a breach of Christian character. It does betray on their part an alienation from God, a dislike of Christian duty, a desire not to be subject to the law of God; for the carnal heart is not subject to the law of God, neither indeed can be. Can we extend to such characters the hand of fellowship? We cannot."[25]

With his use of such words as "duty" and "law" Smith revealed the legalistic emphasis of his understanding of Christianity that in turn led to a thoroughgoing separatist sectarianism.

CURRENT EVENTS AND THE LAST DAYS

During the late 1850s the United States, torn apart politically by the issue of slavery, moved step by step toward the Civil War. Smith, of course, did not know specifically where events would lead, but, based on his interpretation of prophecy, he expected no good result. In 1857, after the Supreme Court declared in the Dred Scott decision that African Americans could not be citizens and struck down the 36° 30' dividing line across the West established by the Missouri Compromise of 1820, Uriah commented that irrevocable conflict existed between the principles of the Declaration of Independence and slavery. "In the institution of slavery is more especially manifested, thus far, the dragon spirit that dwells in the heart of this hypocritical nation." He expected even worse things to come. But being against slavery did not make him an abolitionist. His philosophy of separation from society required that he eschew politics. When a subscriber wrote saying that he was ending his subscription to the *Review* so that he could use the money to support abolition, Uriah replied that while the journal had always regarded slavery as an evil, nothing could be done about it.[26]

Smith expressed his pessimism regarding the possibility of reform more fully in 1858 in a comment following the reprinting of an excerpt from Abraham Lincoln's speech to the Illinois Republican state convention. He stated that Lincoln was capable of judging "the design and tendency of legislative action the position which our government at present occupies with regard to the diabolical institution of American slavery, and the direction in which it is tending on the question. He who looks for good, or hopes for reform in the legislative or executive departments of this government, is doomed, we think, to utter and hopeless disappointment. . . . But if the house does not fall, what reason have we to look for a nation whose tendency is so manifestly downward to become hostile to the spirit and encroachments of slavery? If it shall cease to maintain its dragonic character, then we mistake the impact of the prophetic delineation."[27]

As 1859 drew to a close, Smith called attention to John Brown's attack on the federal arsenal at Harper's Ferry. "The political horizon of our own county is also increasingly stormy. The late affair at Harper's Ferry—the abortive attempt at insurrection by Capt. Brown—has rolled a wave of perturbation over the whole heart of the South. It was in itself a comparatively small matter; but it was to them like a spark in a powder mill. At the thoughts of what it might portend, they stood aghast. The spark was quenched before it had kindled to an explosion; but who shall tell what we may next expect? Or who, save the student of prophecy and the child of God, may know for what to prepare?"[28]

Smith's frequent references to prophecy indicate that he interpreted events within the framework of his premillennial historicist prophetic understanding. As early as 1856 he compared his own time to the days of Lot and concluded that "the admonition of every fulfilling sign [of prophecy] is, Escape for thy life!" As society fell ever more deeply into evil, he expected that "the fires of persecution will burn fiercely against the people of God" and that the wrath of God would then come upon the wicked. The following year he drew attention to spiritualism, the doctrine of immortality, and increasing crime as signs that he was living in the last days. "The next dispensation," he said, "will not only usher in the day of life but the night of death. Then the night also cometh. A night to sin and sinners." Increasingly apocalyptic in his outlook, in 1859 Smith saw an impending conflict between God's people and the wicked: "The people of God should stand together. In unity there is strength. Bad men are combining. The wicked are being gathered into bundles preparatory to the great burning. The ranks of our enemies are filling up and closing in on every hand. Let the good also associate, come into the unity of faith, and stand shoulder to shoulder against the powers of darkness."[29]

With such an apocalyptic framework for his understanding of society and the role of the church, it is not surprising that he saw no hope of eradicating slavery and advocated that the people of God should separate themselves entirely from their surrounding culture.

TENSION WITH THE WHITES

Although it did not appear in the pages of the *Review*, tensions between Smith and James and Ellen White began to appear in the late 1850s. The specific issues are unclear, but apparently James was critical of the operation of the *Review* office, and Smith and others began complaining about how they were being treated. An 1857 letter from Ellen White to Uriah implied that Smith was thinking about leaving the *Review*. "God has not selected or designed Brother [J. H.] Waggoner for the office to occupy your place," she wrote. "Let your influence tell in the meeting, tell in the office, and your own soul will flourish, and a saving, gathering influence will be shed around." She observed that James and Waggoner had "erred in not freely talking their fears to you" and said that Uriah and his wife, Harriet, did not fully understand things and acted too quickly. Mrs. White called on James and Uriah to have one interest and be "true yoke-fellows" and concluded by counseling Harriet to provide support for Uriah. "Never act or talk on the doubtful side," she advised, "but let the weight of your words and acts be to strengthen faith, to dispel doubts."[30]

But problems continued. In June 1860 Ellen White wrote to Harriet stating that she had been shown in vision that James and Uriah were "a distance apart" rather than united. "Darkness was in the office." She accused Uriah of being in the wrong when he wrote letters to Waggoner criticizing her husband.

"There was occasion for Brother White's feelings and Brother Waggoner's, but their feelings were too strong and their course was wrong in not going directly to Uriah and talking over matters with him. But Uriah's and your wrong was still greater in carrying the matter to others and writing to Waukon before speaking to James upon the matter."

Waukon, Iowa, was the home of Harriet's family, who for several years had been unhappy with the Whites. In 1850 the Whites had lived for a time with the Edward Andrews family in Paris, Maine. Encouraged by Harriet's father, Cyprian Stevens, who also lived in Paris, Andrews claimed that James had defrauded him of $8.00. Even though the incident had occurred a decade previously, and both the Andrews and Stevens families had moved to Waukon, the dispute continued to poison relationships with the Whites. Ellen now brought this situation to bear on the current controversy. "The influence and feelings which existed in Paris has affected your judgment and still sways your mind," she told Harriet. "You have received and cherished feelings that Brother White was too hard and severe, and if one is censured or has plain matters of facts laid upon them, they complain of Brother White's severity. You stand all ready to sympathize with them."[31]

Another letter from Ellen written about the same time criticized Harriet even more strongly and again blamed her attitudes on the situation in Paris. Mrs. White accused her of taking an active part in the jealousy and suspicion of James by Battle Creek church members. "I saw that a great trial was before the church at Battle Creek. I saw that James must be careful whom he trusted or confided in, for he was watched by some of his brethren at Battle Creek, and watched by those in the office—especially by you, Uriah, and Fletcher [Byington]." She told Harriet that her feelings were in complete rebellion against James "and if you had felt aggrieved and freely opened your mind to him you would have been convinced that your feelings arose from prejudice, misunderstanding, and misconstruction of his words." Further, she stated that Harriet's feelings, actions, and words had been wrong and "had been under the control of Satan." Accusing her of being both angry and selfish, Ellen again brought in the family connection.

"The present truth has rested very lightly upon you, and selfishness has woven itself closely with all you do. It is the natural besetment of your family, and it is a sin which God has rebuked them for but which they would not confess. You have never realized it. Your influence, instead of helping Uriah, has hindered."

But Ellen White was not finished, declaring "that the Lord would have a shrewd manager in the office, one who will reprove, one who is keenly sensitive to wrong, and who feels that the cause of God is a part of him. Uriah and you have not felt this as you should." Although she admitted that James was severe, he "does not hide things in his heart. If an unconsecrated one is reproved by Brother White you sympathize with him, confide in him." Again she brought up the Paris link, seeing it as extending to Rochester and Battle Creek. "If Uriah and James are connected in that office, their interests are one and the barrier that has been placed between them must be broken down, the reserve on the part of Uriah and yourself must be broken down, the exclusive course Uriah has pursued must be broken down, and they be in perfect union or not labor in connection at all." She added that both Uriah and Harriet had been "at war" with her husband and had not heeded the reproof given two years previously. "Your feelings of selfishness would lead you to tear Uriah from the office," Ellen concluded, "that you might enjoy his company more exclusively yourself."[32]

That was strong stuff. Unfortunately, we have no record of a response by either Uriah or Harriet, but one can imagine that such criticism stung the young wife. The conflict, whatever the specific issue might have been, seems to have died away shortly thereafter. But it was not the end of tension between the Smiths and the Whites.

---

[1] GRK, *Joseph Bates*, pp. 174-177; GWA, "A Sketch of the Battle Creek Sabbath School From Its Commencement to October 1, 1901," *Sabbath School Worker*, February 1947, pp. 6-8. MRH ("George Washington Amadon" [M.A. project, School of Graduate Studies, Andrews University, March 1976], p. 35), states that the church had 100 members by 1857.

[2] MRH, *Flames*, p. 28; EFD, *Yours*, p. 30; GW, *James White*, p. 86; marriage certificate, Uriah Smith and Harriet N. Stevens.

[3] I have drawn the early history of Battle Creek from the following: E. W. Roberts, *Pioneer Days in Old Battle Creek: An Illustrated and Descriptive Atlas of a City in the Making* (Battle Creek, Mich.: Battle Creek Central National Bank and Trust Company, 1951), pp. 13-40; Berenice Bryant Lowe, *Tales of Battle Creek* (n.p.: Albert and Louise B. Miller Foundation, 1976), pp. 10, 51, 61, 62, 64, 67, 135; Larry B. Massie and Peter J. Schmidt, *Battle Creek: The Place Behind the Products, An Illustrated History* (Woodland Hills, Calif.: Windsor Publications, 1984), pp. 25, 29.

[4] Massie and Schmidt, pp. 24, 29; Kathleen Mitchell, "The Population Structure of Battle Creek, Michigan, 1850-1870" (research project, Department of History and Political Science, Andrews University, 1973).

[5] Massie and Schmidt, pp. 75, 76.

[6] Lowe, pp. 100, 114, 131, 169; Massie and Schmidt, pp. 39-41.

[7] Noel L. Braithwaite, "West End Settlement, 1852-1863: A Reconstruction" (research project, Seventh-day Adventist Theological Seminary, Andrews University, 1973).

[8] *RH*, Jan. 31, 1856, p. 140; Jan. 3, 1856, p. 108; May 14, 1857, p. 12; June 3, 1858, p. 24; May 21, 1857, p. 20.

[9] *RH*, Jan. 17, 1856, p. 124.

[10] *RH*, Apr. 16, 1857, pp. 188, 192; July 30, 1857, p. 104; Oct. 15, 1857, p. 188; MRH, *Flames*, p. 29.

[11] *RH*, Apr. 7, 1903, p. 8.

[12] *RH*, June 11, 1857, pp. 44, 45; Dec. 17, 1857, pp. 41, 42; Dec. 9, 1858, p. 20; May 28, 1857, p. 28.

[13] *RH*, Jan. 17, 1856, p. 124; Mar. 13, 1856, p. 188; June 25, 1857, p. 61; Dec. 2, 1858, p. 12; Feb. 7, 1856, p. 152.

[14] *RH*, Feb. 14, 1856, p. 156; Jan. 1, 1857, pp. 68, 69; Mar. 24, 1859, p. 140.

[15] *RH*, July 14, 1859, p. 60.

[16] *RH*, Dec. 11, 1855, p. 84; July 23, 1857, pp. 92, 93; Aug. 5, 1858, p. 92; Aug. 12, 1858, p. 100; Aug. 11, 1859, p. 92; Apr. 24, 1856, p. 12.

[17] *RH*, Dec. 18, 1855, p. 92; Jan. 13, 1859, p. 60; May 5, 1859, p. 188; Aug. 20, 1857, pp. 124, 125; July 30, 1857, p. 100; May 1, 1856, p. 20.

[18] *RH*, Oct. 27, 1859, p. 180.

[19] *RH*, Jan. 15, 1857, p. 84; Sept. 24, 1857, p. 164.

[20] *RH*, Jan. 7, 1858, p. 72; Nov. 12, 1857, p. 4.

[21] *RH*, Feb. 26, 1857, p. 132; May 14, 1857, p. 12; Nov. 4, 1858, p. 188; Apr. 30, 1857, pp. 204, 205,

[22] *RH*, Feb. 7, 1856, p. 148; Nov. 25, 1858, p. 4; June 17, 1858, p. 36.

[23] *RH*, Nov. 18, 1858, p. 204.

[24] *RH*, July 1, 1858, p. 52.

[25] *RH*, June 16, 1859, p. 28.

[26] *RH*, Mar. 19, 1857, pp. 156, 157; Mar. 10, 1859, p. 124.

[27] *RH*, Sept, 2, 1858, p. 124.

[28] *RH*, Nov. 17, 1859, p. 204.

[29] *RH*, Jan. 10, 1856, p. 116; Mar. 6, 1856, p. 180; Apr. 10, 1856, p. 4; May 7, 1857, p. 4; Sept. 3, 1857, p. 140; Apr. 28, 1859, p. 180.

[30] EGW to US, Oct. 8, 1857.

[31] EGW to HS, June 1860; GW, pp. 62, 63.

[32] EGW to HS, June 1860.

CHAPTER IV

ORGANIZATION
AND ITS DISCONTENTS, 1860–1870

As the 1860s dawned, both the growing Sabbatarian Adventist move-ment and the United States faced a crossroads in their histories. Up to this point, the Sabbatarians were a loosely knitted body of believers organized into small, independent congregations and tied together largely by the traveling ministries of Ellen and James White, Joseph Bates, John N. Loughborough, and others, as well as the printed word, particularly Uriah Smith's *Review*. Increasingly, however, it was becoming apparent that the movement needed some form of further organizational structure.

Meanwhile, the American nation faced an even more severe crisis. The election of Abraham Lincoln as president in 1860 brought the acceler-ating debate over slavery to a head. In December South Carolina led the Southern states in declaring secession, followed soon by other states of the Deep South (Mississippi, Florida, Alabama, Georgia, and Louisiana), who formed a new government in February 1861, the Confederate States of America, with its capital in Montgomery, Alabama. Texas joined the new nation in March. After the inauguration of Lincoln as president of the United States in March, the Confederacy responded in April by cap-turing Fort Sumter, located in Charleston, South Carolina. Lincoln then called for volunteers to suppress the insurrection, which provoked the states of the Upper South (Virginia, Arkansas, Tennessee, and North Carolina) to secede and unite with the Confederacy. Subsequently the Confederacy moved its capital to Richmond, Virginia. Although both sides expected the conflict to be short, the American Civil War was un-der way.

MOVING TOWARD ORGANIZATION

Partly because their experience as Millerites expelled from their churches in 1843 and 1844, many Sabbatarian Adventists opposed any form of church structure beyond the local congregation. They believed it would constitute an apostate, world-conforming "Babylon." Nonetheless, the Whites and several of the itinerating ministers recognized problems that organization could address. They included the financial support of the ministry and evangelism, certification of preachers, the holding of church property, and ownership of the publishing enterprise.[1]

As early as 1851 James White began calling for "church order," including the disciplining of erring church members, and during the next few years local congregations appointed deacons. In 1853 Ellen White wrote a Testimony on "church order," and James published four articles in the *Review* on "gospel order," followed in the spring by a long editorial on the same subject.

After the publishing house moved to Battle Creek in 1855, James White, who technically owned the enterprise, brought to the attention of the publishing board the need for legal incorporation. Meanwhile other issues emerged, including evangelism, which now had the added expense of tents, and the ownership of meetinghouses. In 1859, in an effort to provide more regular financial support for the ministry rather than relying on constant appeals for funds through the *Review*, a Battle Creek conference adopted a plan known as "Systematic Benevolence," which suggested donations scaled to the economic situation of members. Gradually the new approach became established in the local congregations, serving as the primary system of financial support until the adoption of tithing in the late 1870s.

Rudimentary steps toward organization continued. In 1857 the leadership established a Committee of Revision to oversee the publication of books, and two years later James White proposed that yearly state meetings take place. With some local congregations taking steps to establish legal organization, he called a meeting in Battle Creek to choose a name for the church and settle the issues of property holding and ownership of the publishing house. On Saturday evening, September 29, 1860, the group convened, electing Joseph Bates chair and Uriah Smith secretary. After several days of debate, the conference adopted the name Seventh-day

Adventist. Sabbatarian Adventists had achieved the first major step toward organization despite strong opposition.

The following May the next step took place, when another conference organized the Seventh-day Adventist Publishing Association, formed as a joint-stock company under Michigan law and thereby becoming the first legal entity of the fledgling church. The same 1861 meeting recommended that the churches in Michigan form a state conference, which completed its organization in October 1862. Other states followed, so that by early 1863 there existed six state conferences with a total of 3,500 members, 125 churches, and 22 ordained ministers. Such efforts culminated in May 1863 with another meeting of 20 credentialed delegates representing all conferences except Vermont. They voted to unite the state conferences into a General Conference that would hold annual sessions and have three executive officers (president, secretary, and treasurer). After James White declined to serve as president, the session elected John Byington, a self-supporting preacher, to that office, along with Uriah Smith as secretary, and E. S. Walker as treasurer.

SMITH AND ORGANIZATION

As is apparent from his participation in all of the 1860s meetings that culminated in the organization of the new denomination, Uriah Smith supported the Whites in their efforts. In September 1860, shortly before the session that chose the church's name, he published an editorial in the *Review* supporting "a harmony of feeling and a unanimity of sentiment." Clearly criticizing those who opposed organization, he stated that "individual feelings, individual prejudices, and individual views must be held in abeyance to the voice of the body." He concluded that union was "essential to our progress as a people."[2]

In addition to serving as secretary for the organizational meetings, Uriah was also elected to several offices. The 1861 meeting of the publishing association appointed him treasurer, while the following year the Michigan Conference session selected him for a similar position, and in 1863 made him president. That same year the General Conference session chose him as secretary. In addition to his editorial duties at the *Review*, a position to which he was reappointed at a salary of $12.00 per week, it appears that Smith had plenty to occupy his time and that the new denomination regarded his services as indispensable. Then in 1864, when the Michigan Conference elected him to a second term as president, it also recommended that he be ordained to the gospel ministry, a privilege that he declined for another 10 years. For the next several years Smith found himself repeatedly elected to various positions and committees, particularly those handling publication matters.[3]

Despite (or perhaps because of) organization, problems appeared in Iowa, which had formed as a conference in 1863. The president and secretary-treasurer of the conference, B. F. Snook and William H. Brinkerhoff, became increasingly critical of the Whites and the church in Battle Creek. Although Smith was not directly involved in handling the situation, he supported strong steps against what many perceived as "rebellion." After receiving a letter from two members in Iowa, Uriah wrote to James White stating that if the report was correct, "there is deep-dyed iniquity at work in that State. If the Iowa ministers come to Battle Creek to play the spy and then go back to lie and deceive the flock, who are not able to contradict their reports, it is time that something should be done." He encouraged James to go to Iowa "and if you find there any crooked sticks, we hope you will straighten them, if it breaks their necks." Also he reported a proposal that at the next General Conference session delegates be required to take an "Oath of Allegiance to the cause of Present Truth, or be sent home as rebels before the meeting commences." Clearly he believed that the organizational integrity of the new denomination faced grave threats. Neither the Whites nor John N. Loughborough were able to settle the conflict, but George I. Butler was soon elected president of the Iowa Conference and through strenuous efforts brought the matter to an end, although about a third of the members and churches in the state followed Snook and Brinkerhoff out of the denomination.[4]

EDITOR

Despite his other job assignments, Smith's principal responsibility remained editing the *Review*. He did not take the position lightly. As he stated in 1860, "every lover of truth should indeed value the *Review* next to his Bible," for it was the only publication devoted to the exposition of Bible truth.[5] Several months later he put the case for the *Review* even more strongly: "We have truths which we know are in advance of any yet apparent among any other people. When the *Review* goes out, it goes with an object, it goes out to teach truths that are definite and distinct, truths which are to prepare men for the great crisis before us, ripening them for the harvest of the earth, truths upon which God has set His seal, truth which it is the only messenger in the land engaged in proclaiming."[6]

Introducing a new volume of the paper in 1865, Uriah again asserted its purpose in no uncertain terms. "May the *Review* expose uncompromisingly all error, and hold up faithfully the truth. May it reveal and warn against the by-paths of fanaticism and sin, while continually pointing forward to the strait and shining path that leads to glory."[7]

Of the points Smith referred to, the Sabbath was most significant. In advocating the doctrine, he developed no new arguments but took every opportunity to respond to Adventism's critics. Replying in 1860 to a tract by Luther Lee, a Methodist minister, he restated the now-familiar Adventist arguments that there existed no biblical evidence for a change of law, that the Sabbath originated with Creation week, and that the purpose of the Sabbath is for humans to remember their Creator. "It is thus clear that by the substitution of any day of the week for the seventh," he observed, "both the *reason* for the institution, and the *object* for which it is designed, are completely obliterated, and the institution destroyed."[8]

Four years later he similarly reviewed a work by former Sabbath advocate T. M. Preble published in the *World's Crisis*. Smith observed that Preble had had only a faint understanding regarding the Sabbath in the 1840s, which explained why he now regarded it as part of the Jewish ceremonial system. Once again he noted that the Sabbath originated in Creation week before the Fall, and remains a requirement. Although he sought to avoid legalism by saying that the law can be fulfilled only through Christ, he also declared that "Christ does not make us righteous by breaking down God's great standard of righteousness, so that it cannot be shown who is a sinner, but by opening a way whereby our characters can be made to conform to that standard." Although the Pharisees had lowered the standard of the law, Christ stripped "off the traditions of the Pharisees, and [affirmed] the strictness of the old." Furthermore, the disciples kept the Sabbath, Jesus urged obedience to the law, and both Christ and Paul observed the Sabbath. "Suppose then," he concluded, "that the Sabbath is mentioned only historically, such historical facts as these cannot be ignored, and they settle the whole question, they cover the whole ground, and are all that the most fervent lover of the Sabbath could desire."[9]

A second major concern that Smith expressed during the early 1860s was the "state of the dead." Modern spiritualism had emerged with the Fox sisters in Rochester, New York, in 1848 and competed with Adventism and other new religions for the attention of Americans. The threat of spiritualism became especially clear after a leading Adventist minister, Moses Hull, who had debated spiritualists in Battle Creek, defected to their ranks in late 1863. Thus the Adventist advocacy of "soul sleep," known theologically as "conditional immortality," was something that Uriah took seriously.[10]

Adventism's basic position, as expounded by Smith, was that "man was created, not immortal, but '*to be* immortal,' if he will fulfill the will of his Creator, and comply with the conditions upon which life is suspended." Uriah also felt that the doctrine of hell (or "eternal misery," as he called it), which accompanied the belief in natural immortality, drove many people from Christianity, because it seemed so unjust. "Thus is Christianity wounded in the house of its friends," he observed.[11] Smith expanded his ideas in a small book entitled *Which, Mortal or Immortal?* published in 1865. Probably prompted in part by the Hull apostasy, he stated that the subject was especially important because of the spiritualist movement. Furthermore, "upon our views of man's nature depends, in a very great extent, our views of life, death, resurrection, heaven, hell, and all other subjects, in short, of divine revelation." Through the first half of the book he sought to refute the philosophical and biblical arguments in favor of immortality and then constructed an argument for soul sleep based on Scripture. After quoting various texts supporting an unconscious state in death, he emphasized a literal resurrection, an idea he believed incompatible with natural immortality, noted that the wicked would be "*consumed and devoured by fire*," and argued that the doctrine of eternal hellfire was a blot on the character of God.[12] He concluded by referring to the serpent's statement in the Garden of Eden that Eve would not die if she ate the fruit of the tree of the knowledge of good and evil. Commenting on the passage, he asserted that "men are growing suspicious of the truth of a declaration, first uttered by a doubtful character in Eden, perpetuated thence through heathenism, and at last through the medium of the mother of harlots, disseminated through all the veins and channels of orthodoxy. But truth will work its way up, however deeply the rubbish may have been heaped upon it; and before the bright rising of its light, all antiquated superstitious and traditionary dogmas will be exposed in their native deformity.[13]

Prophecy, however, was Smith's overriding concern, particularly as national events unfolded after 1860. In an 1860 editorial Uriah stated that "the object of prophecy is to forewarn the world of things to come, in time for the requisite preparation, and to inspire the people of God with fresh courage as they see the time for the full fruition of their hope drawing nigh. . . .

"Prophecy belongs to that portion of the Bible which may properly be denominated a revelation. It is designed to reveal to us things of which we could not in any other way gain information."[14]

With prophecy primarily predictive in nature, it necessarily needed an interpreter, a responsibility Uriah was happy to assume. He believed that those who were humble and teachable and sought the aid of the Holy Spirit could accurately understand what was written. Calling attention to the Old Testament prophets Daniel, Hosea, Habakkuk, Zephaniah, and Malachi, and the New Testament book of Revelation, he stated that they all "forewarned us of the approach of that great day which bears at once the double freight of vengeance and mercy—vengeance and destruction to His [God's] foes, but mercy and salvation to all His people."[15]

Convinced that the last days were at hand, he in somber and even poetic language sought to impress upon his readers the serious times in which they lived. "As the shades of twilight deepen down gradually into the darkness of night, and as the coming tempest casts a deeper and deeper shadow over the land, so the signs of the times are continually thickening around us, and more and more solemn are the portents of coming events on every side," he wrote in November 1860. "The time draweth near when the King of kings shall visit this revolted province, take the righteous to Himself, and gather out all those who do iniquity and who would not have him to reign over them. We even now hear the distant sound of His approaching chariot-wheels. Signs betoken His return."[16]

The following year he declared that "the crisis is right upon us. Decision must now be made for eternal life or everlasting death." In 1864 he continued the theme of preparation for the end, saying that people were living in a time of shaping and refining their characters until "the great Refiner can see His perfect image reflected from His work." Exhibiting his belief that obedience was the key to salvation, he called on Adventists to receive and follow the Testimonies of Ellen White. Again in 1865 he stated that the student of prophecy recognizes that they are living in the last days, for evil and unbelief were increasing. At no time did Smith express any doubt, despite the continuing passage of time, regarding his belief that the last days were quickly approaching.[17]

THE CIVIL WAR

It was within this apocalyptic framework, combined with his Yankee abolitionist sympathies, that Smith understood the Civil War. Soon after armed conflict broke out he told his readers that they should not expect to find much information on the "cruel war" in the pages of the *Review*. He would try not to let himself get absorbed by the controversy or grow unduly excited about it. Rather, "what we should ever keep before our minds is that every new development of the signs of the times is a fresh evidence that the end of all things and the consummation of our glorious hope are right upon us." Three weeks later he compared secession with the "first seceder," Satan, and noted that "all rightminded and enlightened citizens" condemned the Southern rebellion. "One thing you know: you have had fair warning that this [spirited] rebellion shall be crushed, and the rebels dealt with according to the rigors of God's law, which says that the soul that sinneth it shall die."[18]

In November 1861 he explained the war in a lengthy editorial. He identified slavery as the only reason for the conflict and criticized the United States government for attempting to ignore such a "diabolical iniquity." "Until the North shall cleanse its hands from all the stains of this sin," he argued, "and take a bold stand of uncompromising opposition to its very existence, and seize upon every opportunity to abolish and crush it out, God cannot make bare His arm nor manifest His power to aid them in the struggle." The Lord, he said, was chastising the nation because of slavery and could not be expected to "put forth His hand to build up that nation" until it was clear that it had cleared slavery from the land.[19]

Early in 1862 he called Northerners who supported slavery "semi-traitors," for their efforts undermined the Union cause, producing "inefficiency" and "neglect" to pursue "advantages." A few months later, shortly before the Battle of Antietam and the Emancipation Proclamation, he said that the nation was "receiving a just chastisement" for its "sin of slavery." Because the Lincoln administration was slow in moving against slavery, a policy of which God could not approve, "the nation is learning its present lesson in justice at a fearful cost."[20]

In mid-1863 Smith perceived a contradiction in the nation's spirit, with suffering and death seemingly doing little to stimulate serious reflection and avoidance of pleasure seeking. "God is chastening the nation for its sins, yet who thinks of being humbled. While a deplorable civil war is desolating a large portion of the country, and bereavement, sorrow, and mourning are in tens of thousands of families, the rage for amusement and pleasure, and a disposition to throw off every serious feeling, was never so great, and the exhibitions of the pride of life never so extensive and disgusting."

He spoke of the wealth some were making from the war and the luxuries they purchased, concluding that "the apostle is also careful to state that these days are the last days of this world's existence, and what if our own times answer the description."[21]

By 1865 Uriah noted the progress against slavery, begun by the Emancipation Proclamation, stating that "the nation has been, though slowly, committing itself on the side of right." With this change in policy, God could now act. "And now we ask, Is not the nation taking a position where God can favor it, and crown its efforts with success? Let the late Union victories, and the rebel disasters, answer. Let the crumbling power of the Confederacy answer. Let the fall of Savannah, Wilmington, and Charleston answer. Let the giant grip which Grant holds upon the demon of rebellion before Petersburg and Richmond, while Sherman by his triumphant march through the heart of Georgia and South Carolina deals death-blows to its very vitals, answer."[22]

On April 11 Smith expressed thanks to God "for the visible manifestation of His hand in our national affairs," but warned that there would be no permanent peace. As if confirming his prediction, a week later he was commenting on the assassination of President Abraham Lincoln. "But the murder of our own humane and amiable president has scarcely a parallel in the dark annals of any nation," he lamented. "May we not fear that the quiet and happiness of the nation are gone forever." Although the war had ended, events seemed to confirm the Adventist conviction that progress was a delusion and the world was sinking ever further into confusion and darkness.[23]

DEFENDING THE WHITES

Despite their success in pushing the Sabbatarian Adventists to organize, the Whites encountered severe criticism both during and after the process. As noted previously, James frequently encountered charges that he was enriching himself at the young movement's expense. Finally, the Battle Creek church called a meeting in March 1863, chaired by Smith, which appointed him, G. W. Amadon, and E. S. Walker as a committee to investigate the rumors regarding White's business affairs. Two months later the General Conference also authorized the committee. Smith chaired the investigation, which called for people to bring forth facts to support the accusations against White. Although the invitation appeared in the *Review* during a five-month period, the committee received nothing to confirm the charges. After the publication of a second notice, the committee reported that nothing had emerged to "sustain charges against Bro. White, or justify complaints." Since the committee had no negative evidence, it could "therefore only present some of the testimonials in his [James White's] behalf, to represent the feelings of those toward him who are of the day, not of the night, and who do not fear to come to the light lest their deeds should be made manifest." It observed that such testimonies "show that his course has been almost one continued refusal to accept of means that have been urged upon him, with repeated cautions to those who in the liberality of their hearts desired to contribute to advance the cause of truth which they loved, not to go beyond their ability in so doing." The committee concluded its report by "heartily" commending "Bro. White to the confidence and sympathy of Christians everywhere."[24]

About the same time, Ellen White was also encountering severe criticism, particularly from the "rebels" in Iowa, as well as critics outside the Seventh-day Adventist movement. In response, Smith laid the foundations for his later full-fledged defense of Ellen White. At the moment he sought primarily to establish that Adventists followed the "Bible and the Bible alone," rather than White's writings, and that Scripture itself made a place for "gifts of the spirit." "We do not, then, discard, but obey, the Bible by endorsing the visions," he argued in January 1863. He further asserted that the new denomination's leaders had from the beginning "advocated the doctrine of spiritual gifts in the Christian church, and endorsed Sister White's visions as one of those gifts."[25]

Near the end of the year he explained the purpose of the spiritual gifts. "Thus the object of these gifts is shown to be not merely to establish the Christian church at its beginning, as some contend, but to aid the ministry, edify, unite, and perfect the church all through her pilgrimage; and to continue as long as the church needs comforting, edifying, and perfecting; and until the unity of the faith shall be attained."[26] Within a few years Smith would develop a much more extensive defense of Ellen White, but the arguments he presented in 1863 provided the foundation.

Uriah also tried to protect Ellen White in another way. In 1863 he and George Amadon appealed to readers of the *Review* not to expect answers to every letter that they wrote to her or to try to visit the family whenever they were in Battle Creek. "Brethren, others, as well as Bro. White, beg a portion of your company when in Battle Creek. Inquire for U. Smith or G. W. Amadon, who will entertain you or direct you where you may be entertained." Let the Whites rest, they urged.[27]

PERSONAL LIFE

Although it must have seemed that Smith's entire life was bound up with the *Review* and denominational organization, he managed to carve out some time for himself. In 1861 his first son, Uriah Wilton, was born, followed by Leon Alberti two years later. The same year that Leon was born, Uriah patented his first invention, an artificial leg. Prior to this time he wore a cork leg with a foot that had no joint. As John N. Loughborough recalled many years later, Uriah told him "how awkward it is to have a foot with no joint for the toes! It is hard to kneel and rise with such a straight foot." Believing that a leg could be made with the appropriate joints, Smith went to work and succeeded in producing one whose patent he sold to George Rhorer, a manufacturer of cork legs located in Cincinnati. The advertisement for the leg stated: "Nature Imitated. Smith's Artificial Leg. Unparalleled Simplicity of Construction. A Perfect Action Secured Without Bolt or Spring." Among the advantages claimed for the prothesis were that the knee joint would "bend back to the full extent of the natural limb," "A solid and continuous support of wood is obtained from the body to the ground," "all springs in the leg are disposed with," and "lightness." It sold for $75 with a plain finish and $100 with an "extra finish." Presumably Civil War injuries helped create a market. Proceeds from the invention enabled Smith to purchase a new home next door to the Review and Herald building.[28]

Harriet kept a diary during 1866 that gives a few glimpses into their family life. On February 3 she recorded doing washing Saturday evening, with "Uriah turning the machine." In March, after visiting Martha Amadon and her new baby, she stated that she "felt as I returned through the cold and sleet that I had a dear and happy retreat from the world without in my beloved home with my precious children and beloved husband." She occasionally mentioned health matters, commenting in March that she had administered a "water treatment" on Uriah for a cold and the following month expressed a more general concern over his health. During May she wrote that she had a "conversation with Uriah in relation to pecuniary matters. I am sorry to see him cumbered with debt. I fear I am not as careful as I should be in the use of means." From May to June her husband traveled constantly, and she frequently expressed appreciation for his letters, saying such things as being "cheered" by a letter and receiving another "letter from my faithful Uriah." That June she said that "the thought of meeting him soon is happiness indeed." Clearly she and her husband had a close emotional bond.

The diary also recorded lesser matters. In April Harriet told of looking "up articles of clothing for the destitute Negro freedmen. Found 20 pieces or more." That same month she wrote that Uriah commented that her new hat was too small. Somewhat surprisingly, given Adventist attitudes toward entertainment and her husband's frequent editorials condemning such activities, in October she told of taking her boys to a fair at which they enjoyed the horse trotting and "went into a side show for their jokes." In December she reported that she attended an exhibition at which she saw "the Siamese twins [the conjoined Chang and Eng Bunker], the Carolina twins [the conjoined Millie and Christine McCoy, known as "The Two-headed Nightingale" and "The Eighth Wonder of the World"], the wild Australians [Aborigines], and the Scottish queen [probably a reenactment of Mary, Queen of Scots]. Felt well paid for going." That same month she made some Christmas purchases and on December 31 had turkey "in common with others to celebrate the new year." Throughout the year she also made frequent references to sewing for extra income, cooking, and dealing with minor family illnesses, all of which led her to sometimes skip "meeting," presumably a reference to Sabbath services. Unfortunately, Harriet did not maintain her diary in subsequent years, and we therefore have limited glimpses into her family life.[29]

HEALTH ISSUES

The long hours, financial pressures, and personal and theological conflicts eventually took their toll on the Seventh-day Adventist leaders. Although Joseph Bates, John N. Loughborough, and J. P. Kellogg experimented variously with vegetarianism and hydrotherapy, Adventists had no general concern with health reform until 1863. Ellen White's sons had come down with diphtheria in early 1863, which she treated successfully with hydrotherapy after reading an article, "Diphtheria, Its Causes, Treatment, and Cure," by Dr. James Caleb Jackson, which the *Review* reprinted in its February 17 issue. During the next few months Smith ran two excerpts advocating two meals a day and a vegetarian diet from *Hall's Journal of Health*. It is clear, therefore, that increased interest in health had emerged by mid-1863, at least among the editors of the church paper.[30]

In early June 1863 Ellen White experienced a vision at the Aaron Hilliard home near Otsego, Michigan, in which she received instructions regarding health, including reduction in workload and more temperate eating, drinking, and use of drugs. Adventists should regard water as God's medicine, she learned. Encouraged by Dr. H. S. Lay, White eventually reported what she had seen and heard about two weeks later, but did not publish her account of the vision for another year and a half. Meanwhile, she traveled extensively, talking about the need for health reform. Unfortunately, both Henry and Willie came down with pneumonia in 1863 and 1864, with Henry dying in December 1863. Smith preached the funeral sermon in which he drew a lesson for the young: "I would then say to them, Look upon these relics of mortality, these emblems of the grave, and ask yourselves if you have an guarantee of life which he had not."[31]

The J. N. Andrews family had sent their son to Dr. Jackson's water cure,

Our Home on the Hillside, in Dansville, New York, and may have suggested that the Whites visit the institution. In September 1864 they began a stay of three weeks at the Home, observing the hydrotherapy techniques and listening to Jackson's lectures. Impressed by what they saw, James and Ellen returned to Battle Creek enthusiastic promoters of health reform. Despite their newfound advocacy, James White and other Adventist leaders began to experience illness. Most serious of all, James suffered a stroke on August 15, 1865, after which Ellen White, Uriah and Harriet Smith, M. J. and Cornelia Cornell, and Martha Amadon took care of him for several weeks at his home. With only limited improvement in her husband's health, Ellen decided to take him to Dr. Jackson's establishment.[32]

On September 14 "a Seventh-day invalid party" composed of James and Ellen White, J. N. Loughborough, Uriah Smith, Dr. H. S. Lay, and Sister M. F. Maxson boarded the train at the Battle Creek station. The *Review* described them as "overworked and overburdened servants of the Lord."[33] Apparently not afflicted with any particular illness, Smith seems to have accompanied the group because of a need for a vacation. Writing to his *Review* readers, he noted that he had been confined to the paper's office for 10 years, his largest absence having been "but a few days." Advised by friends about the need for some relaxation from office duties, he undertook the journey to Dansville, leaving the *Review* in the hands of George Amadon and Adelia Van Horn. The group arrived in Rochester at 7:00 a.m. on September 15 and spent the Sabbath there. Delayed leaving the city by inclement weather, they did not arrive in Dansville until September 20, having taken the train to Wayland and completing the trip by stagecoach.[34]

Smith reported that they had difficulty procuring rooms but received a cordial welcome from Dr. Jackson. After physical examinations, Jackson said that James White would need six to eight months for recovery and John N. Loughborough five to six months. "But the editor of the *Review*, unfortunately for its readers, is to be let off in five or six weeks." The ministers, including D. T. Bourdeau, who had joined the group from Vermont, met three times each day to pray for James. The General Conference had set aside October 14 as a day of fasting and prayer for White, and Loughborough, Smith, and Bourdeau prayed for their leader throughout the afternoon in a grove near Our Home. Smith reported that he was leaving Dansville on October 17 after a "most pleasant and agreeable" stay, although he could not participate in the amusements it provided. "We leave, feeling refreshed and invigorated by our stay, though short, and persuaded, from what we have seen, heard, and experienced, that whoever is within reach of hygienic influences can receive the full benefit of such influence at that place." He also informed his readers that Loughborough and Bordeau were improving.[35]

Before returning to Battle Creek, Uriah traveled to West Wilton, New Hampshire, to visit his mother, arriving there on October 19. While he was in West Wilton, J. N. Andrews invited him to attend a debate in Portland, Maine, between M. E. Cornell and T. M. Preble regarding the Sabbath, beginning on November 6 and lasting eight sessions. It was Smith's first visit to Maine, and he expressed delight at meeting the company of Sabbathkeepers. On Sabbath, November 11, and Sunday, November 12, Andrews spoke three times, while Cornell and a Brother Howard spoke once each. On the thirteenth Smith visited the residence of the Howlands, early Sabbatarian believers, in Topsham, returning to Portland the next day. Although planning to leave on the fifteenth, he received a request to conduct a funeral service. He spent the following Sabbath in West Wilton, leaving on the twenty-seventh for Battle Creek and arriving there on December 5. "We return refreshed in body and mind," he wrote, "to engage with new vigor in a work which we love, and in which our whole interest is centered."[36]

But James White did not improve, and Ellen became increasingly dissatisfied with Our Home. She did not like the dancing, card playing, and other amusements to which Smith had alluded, but, more important, she did not agree with the complete bed rest that Dr. Jackson had prescribed for her husband. On December 5, after James had suffered a particularly bad night, the Whites left for Rochester, where they stayed with Adventist friends for the next three weeks. On Christmas Eve Ellen experienced a vision revealing to her that Adventists should establish their own water-cure establishment, one free of Dansville's evil influences. On New Year's Day, 1866, the Whites took the train from Rochester to Battle Creek where James gradually regained some of his strength. A year later, in the spring of 1867, they purchased a farm in Greenville, Michigan, which allowed Ellen to push her husband into more vigorous activity.[37]

THE WESTERN HEALTH REFORM INSTITUTE

At the General Conference session in May 1866 Ellen White called on the church to establish its own water cure. John N. Loughborough, president of the Michigan Conference, headed the fund-raising drive, and within a short time the denomination purchased property on the outskirts of Battle Creek. During September the *Review* reported the opening of the Western Health Reform Institute. Meanwhile, Smith had placed his paper clearly behind the project. In June he wrote that "the great subject of health reform is getting to be well defined and clear, by the light of which all will be enabled to adjust their labors to their physical capabilities, and thus have the surest guarantee against breaking down and becoming inefficient in the future."[38]

By January 1867 the institute had filled to capacity and its director, Horatio S. Lay, proposed to *Review* readers the construction of a new building that could house an additional 100 patients. At the end of the month Uriah Smith called for 1,000 people to buy a $25 share each. "A large new building is essential to the future success of the Institute," he observed, "and now is the time to be getting the materials for the same." A few days later he wrote to Ellen White, stating that he, Loughborough, George Amadon, and J. M. Aldrich had consulted together regarding the institute and agreed that the Adventist people were waiting for her to address a testimony on the subject, particularly dealing with the issue of whether it was part of the Adventist Church's mission or simply an enterprise for investment.[39]

Ellen White responded by stating that "the health reform, I was shown, is a part of the third angel's message and is just as closely connected with it as are the arm and hand with the human body." She further said that Sabbatarians should "provide a home for the afflicted and those who wish to learn how to take care of their bodies that they may prevent sickness" and not be forced to "go to popular water cure institutions for the recovery of health, where there is no sympathy for our faith." It was sufficient endorsement for the leaders to move ahead. Reflecting White's perspective, Smith, in response to a *Review* reader who suggested that the new emphasis indicated that Adventists did not really believe that Jesus was returning soon, responded that health reform was indeed part of the preparation for His coming. On April 9 he signed articles of incorporation and purchased two shares of stock at $25 each. A meeting of the stockholders took place at the *Review* office on April 25, chaired by J. N. Loughborough with Smith serving as secretary. The stockholders then elected Loughborough president of the association and Uriah as secretary, along with five other directors. Smith further served on a committee to prepare a stock book and procure a seal.[40]

By the middle of August construction had finished the basement and first floor of the new building. Although they had purchased sufficient lumber to complete the three stories, money for other construction had run out. The directors planned to make another plea to the church membership to buy stock. But hardly had the project begun when Ellen White began to express reservations. In May she had written another testimony expressing her "alarm" that the leaders were moving ahead too quickly. "We should have such an institution," she stated, "small at its commencement and cautiously increased, as good physicians and helpers could be procured and means raised." In writing her earlier testimony she had "yielded my judgment to that of others. . . . In this I did wrong." Her message apparently took the directors by surprise, and E. S. Walker, the secretary, wrote to James White in September, protesting that to stop the project now would result in the loss of considerable money, and requesting his support for at least putting a roof over the building. James, however, insisted that the entire structure be torn down, something that was soon completed.[41]

BECOMING A PREACHER

Although Smith claimed that he had no talent for preaching, he soon found himself drawn into that role. In 1865 a stranger arrived at the *Review* office requesting an Adventist minister to conduct a funeral service in Climax Prairie (now Climax, Michigan). Because all of the ministers were out of town, someone suggested Smith, who eventually accepted the invitation. "I am not a preacher," he said, "but under the circumstances I will go and read a few scriptures, and excuse the matter." Later the individual who had made the request reported that "if that man's talk is an excuse for a sermon, we don't know what a sermon would be, for that excuse was the best funeral discourse we ever heard."[42]

Gradually, despite his inclinations but encouraged by Ellen White, who thought that he needed personal contact with the people, Smith increasingly engaged in public speaking. An 1867 meeting in Wisconsin prompted attendees to adopt a resolution stating "that we consider it a great privilege to be favored with a visit from our much esteemed Bro. U. Smith." That same year he commented that he had left a meeting at Mount Pleasant, Iowa, attended by some 1,000 people on Sunday, "feeling also rested and refreshed by the brief relaxation we have enjoyed."[43] In October he had crossed the Mississippi River at Rock Island, Illinois, to breathe "the pure air of Iowa and [set] our eyes on its boundless prairies." After attending the meeting at Pilot Grove, he reported to the *Review*, "It has been a great privilege to us to see the faces of many friends of the truth, with whose names we have long been familiar. May an acquaintance, commenced through the *Review,* that good medium of communication among the little flock, and now strengthened by the privilege of seeing each other's face, and grasping the friendly hand, be perpetuated forever in the kingdom of heaven."[44]

Clearly, getting away from the confines of Battle Creek and the *Review* office did Smith good, although after the Johnstown Center meeting in September he wrote Harriett regarding some health issues. "The first two days of the meeting I had some difficulty not with a 'little indigestion,' but with a little poor circulation, cold feet, and toward the close of the day and until bedtime, quite a severe headache. Sabbath morning I put on my drawers, which has helped the matter right along."[45]

In June 1868, Smith traveled to the Whites' home in Greenville, about 70 miles north of Battle Creek, where he stayed for a few weeks to help James in the writing of *Life Incidents*. With the Whites, Smith also attended a July meeting at Wright, Michigan, that introduced a discussion of camp meetings. Because such meetings were frequently accompanied with rowdy behavior, Adventists had been reluctant to adopt them. But they apparently overcame their skepticism, for what has been traditionally regarded as the first official Seventh-day Adventist camp meeting took place at Wright the following September. That same year, Smith reported attending meetings in Bushnell and Greenville, Michigan.[46]

In 1869 he traveled frequently with the Whites, J. N. Andrews, and W. H. Littlejohn, a blind Adventist minister. Reporting on a meeting in Orange, Michigan, which he described as part of an experiment whereby two-day meetings would convene in several places across the state, he observed that the attendance was not as large as hoped. Nonetheless, he said that "the brethren and sisters present seem to be firmly established in the truth, but have to regret a backwardness and lack of energy in the work. But all feel that it is time we all awake from the state of stupor, and discharge the high responsibilities rolled upon us by the knowledge of the truth."[47]

After going to Alaiedon, Michigan, with Littlejohn, he observed that the believers there needed the visit of a minister. Other meetings took the two men to Greenville, St. Charles, and Owosso. At the latter town Uriah reported that they gave 27 discourses, sold $13.04 in books, and had an attendance that ranged between 50 and 300, despite the fact that some local ministers forbade their church members to attend. Smith also participated in what he described as the second camp meeting of the season, which had eight "preaching brethren" present and drew 1,500 to its Sunday services. Although he observed that some attendees at the camp meeting came late and some left early, there was a "deep feeling in the congregation," especially on Sabbath.[48]

Despite their benefits, the separation from his family that such camp meeting tours entailed were hard on both Uriah and his wife. In September 1870 he invited her to join him for the weekend. "There will be a bed in the Ings' tent," he said. With wry humor he pleaded, "Now come. There are other bipeds no better looking than I, who have the privilege of having their wives with them at camp meeting, [and] I would like to have mine here to . . . I think it would do you good to come [and] that you would enjoy it." Whether she joined him is not known. The following year she expressed a desire to be with Uriah, but was dealing with illness at home. In addition to a toothache of her own, both Annie (Uriah and Harriet's daughter) and Wilton had come down with the measles. Annie was getting both "better and crosser," she reported. "She is now just getting so that I can live with her at great effort." Harriet said that she had just read Mark Twain's *Innocents Abroad,* and that if Uriah were there she would "enquire how to account for such great armies [and] battles as the Bible speaks of raised in so small a territory."[49]

DEFENDING THE WHITES, AGAIN

During their time in Greenville, tensions accumulated between the Whites and the Battle Creek church. In March 1867 Ellen had written a testimony criticizing Review and Herald publishing house employees for conducting private business affairs and warned that Satan was seeking to gain a foothold in the office. The following May she composed another testimony admonishing the workers for "lightness and folly, joking and laughing." She felt, however, that neither testimony had had its intended effect.[50]

Reporting on her experiences between April and October 1867, she noted that "jealousy still existed" in the Battle Creek church. When they could not sell their home in Battle Creek, James had written to various people in an effort to borrow money. "For this they condemned him and charged him with the sin of grasping for money." During the annual General Conference session, "most looked upon us, especially my husband, with suspicion. Some persons of influence manifested a disposition to crush us." Clearly, relations with the congregation's membership were not good.[51]

In September 1867 the Whites addressed the church, speaking "freely of the wrongs that have been insinuating themselves into our midst. A good blow was struck at some of the things which are sapping the vitality of the church, such as amusements, an unsanctified passion for music and other things through which there is a growing connection between us and the world." The following month the Whites returned for a series of 12 meetings. "There has not been anything which has seemed to be too excited and flashy," Smith reported, "but a calm and candid consideration of wrongs which have led to spiritual declension, and an earnest and persistent purpose to put them away." At the close of the meetings the church leaders wrote a letter to the Whites confessing their wrongs. Signed by a committee of six, it had been unanimously adopted by the Battle Creek church on October 21, 1867. "We now accept with deep sorrow of heart the reproof given us in this testimony," it stated, "and we ask that wherein we have erred from the right, through our lack of spiritual discernment, we may find forgiveness of God and His people." Nearly a year later, on September 7, 1868, the church passed a resolution inviting the Whites to return to Battle Creek "to lead out in the work of the Third Message" and expressing regret "that lack of sympathy on our part in their affliction was one great cause of their removal from us."[52]

Meanwhile, Smith had been working on a more complete defense of

Ellen White against both Adventist and outside detractors. In 1866 he had read much of his manuscript to the General and Michigan state conferences, at which it received the approval of the "ministering brethren." He stated that he had not consulted with Ellen White. Rather, "we take the visions as they are published, and base our explanation of any apparent discrepancy on the language as it stands." He then ran a series of articles ("The Visions—Objections Answered") between June 12 and July 31, 1866, followed by occasional additional ones. In September of that year, for instance, he stated that "we are confident that we can show that there is no discrepancy whatever between the teachings of the visions and the Bible." The following year he declared that "whatever theory enters into our system of belief, we prove by the Bible and the Bible alone. The visions are not given for the purpose of establishing a rule of faith, and are not designed to be quoted for that purpose." And in 1868, about the time of the publication of his book, he said that the "work of the visions is to correct errors, restrain from sin, expose hidden evils, and their self-deception from the sinner and the careless professor." Uriah had composed his book upon such assumptions.[53]

The Visions of Mrs. E. G. White, published in 1868, began with some general, foundational points. Smith affirmed that Adventists not only believed in the gifts of the Spirit, but considered them to be as important as the doctrines of revelation and the Sabbath, among others. The gifts manifested themselves in the visions of Ellen White, he asserted. "Every test which can be brought to bear upon such manifestations, proves these genuine. The evidence which supports them, internal and external, is conclusive. They agree with the Word of God, and with themselves. They are given, unless those best qualified to judge are invariably deceived, when the Spirit of God is especially present. They are free from the disgusting contortions and grimaces which attend the counterfeit manifestations of spiritualism. Calm, dignified, impressive, they commend themselves to every beholder, as the very opposite of that which is false or fanatical. The instrument is herself above jugglery or deceit."

Not only were the visions not caused by mesmerism or disease, as some charged, but they also produced good results (or "fruit" in Smith's parlance), promoting pure morality, leading people to the Bible and Christ, and bringing "comfort and consolation to many hearts."[54]

The author argued that the Bible teaches that although visions are a gift of the Spirit for the last days, one should not consider them an addition to the Bible. "Any subsequent instruction given by the Lord to His people through visions, dreams, tongues, or any of the operations of His Spirit would no more be an addition to the book of Revelation than the Revelation was an addition to the book of Daniel."[55]

After these general points, much of the remainder of the book addressed specific objections to Ellen White's writings. A few examples will illustrate Smith's style of argument. With regard to the "shut door," he denied that the visions taught that it represented the end of probation. "Again, on pp. 24 and 25, of *Experiences and Views,* we have a vision of the open and shut door. This plainly sets forth the fact that when the door of the holy place of the sanctuary in heaven was closed, the door into the Most Holy Place was opened, and since that time, the commandments have been shining out to God's people, and they are being tested on the Sabbath question."[56]

Responding to charges that White had said slavery would never cease, he stated that Ellen White had only said that it looked "like an impossibility" that slavery would be done away with. Furthermore, "men of quite as much erudition and scope of discernment as any who are now engaged in a petty warfare against the visions assert and reiterate, from personal knowledge of things in the South, that slavery is as much a fact today, in some portions of those states, as it was five years ago; that it is abolished only in name. It is beginning to *look* even to some of these like an impossibility, under the present state of things, for it to be done away."[57]

As a final example, he sought to explain White's statement regarding the "amalgamation" of man and beast. The visions, he stated, do not teach that some human beings are not human. "If they did, they could easily be silenced by a reference to such cases as the wild Bushmen of Africa, some tribes of the Hottentots, and perhaps the Digger Indians of our own country, etc. Moreover, naturalists affirm that the line of demarcation between the human and animal races is lost in confusion. It is impossible, as they affirm, to tell just where the human ends and the animal begins. Can we suppose that this was so ordained of God in the beginning? Rather has not sin marred the boundaries of these two kingdoms?"[58]

Smith went on to explain that "we are to take all races and peoples as we find them. And those who manifest sufficient powers of mind to show that they are moral and accountable beings are of course to be esteemed as objects of regard and philanthropic effort. We are bound to labor, so far as in our power, for the improvement of their mental, moral, and physical condition. Whatever race of men we may take, Bushmen, Hottentots, Patagonians, or any class of people, however low they may apparently be in the scale of humanity, their mental capabilities are in every instance the basis on which we are to work, and by which we determine whether they are subjects of moral government or not."[59]

Uriah closed his arguments by reasserting that the visions did not replace the Bible. We must, he said, judge all things by the Bible. "All gifts of the Spirit in the church must be thus tested. Now it is evident that that which tests occupies a higher position than that which is tested by it. This, in one word, expresses our view of the relative position which the Bible and the visions sustain to each other. But when a manifestation accords with the Word, and gives every evidence that it is a genuine manifestation of the Spirit of God, we submit it to the objector himself to say how far we may regard it lightly or despise or transgress its teachings with impunity."[60]

Overall, Smith focused on close arguments about the language of Ellen White, mostly in *Experience and Views*, usually contending that the objector was misinterpreting her, ignoring the context of a statement, or overlooking relevant facts. The volume ended with an appendix that included several testimonies from associates regarding Ellen White and her work.

But she was not the only issue. Her husband also continued to face accusations of personally profiting from church activities. Similar to his actions in 1863, Uriah again stepped forward, this time with J. H. Waggoner and J. N. Andrews, to examine White's case and prepare a response. As done previously, the committee ran announcements in the *Review and Herald* inviting people to bring forth evidence against James. Once again they did not receive any negative responses. In its resulting pamphlet, published in 1870, the committee stated that although White had sold Bibles and Bible concordances, dictionaries, and atlases to supplement his income, he had not "appropriated any of the [denominational] funds passing through his hands to his own personal benefit. Every dollar of such money he has scrupulously accounted for to the proper persons appointed by our Association or General Conference to receive and examine such accounts." The pamphlet quoted a General Conference action on March 15, 1870, to "express our high regard for the labors of Bro. James White, not only as a minister and a writer, but also for his efficient management of our publishing department; and we further express our perfect confidence in his integrity as an honest man and a devoted Christian; and we request him to accept the oversight of our business affairs for the coming year." In the mind of the committee, White stood vindicated.[61]

Unfortunately for Smith, his efforts to defend the Whites did not protect him from the difficulties of working with James, whose personality his strokes had negatively affected. Consequently, for the next few years, Uriah endured a particularly difficult time.

---

[1] The following account of the development of Seventh-day Adventist organization is drawn largely from Godfrey T. Anderson, "Sectarianism and Organization, 1846-1864," in *Adventism in America: A History*, ed. Gary Land (Grand Rapids: Wm. B. Eerdmans, 1986), pp. 46-65.

[2] *RH*, Sept. 4, 1860, p. 124.

[3] *RH*, Oct. 9, 1860, pp. 161-163; Oct. 16, 1860, pp. 169-171; Oct. 23, 1860, pp. 177-179; May 28, 1861, p. 16; Apr. 30, 1861, p. 189; Oct. 8, 1861, pp. 148, 149; Oct. 14, 1862, pp. 156, 157; *RH*, May 26, 1863, p. 206; May 31, 1864, pp. 1, 2, 6; May 23, 1865, pp. 196-198.

[4] US to JW, June 13, 1865; *RH*, Jan. 23, 1866, p. 63; Emmett K. VandeVere, "Years of Expansion, 1865-1885," in *Adventism in America*, ed. Land, p. 75.

[5] *RH*, Nov. 20, 1860, p. 4.

[6] *RH*, May 21, 1861, p. 4.

[7] *RH*, June 6, 1865, p. 4.

[8] *RH*, Nov. 27, 1860, p.12.

[9] *RH*, Mar. 29, 1864, pp. 137, 138; Apr. 19, 1864, p. 163; May 17, 1864, p. 194; May 31, 1864, p.5.

[10] *RH*, Mar. 25, 1862, p. 133; Jan. 5, 1864, pp. 45, 46; Jan. 12, 1864, p. 56. For the history of spiritualism, see Ruth Brandon, *The Spiritualists: The Passion for the Occult in the Nineteenth and Twentieth Centuries* (New York: Knopf, 1983).

[11] *RH*, July 30, 1861, p. 68; Jan. 28, 1862, p. 69.

[12] US, *Which, Mortal or Immortal? or, An Inquiry Into the Present Constitution and Future Condition of Man*, 3rd ed. (Battle Creek, Mich.: Steam Press of the Seventh-day Adventist Pub. Assn., 1865), pp. iv, 7, 75-103.

[13] *Ibid.*, p. 111.

[14] *RH*, May 29, 1860, p. 1.

[15] *Ibid.*; *RH*, Aug. 13, 1861, p. 86.

[16] *RH*, Nov. 13, 1860, p. 204.

[17] *RH*, Apr. 29, 1861, p. 157; Sept. 6, 1864, p. 116; July 11, 1865, p. 45.

[18] *RH*, May 7, 1861, p. 196; May 28, 1861, pp. 12, 13. For a one-volume history of the American Civil War, see James M. McPherson, *Battle Cry of Freedom: The Civil War Era* (New York: Oxford Univ. Press, 1988).

[19] *RH*, Nov. 12, 1861, pp. 188, 189.

[20] *RH*, Feb. 4. 1862, pp. 77, 78; Aug. 12, 1862, p. 85.

[21] *RH*, July 7, 1863, p. 44.

[22] *RH*, Mar. 14, 1865, p. 116.

[23] *RH*, Apr. 11, 1865, p. 148; Apr. 18, 1865, p. 156.

[24] *RH*, Mar. 31, 1863, p. 141; Aug. 18, 1863, p. 96; US, GWA, and E. S. Walker, *Vindication of the Business Career of Elder James White* (Battle Creek, Mich.: Steam Press of the Seventh-day Adventist Pub. Assn., 1863), pp. 9, 38, 39.

[25] *RH*, Jan. 13, 1863, pp. 52, 53.

[26] *RH*, Dec. 8, 1863, p. 12.

[27] *RH*, Aug. 4, 1863, pp. 77, 78.

[28] *RH*, Apr. 7, 1903, p. 8. The patent, no. 39,361, and a copy of the advertisement are located in the Smith/Bovee Collection, Box 3, Fld. 45. Barbara J. Becker reprints an October 24, 1863, *Scientific American* article on Smith's artificial leg (faculty.humanities. uci.edu/ bjbecker/NatureandArtifice/lecture19.html). Three years later Smith patented "Smith's Parallel Ruler," which "combines within itself an improved parallel ruler, square, quadrant, calipers, and compasses." The invention does not appear to have been manufactured.

[29] HS, diary, 1866.

[30] Unless otherwise noted, the following account is based on R. L. Numbers, *Prophetess of Health*, pp. 127-155.

[31] *RH*, Dec 15, 1863, p. 24; US, "An Address at the Funeral of Henry N. White, Battle Creek, Michigan, December 21, 1863," in *An Appeal to Youth* (n.p., n.d.), p. 11.

[32] *RH*, Aug. 22, 1865, p. 96; Nov. 7, 1865, p. 180.

[33] *RH*, Sept. 19, 1865, p. 128.

[34] *RH*, Sept. 26, 1865, pp. 132, 136.

[35] *RH*, Oct. 3, 1865, p. 140; Oct. 24, 1865, p. 164.

[36] *RH*, Oct. 31, 1865, p. 172; Dec. 12, 1865, p. 12.

[37] Numbers, pp. 153, 154.

[38] *RH*, Sept. 11, 1866, p. 116; June 5, 1866, p. 4. For the early history of the Western Health Reform Institute, see Numbers, pp. 156-183.

[39] *RH,* Jan. 29, 1867, p. 90; US to EGW, Feb. 5, 1867.

[40] EGW, *Testimonies for the Church* (Mountain View, Calif.: Pacific Press Pub. Assn., 1948), vol. 1, pp. 486, 489; *RH*, Mar. 5, 1867, p. 150; May 28, 1867, pp. 279-281.

[41] EGW, *Testimonies*, vol. 1, pp. 558, 563. Although E. S. Walker signed himself as secretary of the Western Health Reform Institute in an appeal for money (*RH*, Aug. 27, 1867, p. 169), I have been unable to find a record of when he took over that position.

[42] *RH*, May 5, 1903, p. 8.

[43] *RH*, Oct. 1, 1867, p. 248; Oct. 15, 1867, p. 280.

[44] *RH*, Oct. 8, 1867, p. 264.

[45] US to HS, Sept. 23, 1867.

[46] *RH*, June 23, 1868, p. 8; July 14, 1868, p. 56; Sept. 15, 1868, p. 172; July 6 [7], 1868, pp. 40, 41; July 21, 1868, p. 72.

[47] *RH*, June 22, 1869, p. 207.

[48] *RH*, June 29, 1869, p. 8; July 6, 1869, p. 16; July 27, 1869, p. 37; Aug. 24, 1869, p. 72; Aug. 31, 1869, pp. 77, 78.

[49] US to HS, Sept. 27 [1870]; HS to US, [no day or month], 1871.

[50] EGW, *Testimonies*, vol. 1, pp. 585-592.

[51] *Ibid.*, pp. 592-597.

[52] *Ibid.*, pp. 609-612; *RH,* Oct. 22, 1867, p. 292; Battle Creek church to JW and EGW, Sept. 7, 1868.

[53] *RH*, June 12, 1866, p. 16; June 12, 1866, pp. 9, 10; June 19, 1866, pp. 17-19; June 26, 1866, pp. 25-27; July 3, 1866, pp. 33, 34; July 10, 1866, pp. 41, 42; July 31, 1866, pp. 65-67; Sept. 25, 1866, p. 132; July 30, 1867, p. 104; Sept. 29, 1868, p. 188.

[54] US, *The Visions of Mrs. E. G. White: A Manifestation of Spiritual Gifts According to the Scriptures* (Battle Creek, Mich.: Steam Press of the Seventh-day Adventist Pub. Assn., 1868), pp. 3-7.

[55] *Ibid.*, p. 15.

[56] *Ibid.*, pp. 20, 38.

[57] *Ibid.*, pp. 52, 53.

[58] *Ibid*, p. 103.

[59] *Ibid.*, p. 104.

[60] *Ibid.*, pp. 127, 128.

[61] J. H. Waggoner, J. N. Andrews, US, *Defense of Eld. James White and Wife—Vindication of Their Moral and Christian Character* (Battle Creek, Mich.: Steam Press of the Seventh-day Adventist Pub. Assn., 1870), pp. 7, 9, 22, 23, 77.

CHAPTER V

TRIALS AND RECONCILIATION, 1870-1880

When the 1867 General Conference session did not reelect James White as president of the church, he resigned his position as head of the publishing board, and J. M. Aldrich replaced him. During the next two years the publishing association raised salaries significantly without compensating with the prices of its publications. Consequently, debts piled high. When once again elected church president, White discovered the financial problems, and he worked frantically to improve the situation. Aldrich resigned within a few months, and White took over the publishing operation. In the process of stabilizing the financial situation, he seems to have held Smith responsible for many of the problems. Unfortunately, with one exception, we have only Smith's letters and thus know only his side of the story.

CONFLICT WITH JAMES WHITE

In April 1869 Uriah responded to a letter from James that apparently asserted that the church was driving him to "poverty and beggary." Smith pointed out that the General Conference had pledged him the sum of $18 a week, which he could have drawn on at any time. More personally, James also charged Smith with taking a neutral stand regarding publishing house issues. Smith protested that "if you mean that where I have clearly perceived the right, I have shrunk from standing up for it from personal consideration, or from fear of my reputation, or from any motive of this kind, I do NOT plead guilty to the charge. If you mean that, in cases where I could not be positive one way or the other, I have not taken either side, as in the case of your conversation with Bro. Aldrich respecting his leaving the office, I do not see how I could do otherwise. You are positive that it is as you have it, and he is equally positive that it is the other way. It would be presumption in me to undertake to decide whose memory is correct in the matter, so in such cases, I advocate neither one side nor the other."

White had also accused Harriet of having "studiously" occupied "neutral ground." Uriah responded that family matters occupied her time and that her understanding of the situation would have come from Smith himself. Finally, regarding the Health Reform Institute, he said that "the board overruled Aldrich regarding building of the institute. All charges should go against Smith and the rest of the board."[1]

A few days later Uriah wrote to Ellen White, telling her that he had read her most recent letter with "very painful feelings. I fail to find in it a single syllable of anything else but censure, condemnation, and distrust. I do not say that we are not deserving of all this; but if we are, what grounds of courage have we for any further efforts?" He further stated that for the past several years he and Harriet had tried to be friends with and had defended the Whites, but now that he was "being accused of having no elements of hope in my case, no backbone, no principle underlying my actions, etc., I can but feel grieved to say the least. And the question will force itself upon my mind, 'What have I to hope for? And why may I not as well quit at once?'" After explaining that others had determined the wages of Homer Aldrich and Charles Jones, he went on to say, "That the Lord has been with you, blessed your labors, called you out to lead, etc., I have not doubted nor questioned. We do not need more evidence of this. But this is not saying that you cannot, in particular things, err and misjudge. And now, since you have no confidence in us, and say you cannot trust us, and have no hope that we will do any better in the future, I see no other issue but that we should vacate our places in favor of those who can fill them. Self-respect, to say nothing of the interests of the cause, demands that we should do so. And I for one am ready to do this, rather than that you should longer be burdened, and the cause hindered by my lack of discernment and misjudgment."[2]

In early May, Smith wrote again to James White, commenting that rather than talking directly with them, he had sent letters to him and Ellen, because they were 80 miles away. "It is simply because of the sharp letter of yourself and Sister White to me since you went away. It is this that has drawn them out. I never designed to make them known to anybody, but your letters compelled me to say something or receive censure for things to which I do not plead guilty. What I have said has been simply in self-defense." He had not spoken publicly, because he did not want to be perceived as opposing James. "But of two things I am certain— "(1) that your place is in Battle Creek, and (2) that if we cannot co-operate, it is my place to leave, not yours."[3]

The only letter that we have from James regarding the controversy is an undated fragment that appears to have been composed about this time. We also do not know to whom it was directed, but it very strongly condemned Smith's actions and attitude: "Bro. Smith has shown but little patience and forbearance toward me in this matter. However wrong it might be proved that I have been one who has caused . . . so much suffering much of the time for more than fifteen years (the numerous testimonies are sufficient authority), while at the same time I have been trying to help him in every way possible, would appear to good advantage in manifesting some degree of patience and forbearance towards me in my feebleness and overwhelming discouragement. Bro. Smith has made a bad mistake and is making work for bitter repentance. The summer in which he resisted the spirit of grace at your house at the time of the conference was fearful. Bear this in mind, I have not had, neither have I any controversy with Bro. Smith. If he had not risen up against me for my references to the past which I regard wholly without cause and simply the temptations of Satan, we might now be enjoying the sweetest union."[4]

In what would become a pattern through the years, after his strong protests, by May 22 Smith reversed course, writing to Ellen White that he regretted his letter of May 5, "and not only this, but for what lies back of this, namely my blindness and lack of the spirit in the work." He further stated that he now understood the testimony to Aldrich, "and there is now no point on which I have the slightest difficulty with the visions." Furthermore, he apologized for his letters to James White.[5]

Despite the apologies, Uriah left the *Review* for several months and appears to have made his living as a freelance engraver. In November he wrote to James that he had taken up engraving as a means of supporting his family but had no intention of leaving "the service of the Lord." Expressing a desire to find a position that would allow him time to write for the church, for he believed that was where his talents lay, he again apologized for his past actions.

"I have no other feelings, I believe, but those of sincere contrition—regret for my past errors, and an intense desire to remedy them so far as I can, and meet the mind of the Spirit, which I know will relieve your feelings and those of Sr. White in my case. I freely offer all I have toward making up for my wrongs in respect to means. Some days since, I gave the association my note for $450. If this is not enough for the association, I offer the remainder of my property to the institute to offset, so far as it will go, bad management there."[6]

Uriah's absence was hard on Harriet, who wrote in her diary that the "past year has been the darkest, saddest year of my life." She went on to say that she felt "bad because Uriah feels so about returning to the office. I want to see him engaged in the cause of truth in some way, but I will try to pray for him and say little." Meanwhile, she had to deal with numerous family illnesses.[7]

CONTINUING CONFLICT

Problems persisted. The Battle Creek church experienced internal conflict, apparently over dress and health reform, though the issues are not clear. Sometime in 1869 Smith and George Amadon began circulating a document that satirized the behavior and/or standards of the church membership, thereby further stirring the cauldron of emotions. They said that "the children all wear copper-toed shoes, just the height of fashion and highly popular. The men wear agate shirt buttons, a material which bears the same name as that which adorns the foundations of the New Jerusalem! Oh, how fallen! Many of the church use Bibles with gilt edges, just such gold is forbidden in . . . [1 Timothy 2:9]."

Furthermore, "nearly every family of the Battle Creek church have their tables varnished, when good substantial paint would answer every purpose. Many of the sisters wear strings on their bonnets fifteen or twenty inches long, when those of eight or ten inches would answer every practicable purpose. . . .

"And in the culinary department, some are running to the same excess of riot. Why, there are some in this church who have spent $50 or $60 for cooking stoves, when they might get an article that would answer to bake our gems and boil our mush for $20 or $30, and so much would be saved to advance the precious cause of truth, or help to raise the pay of the self-sacrificing minister to $12 per week. Oh, the extravagance and worldly-mindedness of this professed church who ought to be lights and patterns to all. . . .

"And we must confess also that there are some in this church who wear 'artificials.' Three have fallen into that sin. And worst of all, these are brethren! Think of brethren wearing artificials, and it is a fact that Brethren Smith, Lockwood, and Byington all wear 'artificials'—legs."[8]

More seriously and regretfully, in October 1869 Amadon wrote in a letter that "these are solemn times for the church in [Battle] Creek. A few of us begin to realize more fully than ever before the terrible work of iniquity that we have been engaged in in regard to Bro. White. For one, I feel that a confession is due you for the mean [and] wicked way that I lent my influence against those afflicted servants of God, at the time you were in [Battle] Creek, in the winter of 1866-7. It was all wrong, it was wicked [and] unbrotherly. What a strange lack of charity, what an unholy zeal, what lack of Christian sympathy, what random gossip [and] talk. I am very sorry for my sin in the sight of God. . . . I have been exalted, puffed up of the devil, jealous, censuring, backbity, hypocritical, [and] wicked. Oh, the depths of my way."[9]

The following year the church's leaders apparently decided to address the situation by dropping individuals from membership, reducing the church from about 300 to 400 members to 12. Among those dismissed were the Amadons and the Smiths. Harriet wrote to Ellen White, saying that she was "in perfect sympathy with the steps taken by the conference committee in reorganizing the church so that if possible, the ark of the Lord may once more rest in Battle Creek." She further stated that she "felt anxious that Uriah should go forward and join the church if there is no objection, and I am not without hope that the time will come when my life shall have proved the genuineness of my conversion to God and my poor name may too be found among the records of His people." They regained their membership in early 1871.[10]

Meanwhile, Smith became ill in October with "bilious fever," which prevented him from editing the *Review* and working on the manuscript of *Thoughts on Daniel*. James White seems to have edited the church paper beginning with the November 8 or 15 issues until Uriah returned for the issue dated December 6. A week later Smith wrote that "through the blessing of the Lord we have recovered from our recent attack of fever, which was brought on by overlabor, and have regained our usual degree of health. During the period of convalescence, by the advice of physician and friends, we spent a few weeks with brethren abroad, visiting Detroit, Mich., Rochester, Lancaster, Parma, and Olcott, NY."

Smith seems to have been well enough to preach at Olcott.[11]

In September 1871 he reported that he had been in Boston assisting J. N. Andrews with his work on the history of the Sabbath, observing that their association was "of the most agreeable character." In addition he commented that the arguments put forward by Sunday advocates "should have convinced them that they were on the tortuous track of error, and not traveling in company with truth." During the 13 weeks that he was away from Battle Creek he presented 23 sermons, visited his mother, and had the pleasure of seeing a second brother accept the Sabbath. Uriah concluded by declaring that he was in excellent health as he took "up the thread of duty in my wonted sphere of office labor."[12]

Ellen White wrote a testimony to the Battle Creek church in December 1871 that explicitly criticized both Uriah and his wife, Harriet. She said that Smith had allowed himself to be crippled by his surroundings and that Harriet had "been a great hindrance to her husband." Apparently referring to the situation that led to the church's dismissal of the Smiths the previous year, she spoke of a letter that Harriet had written and her subsequent "humiliation" and confession. Although White thought that the church should have accepted the confession, she described Harriet in strongly negative terms, as she had some 10 years earlier. With regard to Uriah, she said that "home influences have confused his faith, and clouded his discernment." In addition, Ellen further blamed his "bilious" fever on Smith's failure to follow proper habits of eating, drinking, and exercising. She criticized his consumption of flesh foods and recommended a diet of vegetables, fruits, and grains. We have no record of either Uriah's or Harriet's response.[13]

By September 1872 problems began to appear once again at the Review and Herald publishing house. George I. Butler, General Conference pres-

ident, who resided in Iowa, told James White that he felt a need to go to
Battle Creek, although he suspected that Smith did not want to see him.
In October he reported discord among the Review and Herald employees.
"Indeed," he stated, "the councils had in some instances been pretty warm,
contentious." He concluded that the institution lacked leadership. "I never
saw the beat of their councils—Bacheller in the chair, Uriah looking at a
paper and saying scarcely anything at all. Edson with this and that project
on hand. George and Stephen now and then saying a word, and the sisters,
of course, taking no very active part." Butler concluded that the publishing
house needed a more forceful chairman.[14]

The GC president focused on Smith as both the cause and ultimate solu-
tion to the problem. "It seemed to me he was a sort of center around
which all the dark overhung," Butler wrote to James White, "and unless he
would move, nothing could be done." Butler had a long talk with Smith,
telling him that "he must take hold or suffer loss himself and bring loss
upon others. I told him how his influence had counted against our efforts
so far, by simply doing nothing when he ought to be the first on his feet."
Uriah responded positively to Butler's criticisms and pleas for help. "Well,
that night light came into our meeting," the GC president reported. "Uriah
took a noble stand on health and dress reforms. His wife did also. We had
a good meeting."[15]

Apparently on that same day, Butler met with the Review and Herald
staff, where he publicly urged Smith to step forward. "I knew he could
put things through, for I had seen him. I talked quite awhile, and they
voted him right in. He made some confessions of his not taking hold of
these things in the past and said he now was going to do different." Despite being Butler's handpicked choice, Uriah did not correct the situation
sufficiently to satisfy the church leadership, for in May 1873 James White
wrote that he had come from California to Battle Creek, against his wishes,
to address matters at the publishing house. Unfortunately, from his perspective Andrews, Waggoner, Smith, and even Butler opposed his efforts.
"The crisis has come," he wrote. "I have shown myself willing in coming
from California to make any sacrifice and have come near losing my life
and my best efforts have been resisted, especially by Brother Smith and
Brother Butler."[16]

Harmon Lindsay notified James and Ellen White that the GC president had called a meeting at the church, probably on May 14, "in regard to things in the office and the state of things existing in Brother Smith's case." After a presentation by Butler reporting that the Board of Trustees had held several meetings laboring with Smith, Uriah responded that "he had done all he could do and could not promise to do better in the future. He seemed to rather justify his course." Given the state of affairs, Butler stated, the board "felt it our duty to say to him that as long as he viewed things in this light and took this position, we did not think he had better stay longer." The board then discharged Smith from his position as editor of the *Review*. In retrospect, it appears that Smith, unlike James White and George I. Butler, was not one to assert himself in controversial situations that involved personnel conflicts. Uriah was a man of the pen rather than a decisive executive. White and Butler, it seems, were asking him to do something he was by nature unable to accomplish.[17]

A few days later, on Saturday, May 17, George Amadon noted in his diary that after a good Sabbath school in the morning, attended by Smith, an afternoon meeting had convened to investigate "Bro. Smith's case. Bro. [and] Sr. White [and] Butler occupied the time. Plain, cutting things were said. Bro. Smith said nothing. His wrongs were made very clear to all, as well as those of the rest of us." In July James White essentially placed Lindsay in charge of the publishing house. The following month Butler wrote to the Whites saying that he dreaded attending the Michigan camp meeting, for "I am sure there are whisperings all through the state over Uriah's case." On Monday, September 8, Amadon noted that there was a "presentation of Uriah's case" at what appears to have been an early-morning meeting followed by a social (testimony) meeting and preaching. More than a month later Butler told James White that "as hard-hearted a man as I am supposed to be, I have wept over this state of things."[18]

Despite the continuing controversy, Butler reported that Smith was beginning lectures at the Battle Creek church the next day. Nonetheless, about two weeks afterward Amadon recorded that the "Gen. Conf. Com. [and] picked men" held a session with Smith on November 4 or 5. Two days later he observed that "Bro. Smith is not doing well." On Monday, November 17, Butler, Andrews, Waggoner, Smith, White, and others had another meeting, and the next day Amadon recorded that meetings took place in the afternoon and evening. "A [shift] in the clouds in the afternoon. Darkness on the congregation somewhat in the evening. I am not getting out, though others are, especially Bro. Smith."[19]

During the months of continuing controversy after his dismissal from the *Review,* Smith sought engraving work in the Grand Rapids area, reporting to Harriet in July that his prospects seemed very good. He had a table in the *Democrat* newspaper office and said that people were impressed that he did his own woodcuts. But he seemed to long for Harriet to join him, asking, "Now, are you ready to pull up and come now?" Later that month he told his wife that he had earned $25 the past week "and there is almost any amount more talked up by different parties." Despite his fallout with the denominational leaders, he maintained his interest in the church, visiting Adventist families and speaking at least once. Although Uriah must have traveled back to Battle Creek frequently to attend those numerous meetings concerning his case, Harriet felt his absence. In an undated letter she wrote, "I feel terribly lonesome you may believe [and] long for something different from our present condition. Hasn't the Lord something working for us that will revive our hearts a little?" She concluded by saying that "*somewhere* there is a place for you in the Lord's vineyard, [and] may you find it in His time is my prayer."[20]

From that point on, Amadon's diary reported that Smith preached frequently at the Battle Creek church and conducted his Sabbath school class. By December 1873, now back at the *Review*, Smith expressed thanks to God for James White's work in Battle Creek and, while reporting that the Whites had left for California, stated that he looked forward to their return. In February 1874 he wrote to White thanking him for his encouragement in a recent letter, stating that "this work seems to present to me now an entirely new aspect from what it ever did before; that is, I feel, more than ever before, a constant and living impression that it is in truth the work of God, and the last work for this generation." He concluded by saying that he wished he could do more. "Oh! That I could put three weeks' time into one, and had a hundred extra heads and hands to devote to the work!" Smith's pattern of resistance followed by confession of his alleged wrongs and reconciliation had once again come to the fore. The circle seemed to be closed when the Michigan Conference ordained him to the ministry during its August camp meeting.[21]

Although issues with Smith seem to have largely resolved themselves, the publishing house situation remained problematic. While on a camp meeting tour Uriah hinted at such matters in a letter to Harriet in June 1875, saying that James White "has said nothing to me against [the Battle Creek church]. Nor anything against anyone with which we are particularly concerned, except occasionally a remark about Bro. Butler and Lindsay." About a year later James wrote to his son W. C. White, who was editing the *Signs of the Times* in California, that the latter magazine was "conducted better than the *Review*," saying further that he was glad that "you do not get in a great lot of wishy-washy matter in reports of progress and of meetings. There Brother Smith has made a great mistake." Even more strongly, he reported that Lindsay, whom he had picked two years previously to run the publishing house, had left. "He has proved himself to be a miserable fellow. He would neither do anything, nor let others work. Now Smith, [Sydney] Brownsberger, [H. W.] Kellogg, and your parents have taken hold of matters. And we are bound to put them through." A few days later he said that Lindsay and a Sister Caskell had been "acting like crazy people," and that Lindsay had "abused Smith and John Harvey Kellogg because they had exposed him." Brownsberger, Smith, and Kellogg, he reported, had now decided "to pull off their coats and do as Stephen Smith of New Hampshire did when he went to ring his hogs to keep them from rooting the pasture."

Although White had said he wanted only to be a councilor and "shall attempt no offices," while on his way to meetings in Battle Creek in September he implied to his son that he had engineered events to fix the situation: Smith would call an extra session of the publishing association that would appoint White as president and editor. Seemingly not satisfied unless he was in charge, James now concluded that "things are working well." In April of the following year he reported to his son that "things at Battle Creek are moving well generally. . . . H. W. Kellogg at the *Review* office is splendid."[22]

INTERPRETING REVELATION AND DANIEL

Despite all his problems with the church leadership, Smith devoted much of his spare time beginning in the late 1850s through the early 1870s to writing two books that further developed and systematized the Adventist interpretation of prophecy: *Thoughts, Critical and Practical, on the Book of Revelation* and *Thoughts, Critical and Practical, on the Book of Daniel*, both eventually combined into a single volume popularly known as *Daniel and Revelation*. In these works Smith followed William Miller's historicist approach, revising his conclusions and integrating them with later Seventh-day Adventist understandings. He also buttressed his interpretations by citing, sometimes at great length, biblical translators and expositors such as Albert Barnes, Samuel Thomas Bloomfield, Adam Clarke, and John Wesley, as well as historians, including Jean-Henri Merle d'Aubigné, Edward Gibbon, Niccolò Machiavelli, Johann Lorenz von Mosheim, and Leopold von Ranke. While he was writing an essentially apologetic commentary, such citations, often in the form of quotations, provided authority for some of his interpretations and gave his work a more scholarly character than most previous Adventist writings on the two biblical books. Although some commentators believed that the book of Revelation could not be understood, he asserted the contrary.

"As though God would undertake to make known to mankind some important truths and yet fall into the worse than earthly folly of clothing them in language or in figures which human minds could not comprehend! . . . No, the Revelation will accomplish the object for which it was given, and 'his servants'" will learn therefrom "the things which must shortly come to pass" and which concern their eternal salvation.[23]

Furthermore, Smith did not believe that he was providing a personal interpretation. In a baccalaureate sermon delivered at Battle Creek College a few years after completing the books, Smith spelled out his Baconian understanding of truth drawn from the Scottish commonsense philosophy that permeated mid-nineteenth-century American culture and that had shaped Smith's views from his earliest days as an Adventist. "The truth is all made plain in the Bible. The Bible explains itself," he said.

"The Lord has given His truth to us in so clear terms that it need not be misunderstood. The Word of God is so plain that the wayfaring man, though a fool (in the world's estimation), need not err therein. Then why do men reject it? Simply because they think more of their own wisdom than of the wisdom of God."[24]

In his books and articles Smith believed that he was presenting God's own truth. Such a strong assumption, for that is what it was, provided strength and certainty to his language but also contributed to his unwillingness in later years to reconsider whether his understanding was always correct. At the same time, however, in his text Smith also sometimes used phrases that gave room for the possibility that he might be wrong. For example, when discussing the leopard with four wings and four heads that appears in Daniel 7, he stated, "If we are correct in the application," then the extra wings indicated the rapid expansion of Greece's power. Such qualifying statements suggest that his understanding that the Bible is self-interpreting and that he as commentator is only a reporter needs to be softened somewhat.[25]

The work on Revelation came first, having its origins in Smith's Sabbath school class at the Battle Creek church, where participants studied the biblical book "confident that they had found a better harmony than they had before seen, and clear light on some portions of the book." James White published elements of what became the first nine chapters of the commentary in the *Review*, while late at night Smith wrote the remaining 22 segments, the series beginning in the June 3, 1862, issue and, with interruptions, ending with the February 3, 1863, one. Although the *Review* announced in 1865 that he was revising his material for book publication and Uriah consequently took five weeks off from editing the paper, James White's stroke brought Uriah back to the editorial desk. His own trip with the Whites to Dr. Jackson's water cure further delayed work on the manuscript. Finally the book appeared in April 1867. J. M. Aldrich, associate editor of the *Review*, strongly endorsed the volume, saying that "no Adventist's library is complete without it." James White further stated that it was "a book of thoughts, clothed in the author's happy style, plain, yet critical and practical, coming down to the spiritual wants of the common people, yet elevated and dignified. This standard work should be in the library of every believer."[26]

In 1869 Smith began a commentary on Daniel. Again with interruptions, the work first appeared in the *Review*, beginning in January 1869 and extending through July 1871. He worked on the series during evenings until late at night, probably thereby contributing to the illness he reported in the fall of 1871. After his revision of the articles, the *Review* announced the finished book at the end of December 1872. The next month J. N. Andrews published his endorsement. "It is written in a style which cannot fail to interest all classes of readers," he wrote, "and the truths which it contains are of priceless value. I do therefore most heartily recommend the volume, and wish it a very extended circulation." Uriah continued his biblical exposition with "The United States in the Light of Prophecy," like the previous works first appearing as a series of articles in the *Review*, beginning in October 1871 and ending in February 1872. It appeared as a book in 1874, seemingly with little revision, though shorter than the commentaries.[27]

Smith consistently understood the prophecies as referring to historical periods and events, hence the term "historicism," and believed that a rational structure undergirded and tied them all together. Following and extending the prophet's own interpretation, he stated that the image of King Nebuchadnezzar's dream reported in Daniel 2 refers to "great universal empires:"[28] the head of gold (Babylon), breast and arms of silver (Medo-Persia), belly and thighs of brass (Greece), and legs of iron (Rome). The feet and toes of a mixture of iron and clay represent the 10 kingdoms into which he believed that Rome had splintered: Huns, Ostrogoths, Visigoths, Franks, Vandals, Suevi, Burgundians, Heruli, Anglo-Saxons, and Lombards. The four beasts of Daniel 7 parallel those of Nebuchadnezzar's image and the 10 horns have the same meaning as that image's feet and toes. Smith explained the repetition on the grounds "that additional characteristics may be brought out, and additional facts and features may be presented."[29] For example, the beast with four heads represents Alexander's empire as divided among his four generals: Cassander, Lysimachus, Ptolemy, and Seleucus. According to Smith, the little horn that challenges the host of heaven and oppresses true religion refers to the Papacy, which, following his understanding that a day in prophecy represents a year in historical time, ruled for 1260 years, from A.D. 538, when Justinian's decree to place the pope at the head of all the churches took effect with the removal of the Ostrogoths from Rome, to 1798, when Napoleon's General Berthier captured the pope. "Thus again this power [the Papacy] fulfills to the very letter the specifications of the prophecy, which proves beyond question that the application is correct."[30] Although limited in power, the Papacy would continue to exist until the second coming of Jesus.

The little horn of Daniel 8 represents Rome in both its pagan and papal phases, but it was the latter that most interested Smith. "The papacy is the most God-dishonoring system of iniquity ever devised," he declared, "because in His name it commits its abominations, and practices its orgies of hell in the garb, and under the pretense, of pure and undefiled religion." Again, "Rome meets all the specifications of the prophecy. No other power does meet them."[31] In verse 13 a saint asks how long the prophetic period shall last. The following verse gives as the answer 2300 evenings and mornings, at the end of which the sanctuary shall be cleansed. As with William Miller before him, following the day-year interpretation, Smith understood the 2300 days to mean 2,300 years. Unlike Miller, who interpreted the sanctuary as the earth and the cleansing as Christ's second coming, following Sabbatarian Adventist reinterpretation Uriah argued that the sanctuary of Daniel 8 referred to the sanctuary in heaven described in Hebrews 8 and 9. To understand this cleansing, Smith referred back to the Jewish ceremonies in their sanctuary, the "type" prefiguring future events, in particular the entrance of the high priest into the Most Holy Place to minister before the ark of the covenant in behalf of the people. "In the antitype," which fulfills the "type," Uriah wrote, "when the time comes for the cleansing of the sanctuary, our High Priest, in like manner, enters into the Most Holy Place [of the heavenly sanctuary] to make a final end of His intercessory work in behalf of mankind. We confidently affirm that no other conclusion can be arrived at on this subject, without doing despite to the Holy Word of God." In short, the "cleansing of the sanctuary" refers to the beginning of the final judgment.[32]

According to Smith, Daniel 9 provides information regarding the beginning of the 2300 days. The 70 weeks, or 490 years, in this chapter are, he stated, the first part of the 2300-day prophecy of the previous chapter and starts with Artaxerxes' command in 457 B.C. to Ezra to rebuild Jerusalem and ends with the stoning of Stephen in A.D. 34, which marked "the formal rejection of the gospel of Christ by the Jewish Sanhedrim in the persecution of His disciples, and the turning of the apostles to the Gentiles."[33] Subtracting 490 from 2300 leaves 1,810 years, and counting 1,810 years from A.D. 34 takes one to 1844. "Thus speedily and surely do we find the termination of the 2300 days, when once the seventy weeks have been located."[34]

According to Smith and the Seventh-day Adventist understanding, therefore, God's final judgment began in 1844. "This work," he explained, "involves an examination of every man's character; for it consists in the remission of the sins of those who shall be found worthy to have them remitted, and determines who among the dead shall be raised, and who among the living changed, at the coming of the Lord, and who, of both dead and living, shall be left to have their part in the fearful scenes of the second death."[35]

For Smith, chapters 8 and 9 were the heart of Daniel's prophecies, while the remaining chapters spelled out in more detail the history of Rome as well as that of Egypt and extended as far as the French Revolution and the mid-nineteenth-century "Eastern Question" involving the fate of Turkey. "The Turks will very soon be obliged to make this move [making Jerusalem their temporary capital after being driven from Europe]," he announced. "This movement on the part of Turkey is the signal for the standing up of Michael [Jesus]."[36] A short time will then pass, after which the Second Coming will occur. Smith closed his commentary with a spiritual application, stating that "we now stand upon the borders of the heavenly Canaan, and decisions are being made, assigning to some a place in the eternal kingdom, and barring others forever therefrom. . . . And when this devoted servant of God [Daniel] . . . shall enter upon his reward for well-doing, we too may enter with him into rest, behold his rapture and share his joy."[37]

Although Smith wrote his commentary on Revelation first, his historicist interpretation of the prophecies understood them as dealing with the Christian era, largely following the events described in Daniel. In introducing Revelation he stated that "no other book contains so many chains of prophecy reaching down to the end. In no other book is the grand procession of events that leads us through to the termination of probationary time, and ushers us into the realities of the eternal state, so fully and minutely set forth."[38] The seven churches represent, according to him, seven periods of the Christian church, each of which had a particular characteristic: Ephesus (faithfulness), extending to the end of the first century A.D.; Smyrna (persecution), 200-323; Pergamos (corruption), 323-538; Thyatira (spiritual improvement but continuation of error), 538-1798; Sardis (spiritually dead), 1798-1830s; Philadelphia (brotherly love), 1830s-1844; Laodicea (period of judgment), 1844-end.

The descriptions of the four beasts (Smith preferred the translation "living creatures"), the elders, the one on the throne, and the lamb in Revelation chapters 4 and 5 involve figurative language, but, Uriah asserted, "though the Revelation deals largely in *figures*, it does not deal in fictions. There is reality in all the scenes described."[39] Thus the one on the throne is God, the lamb symbolizes Jesus, and the four living creatures and 24 elders represent those resurrected at the time of Christ's resurrection. Chapter 6 introduces the seven seals, which, according to Smith, depicted the same periods of Christian church history as the seven churches in the early chapters. At the end of earthly time both the heavens and the earth shall shake and the rich and powerful as well as those they rule will recognize that God, not humanity, is in charge. But their pleas for mercy are rejected. "It is too late," he wrote. "They cannot conceal their guilt nor escape the long-delayed vengeance."[40]

Smith understood Revelation 7 as providing further information regarding the sixth seal. Most significant is the "seal of the living God," which refers to the rediscovery of the seventh-day Sabbath. "We conclude," he wrote, ". . . that the angel ascending from the east, having the seal of the living God, is a divine messenger in charge of a work of reform to be carried on among men in reference to the Sabbath of the fourth commandment."[41] This reform, of course, refers to the emergence of Sabbatarian Adventism.

The seven trumpets appear in Revelation 8 and 9 and, in Uriah's view, represent "the principal political and warlike events which were to transpire during the same time" period covered by the seven seals.[42] The first four trumpets refer to the fall of Rome, beginning near the end of the fourth century and extending to the mid-sixth century: first trumpet (the Gothic invasions of the Roman Empire); second trumpet (the conquests of Africa and Italy by the Vandals under Genseric); third trumpet (invasions of Attila the Hun); fourth trumpet (Odoacer, Theodoric, and the ultimate fall of Rome). The prophecy, according to Smith, then turns to the East: fifth trumpet (the rise of Islam and Turkey) and sixth trumpet (the rise of the Ottoman Empire, decline, and loss of independence in 1840).

Revelation 10 and the first portion of chapter 11, according to Smith, constitute a parenthesis between the sixth and seventh trumpets. The opening of the little book refers to the fact that Daniel's prophecies are now understood as revealed by the Advent movement of 1840 to 1844.

When the angel proclaims that "time shall be no more," he is stating that the prophetic time prophecies ended in 1844. The period of the seventh trumpet begins at this point. "Not many years from that date, then, the mystery of God is to be finished," but Scripture gives no specific information regarding when that great event will take place.[43]

The woman of Revelation 12 represents the Christian church while the dragon symbolizes the Papacy. Smith summarized his understanding of the church's history when he declared: "Then we have again brought to view the church in her wilderness state, a time, times and a half, 1260 years, verse 6, the flood of persecution which the devil cast out after the church through the medium of the papacy, the help the church received from the Reformation, which, being espoused by various princes and earthly powers, restrained the spirit and work of persecution, and finally the last assault of the dragon upon the commandment-keeping remnant, just in the future."[44]

The two-horned beast, Smith believed, denoted the United States, one horn representing freedom and the other oppression, which Smith said was coming soon. Revelation 13 closes "leaving the people of God with the powers of earth in deadly array against them, and the decrees of death and banishment from society out upon them, for their adherence to the truth."[45]

Revelation 14 introduces the three angels. The first angel, who proclaims the "everlasting gospel," refers to the Millerite Advent movement, beginning about 1840 and extending to 1844. The second angel announces the fall of Babylon, the "fall" representing the rejection by the mainstream churches of the Millerite message of Christ's soon coming. "But instead of receiving the truth, she clung to her errors," Smith wrote, "and by spreading them among the nations has stood directly in the way of the advancement of the truth in the earth. Thus having grieved the Spirit of God, [that Spirit] has been withdrawn, and a moral fall is the result."[46] The third angel warns against worship of the beast and his image. "This is the issue, then, into which the world is to be brought," Uriah stated. "Refuse the mark of the beast and thus become exposed to the wrath of antichristian, earthly powers; or receive the mark, and brave the unmixed wrath of God."[47] The "mark of the beast" refers to Catholicism's change of the Sabbath from the seventh day to the first day of the week, "an institution put in place of the original institution of Jehovah, and brought forward by the Romish church itself as the badge and token of its power to change the law of the Most High." Observance of Sunday as the Sabbath is the final element separating unfaithful and faithful Christians. Of the remaining angels, the fourth utters a prayer for the church after it has completed its work and probation has ceased. The last two angels address the destruction of the wicked. "Thus closes this chain of prophecy—closes as others close, with the complete triumph of God and Christ over all their foes, and with the glorious salvation that awaits the faithful followers of the Prince of life."[48]

The seven last plagues of Revelation 15 and 16 take place in the future, after humanity's probation has ended. According to Smith, "the work of mercy is closed, and there is no ministration in the sanctuary during the infliction of the plagues; hence they are manifestations of the wrath of God, without any mixture of mercy."[49] He further wrote, "Thus all is finished. The cup of human guilt has been filled up. The last soul has availed itself of the plan of salvation. The books are closed. The number of the saved is completed. The final period is placed to this world's history. The vials of God's wrath are poured out upon a corrupt generation. The wicked have drunk them to the dregs, and sunk into the realm of death for a thousand years. Reader, where do you wish to be found after that great decision?"[50]

Revelation 17 and 18 present the destruction of both the Roman Catholic Church and the apostate Protestant churches. "Like a great millstone, Babylon sinks to rise no more. The various arts and crafts that have been employed in her midst, and have ministered to her desires, shall be practiced no more. The pompous music that has been employed in her imposing but formal and lifeless service dies away forever."[51] Revelation 19 describes the redeemed saints performing a song of triumph as they "behold the complete destruction of that great system of opposition to God and His true worship, comprehended in great Babylon."[52] Then in chapter 20 God confines Satan to the ruined earth for 1,000 years, at the end of which He resurrects the wicked. Satan then rallies them to battle against the Holy City that has come down to earth. In Uriah's summary, "the saints are with Christ in heaven during the thousand years, while the earth lies desolate; . . . at the end of that time the saints and the city come down, the wicked dead are raised, and come up against it; . . . they receive their judgment; and . . . from the purifying fires which destroy them come forth the new heavens, and new earth, to be the abode of the saints throughout endless ages."[53]

Smith closed his discussion of chapter 20 with another appeal to the reader to be sure that their names are registered in the book of life.

After discussing the descriptions of the holy city and the tree of life in Revelation 21 and 22, Uriah assured the reader that "if we keep the commandments of God and the faith of Jesus, we *shall* have right to the tree of life, we *shall* enter in through the gates into the city." He closed his work, saying "Even so come, Lord Jesus."[54]

Smith supplemented his commentaries on Daniel and Revelation with a smaller book entitled *The United States in the Light of Prophecy* in which he argued that the only prophecy symbolizing the United States was the two-horned beast of Revelation 13. Because the text refers to it as "another beast," it cannot therefore refer to the Papacy. "The sum of the argument, then," he concluded, is that "the two-horned beast does not come into the field of this vision previous to the year 1798; that it performs its work while the last generation of men is living on the earth; and that it comes up to the battle of the great day a living power in the full vigor of its strength."[55]

As mentioned but not developed in his commentary on *Revelation*, the two horns represent the "civil republican power of [the] government" and the "Protestant ecclesiastical" power. When he applied the prophecy to the future of the United States, Smith took a pessimistic view. Surveying the American scene, he saw political corruption, apostate Protestantism, spiritualism, infidelity, free love, trade unions, and Communism threatening the country. But most significantly, the Papacy "has fixed its rapacious and bloodthirsty eyes on this land, determined to make it its helpless prey. It already decides the elections in some of our largest cities. It controls the revenues of the most populous state in the union, and appropriates annually hundreds of thousands of dollars raised from Protestant taxes to the support of its own ecclesiastical organizations, and to the furtherance of its own religious and political ends."

He believed that such influences would soon "culminate in a state of anarchy, and a reign of terror as much more frightful than the French Revolution as they are now more widely extended, no man can say." Rather than looking for a union of church and state in America, Smith expected "not a state controlled by the church, and the church in turn supported by the state, but an ecclesiastical establishment empowered to enforce its own decrees by civil penalties," which would take the form of a national Sunday law forcing obedience to the "mark of the beast."[56]

Though it leaves out much, the foregoing summary of Smith's commentaries provides an outline of his understanding of how, in the light of prophecy, history is unfolding. Such a prophetic interpretation underlay virtually all of his views expressed in editorials, articles, and books discussing topics ranging from doctrine to current events. Uriah's interpretations of prophecy also became the standard of orthodoxy within Seventh-day Adventism for several decades and set the stage for some painful controversies both during his lifetime and after.

THE LAST DAYS

Although Smith's editorials in the *Review* frequently dealt with the details of prophetic interpretation explicated in his commentaries, in the weekly paper he was more concerned with awakening within his readers a consciousness that the end of time was near and that they needed to examine their readiness for the judgment. As argued in his commentary, the prophetic time periods had ended with the Advent movement of the 1840s. No time prophecy applied after 1844. Nonetheless, the investigative judgment that began in 1844 could not continue for long. The last days were at hand.[57]

As Uriah observed the world around him, particularly developments in the United States, he saw many signs that the end of all things was near. With colorful and dramatic language in 1871 he described climate conditions in America that indicated humanity's only hope lay in the second coming of Jesus: "While our Western states were kiln-dried by long weeks of cloudless sun, and then swept by fiery cyclones and burning tornadoes, which sent balls of fire like bullets through hickory plough handles, and melted pennies in men's pockets, and took the life of every living thing within reach of their blasting breath, other parts of the country have been soaked with continuous rains, and damaged with uncommon floods."[58]

He also pointed to events as varied as the increasing numbers of ships lost at sea, the growing distribution of Bibles by the American Bible Society and other organizations, discoveries in science and technology, the 1871

revolution in Paris, the activities of the Ku Klux Klan, the adultery trial of
the famous American preacher Henry Ward Beecher, the growth of spiritualism, and the increasing strength of the Papacy. A tower planned for the
1876 Centennial Exposition in Philadelphia reminded him of the Tower of
Babel, erected before the universal destruction of the Flood: "Yet there is in
the human race at the present day," he wrote, "in view of the great achievements of late years, an ill-concealed disposition of self-laudation, an assertion, almost of omnipotence, and independence of any higher power." The
year following the exposition he recounted the number of people killed
and the cost of wars during the previous 25 years. "How heart-sickening
is such an exhibition of selfishness and passion," he commented, "on the
part of those who call themselves reasonable beings."[59]

Smith also called attention to the growing labor movement. In 1874 he
said that "the spirit of Communism" was taking over "larger masses of the
lower people." The railroad strike of 1877 was "part of the . . . impending
conflict between labor and capital, fostered by the spirit of communism,
trades unions, working men's associations, etc., that is abroad in the land,
and is one of the disturbing elements of the troublous times of the last
days." Although critical of labor, Uriah did not side with capital. "It is undoubtedly true that many of the rich . . . have enriched themselves at the
expense of the poor," he wrote. "They have wrung means from the neces-
sities of the needy, that they might gratify and gorge and pet and pamper
themselves. But the poor," he observed, "goaded at length to desperation,
spring upon their oppressors with the fury of a wild beast unchained. And
their long unbalanced accounts will be adjusted, that being paid in blood
which they reward in gold." Two years later he described labor strikes in
England as "utter blindness and folly" that would destroy the country's
prosperity. As noted elsewhere, Smith resisted change, whether in theology or society and, therefore, was unlikely to support the labor movement
in any form. But rather than favoring capitalists over workers, he saw both
involved in a dynamic conflict that presaged the Second Coming.[60]

In fact, he believed that Communism, political corruption, and labor
organizations were moving quickly toward cataclysm: "All the baleful elements which led to the reign of terror in France in 1793 and 4, are now
at work throughout all Europe and America," he announced, "threatening
to precipitate upon the world within a few weeks or months at most, the

direst, because the most widespread, calamities the world has ever seen." Despite his explicit prediction, he made no comment when such calamities did not occur.[61]

Following up his expectations regarding Turkey, explained in his commentary on Revelation, Smith argued in 1877 that the material aid and moral influences upholding the Ottoman Empire were giving way, "presaging the speedy downfall of that semi-barbarous power." A year later he followed closely diplomatic efforts to bolster Turkey. As long as European powers guaranteed its independence, he believed, the empire stood in the way of "hordes" from the East spreading into western Asia and eastern Europe. "But when Turkey falls," he stated, "their way will be prepared, the barrier removed; and why may we not expect the deluging waves of them to flow westward, as at times in the middle ages" in fulfillment of the prophecies of Joel and Revelation. A few weeks later he commented less apocalyptically that "the time has come when the Turkish empire must fall to pieces, and the only question to settle is a satisfactory division of the spoils." Uriah would continue to keep his eye on the "sick man of Europe."[62]

Most ominously, he saw religious liberty threatened in the United States. In 1863, believing that the Civil War was God's punishment of the nation for the sin of slavery, representatives of 11 denominations from seven Northern states proposed revising the wording of the Constitution's preamble so that it included an acknowledgment of God. The following year they organized the Christian Amendment movement, soon renamed the National Reform Association (NRA). The NRA proposed to Congress a constitutional amendment that acknowledged God as the source of government and Jesus Christ as the ruler of nations in order to "constitute a Christian government." Also, efforts took place in several states to establish laws prohibiting labor on Sunday. Then in 1870 Smith drew attention to the call of Methodists in New York for government protection of the Christian Sabbath. "There is a hidden power impelling it [the Sabbath] forward which will soon make it the leading question of the day," he stated. "Let us prepare for the scenes before us." By 1872 he warned that the ultimate purpose of the proposed constitutional amendment was to "control actions" and that it would "remodel the whole framework of our government, and give to it a strong religious cast." In 1874 he cautioned

that preliminary steps were occurring to unify the various apostate Protestant churches, thereby forming the "image to the beast [Catholicism]."
The following year he wrote that "the evidence is continually accumu-
lating strength that the application we make of that portion of prophecy
[Revelation 13] is correct, and that we are soon to see movements on the
part of the government which will put the matter beyond all questioning."
And by 1876 he fully expected that the nation would adopt the Sunday
law amendment. During 1879 he thought that it might be a major issue in
the next year's presidential election and predicted that the nation would
establish an American Sabbath "resting on the sanction of human law."[63]

As a premillennialist who believed that Jesus would come before the
millennium, Uriah held a pessimistic outlook regarding earthly developments. He assumed that slavery would be reinstated when the opportunity
arrived, and counseled his fellow Adventists to avoid affiliation "with that
party which has supported it in the past, and who would again restore it if
they had the power." Indeed, he advised, if anyone voted, they should do
it quietly without a partisan spirit. More broadly, writing in 1874 he found
"general acknowledgment, all over the land, of the unparalleled degener-
acy of our times." Corruption was widespread, he believed, "pervading all
classes of society, the high and low, the rich and poor, [and] almost equal
to the worst local manifestations of ancient times." During 1879 he gave
evidence of moral decline in Germany, the home of the Protestant Reformation, noting an increase in crime, lower church attendance, the growth
of rationalism, and the spread of entertainment. "What does it prove," he
wrote, "but that the Reformation has not been followed out, the advancing
light of truth has not been heeded, and the inevitable moral declension has
followed." In light of the decline in Western culture, he called upon his
readers to meet God's expectations "for piety and holy living." He asked
whether "we, then, come up to the standard? Are we endeavoring to live
as holy lives, as the wicked around us are living abandoned ones? As the
world is growing worse are we growing better? We must be doing this if
we would be among His chosen ones at last." Although he would deny that
he was a legalist, Smith's emphasis on the judgment that would separate
the unsaved from the saved suggests that behavior was the key element.
Surveying the history of the Christian message, he said that the first several
centuries revolved around the crucified and risen Savior, followed by the

Protestant Reformation, which emphasized justification through Christ. The last days, he argued, were now witnessing the preaching of the judgment as heralded by the Advent movement in fulfillment of the prophecy of Revelation 14.[64]

CONTEMPORARY RELIGION

As Smith observed the contemporary religious scene, he similarly saw decline and corruption. In 1874 he stated that the churches were becoming "sadly degenerate in religious things." Three years later he condemned them for accepting such things as dancing and billiards, commenting that "it is not a crossbearing self-denying religion like that preached and taught by the Master." Even the revivals brought about by the preaching of Dwight L. Moody were insufficient, because they left "out the demands of the law, and the work of true conviction of sin, and repentance by godly sorrow for transgression, and forsaking of evil ways with brokenness of heart." The negative reactions of several religious journals to the premillennial prophetic conference of 1878 demonstrated to him the infidelity of the various denominations regarding the doctrine of Christ's second coming, which he believed the Bible plainly taught.[65]

Although highly critical of contemporary Protestantism, Smith spent much more time discussing Roman Catholicism. The number of Roman Catholics in the United States had increased rapidly since the Irish immigration of the 1840s, which had brought in 1.5 million individuals during the famine years between 1845 and 1855. More than 2 million Catholics arrived after 1860.[66] Although Smith offered a unique Adventist prophetic perspective on Catholicism, he was also part of the larger anti-Catholic movement in America, represented in such organizations as the "Know Nothing" or American Party of the 1850s and anti-immigrant associations. Normally apolitical, he in 1871 advocated establishing an educational requirement for voting to limit the influence of the "vicious demagogues and designing priests" who controlled Irish voters for their own purposes. In a statement that reflected the strong anti-immigrant opinion pervading the American public, Uriah wrote that "the intelligent and refined will be more ready to [vote] without being crowded and jostled by a degraded, ignorant, and vicious mass of humanity, and without having to stem a tide of unmitigated filth and drunken obscenity."[67]

Smith, however, was more concerned with the influence and power of the Papacy than he was with the voters who might support it. When the pope criticized King Victor Emmanuel II for lifting restrictions on Jews in Italy in 1870, Uriah called persecution of the Jewish people "one of the foulest blots upon the filthy and blood-begrimed escutcheon of the papal power." Frequently he described Catholicism in strongly expressed negative terms: "man of sin," a "great spiritual despotism," "an unchristian power," and an "iniquitous organization." He believed that "Bible institutions and practices" must be rescued from "the foul heap of Romish superstitions" and described the "corrupt and disreputable" Catholic Church as venting its rage on "the good, the pure, and the true." The church that would be prepared for the Second Coming, he asserted, must free itself from papal errors and corruption, particularly the Sunday Sabbath. Further, he warned against Catholicism's effort to regain political power in Europe. "Against such a move the nations must be forewarned," he wrote in 1875. "A strong undercurrent is at work. A storm is gathering which must soon burst forth." America especially needed warning, for "the growth of this church is no small element in the threatening changes now hanging over this country."[68]

In addition to Catholicism, Smith was also concerned with the growth of spiritualism, particularly in the early to mid-1870s. Modern spiritualism had its American origins with the Fox sisters of Rochester, New York, in the 1840s and gained appeal during and after the American Civil War as mourning families sought solace through communion with their lost sons. Uriah regarded spiritualism as a fulfillment of Hebrews 10:29 and the book of Jude, noting that it came at the exact prophetic time and attacked Christ and Christianity. It was the work of Satan and a counterfeit form of Christianity despite the efforts of its leaders to bring its statements "more into accord with the creeds of orthodoxy." In the fall of 1871 he noted the presidential candidacy of Victoria Woodhull, who advocated both spiritualism and free love, commenting, "It will perhaps do the reader no hurt to try for a moment to imagine what the condition of our country will be when a woman more familiar with familiar sprits, and a more fanatical devotee of the unhallowed intercourse, than even the witch of Endor, shall sit in the chair of its chief executive." He also claimed that spiritualists "brazenly confess themselves adulterers and adulteresses and glory in their cause."

Perhaps recalling the experience of Moses Hull, the Adventist preacher who had debated spiritualists and then joined them, Uriah declared that he would not engage in such debates. "We shall take the high ground," he said, "giving them the widest possible berth in the filthy pool where they have chosen to wallow." Whereas Catholicism threatened society through its religious and political power, spiritualism worked more subtly but no less dangerously, moving like a virulent gangrene through society.[69]

Despite his pessimism regarding human society, whether political, economic, or religious, Smith strongly believed in a hopeful future, for Jesus was literally soon returning to rescue His saints from a fallen world. The Second Coming would end all human enterprises, destroying all the living wicked, and reducing the earth to its "original condition of disorder and chaos." At the same time, for those who live holy lives "the suffering, the humiliation, the warfare, the labor, the cross, the burden of mortality, are about ended," he wrote. "The next to come is the glory, . . . the rest, the crown, the thrill of immortality." Furthermore, he had no doubt that the Second Coming would take place as expected. "The bare *possibility* that such an event is near should arrest attention. The open *probability* that such is the case should excite an absorbing interest. The clear evidences that it is *certainly* so should cause all to act immediately in the work of preparation."[70]

REINFORCING DOCTRINE

Through the pages of the *Review* and his other writings, Smith continually reminded his readers of their doctrinal beliefs, especially the "state of the dead," the Sabbath, and the sanctuary, each of which distinguished Adventists from most of Protestantism. The growing popularity of spiritualism made the Adventist belief that immortality, rather than being natural, was a gift given by God at the resurrection, particularly significant for the time. Uriah explained the Adventist view in *The Testimony of the Bible on the State of the Dead*, published in 1873. Like most of his other books, much of the volume had previously appeared in editorials and articles in the *Review*.[71]

Uriah argued that the Bible's teaching regarding death was "the most effectual antidote" to the "unhallowed delusion" of spiritualism and would also destroy such beliefs as purgatory, saint worship, universalism, and other errors. Because we cannot know what lies beyond the grave until we die, he stated, we are dependent on what God tells us. He noted that the words "immortal" and "immortality" do not appear in the Old Testament. In the New Testament "immortal" appears only once and means "incorruptible," while "immortality" appears five times, always as a contrast between human beings and God. Furthermore, he observed, we find in Scripture no evidence that the word "soul" refers to something that operates both within and outside the body. Therefore, like his fellow Adventists, he advocated what at the time was called "annihilationism" or "soul sleep," the idea that the human being is a unified whole, not divided into body and soul, that begins decomposing at death and, if among the saved, is re-created at the resurrection. Today we would refer to it as "conditional immortality."[72]

Much of his book Smith devoted to analysis of particular passages that allegedly support the idea of natural immortality, including the story of Samuel and the witch of Endor, the Transfiguration, the parable of the rich man and Lazarus, and Jesus' statement to the thief on the cross that "this day you shall be with Me in Paradise." In each case, of course, he sought to demonstrate that the texts did not endorse the idea of natural immortality. Furthermore, he regarded the doctrine of natural immortality as incompatible with the resurrection, for why would immortal souls need resurrecting as bodies. "While we deny that immortality is proved for either man or beast by any vital or mental powers which they may exhibit," he concluded, "our theory finds a superior position for man in his more refined mental and physical organization, whereby he becomes possessed of a higher mental and moral nature, and is the proper recipient of the hope of immortality."[73]

Of all doctrines, Uriah was most interested in the Sabbath and continued to advocate and defend it. With the emergence of efforts to enforce Sunday observance by law, it was all the more important to explain the significance of the seventh-day Sabbath. In 1871 Smith set out the issues: "A truth of unparalleled clearness is given us. God has a controversy with the nations in this respect. He has set His hand to vindicate the claims of His law, against the corruption and presumption of the man of sin. A counterfeit Sabbath [is] soon to be made a civil test in the law of the land, as the true one is now a moral test in the law of God, [and] the people must be enlightened on the subject. And they will be—so enlightened that when they decide against the right, it will be in obedience to the claims of self-interest, in opposition to clear convictions of duty.[74]

Uriah put forward the now-familiar arguments for the seventh-day Sabbath. People had observed it before the issuing of the Decalogue at Sinai. Furthermore, the Ten Commandments were not part of a covenant, an agreement between two parties that either could end at any time. Therefore, they are "binding on all the world, whatever their name or nation." The New Testament reports the disciples observing the Sabbath, while Paul says nothing in any of his epistles about changing it from the seventh day to the first. If the Sabbath was simply a matter of rest, Smith wrote, any day would do. "But there are higher considerations involving the sanctification of the day, the precept and authority of God in its appointment, and its being a memorial of the Creator."[75]

Sunday observance, on the other hand, is a pagan and papal rival of the true Sabbath and constitutes the "mark of the beast." He declared that "Sundaykeepers are driven to take the ground that the Sabbath of the Lord has been abolished, and to introduce this namby-pamby makeshift of first-day into the place of the sacred institution." Thus Sunday becomes a day of rest, he asserted, only as a product of human effort.[76] The time had come, he believed, for the issue of the Sabbath to rise to the fore, dividing the faithful from the unfaithful:

"A great sin lies at the door of Christendom. The law of God is ignored—in too many cases despised. God's Sabbath is trodden down by professedly Christian feet. Of this sin they must repent by turning from it. The time has come for a reform right here. It is laid down in prophecy and must be fulfilled. The judgment hastens on apace. A people must be prepared; and they who are prepared will be found not only loving and trusting Christ, but also loving and obeying God, keeping His law because, like Paul, they delight in it after the inward man."[77]

Smith continued to emphasize the necessity of observing God's law. In perhaps his clearest statement, he argued in 1878 that recognition of the law is the foundation of Christianity. Elsewhere he wrote that the "ten-commandment law is a unit; its ten words are inseparably united, and stand or fall together." It has not been abolished and is binding on all dispensations. Indeed, one little sin can cause an individual to be lost.[78]

At the same time Uriah struggled to reconcile law and gospel. For example, in 1871 he stated that while "justification by faith is our sole dependence, and ever has been, . . . [it does not give us] liberty now to commit any of the sins forbidden by the Ten Commandments." Commenting on an allegorical picture by M. G. Kellogg, he said that it showed the relation of both Christ and the law to each dispensation, "and the problem, so difficult to many minds, how the law and the gospel can exist together, is solved at a glance." The key element is repentance, for it acknowledges both our obligation and failure to obey the law and constitutes the first step toward salvation. "Our part," Smith said, is to "repent and be convicted." God will bring the refreshing while we decide to "repent and be converted." Discussing the issue of predestination, he asserted that human beings are free agents, thereby implying that repentance is a human choice. "It is for every man to say whether he will be predestinated or elected or not," he concluded. He also brought in Paul to support his position. "But Paul's course was first of all to preach repentance, showing that the law they had violated was of long-standing obligation and well-understood principles," Uriah observed. "When Paul said, Repent, they knew what he meant, and on what authority he pronounced them guilty." By emphasizing the need for repentance, Smith sought to reconcile the continuing obligation to obey the law with Christ's willingness to forgive and provide absolution.[79]

The sanctuary was the third major doctrine that he emphasized. Beginning a series of 35 articles that extended from January 6 to August 31, 1876, he urged that, next to Jesus, the sanctuary is the most important element in the plan of salvation, "occupies [the] central position" in the "great wheel of truth," and unites and reveals the relationship of the Mosaic and Christian dispensations. Furthermore, it explains where the Advent movement of 1844 went wrong. "The sanctuary is the one subject which brings order out of chaos," he argued, "points out the mistake, shows where and how it was made, reveals the rock on which so many have foundered, vindicates the past movement, and points out the path to further truth and final triumph."[80]

After a detailed history of the Israelite sanctuary, he noted that its services "came really to an end" at the time of Christ's crucifixion, "for they were no longer of any virtue." He then turned to Jesus' ministry in the heavenly sanctuary, which he believed that the Jewish ceremonies had prefigured. In 1844 Jesus entered heaven's Most Holy Place and began the process of cleansing, which "involves the examination of the records of all the deeds of our lives," Smith explained. "It is an investigative judgment. Every individual of every generation from the beginning of the world thus passes in review before the great tribunal above." Uriah commented that the examination had progressed for almost 32 years and asked, "How much longer can it continue?" Finally, he concluded his series by reasserting that "we are now . . . in the period of the finishing [work]." For Smith, the sanctuary doctrine confirmed that he was living in the last days of earth's history.[81]

As he considered the doctrines espoused by Seventh-day Adventists he expressed great confidence in their truth and vitality. Regarding the various Adventist groups that had emerged from the Millerite movement, he distinguished between those who followed the "advancing light of truth" and those who had rejected "the light, and fallen more or less into bewilderment and confusion." Seventh-day Adventists, he said, had not shifted their views from day to day, as had others. "The positions we hold now are the same as at first," he argued, "only illuminated with greater light, and established in tenfold strength." Observing that 11 prominent ministers had left the "first-day Adventists," he commented that those who have faith in the Advent movement should see "that it is with those who have been led to the keeping of the commandments of God and the faith of Jesus, to prepare for the coming kingdom, that the Lord is working, and the power of His truth is to be found."[82]

But despite the clear truth and power of the Advent message, some who at one point held the faith later departed from it. "Now and then one is shaken from his moorings on present truth," Smith observed, "by the idiotic frothings of such men as [Robert] Ingersoll [a prominent American agnostic], or by the assumptions of science falsely so called, or by the pollutions of spiritualism." But they do so through their own volition, he asserted. "If a person wants to depart, if his desires are in that direction, if the carnal mind which is not subject to the law of God, is allowed to control, he will depart in the very face of circumstances and influences best calculated to lead him heavenward." As he had explained elsewhere, human beings are free agents who decide for themselves whether or not to follow God's truth.[83]

For those who followed Christ faithfully, according to Smith, the doc-trines taught by Scripture revealed that the Christian life was a serious en-deavor that left no room for trivial things. He told his readers, for example, not to read novels. "They poison the mind. They destroy a taste for all that is useful, wholesome and true." At the final judgment one would be un-able to account for time wasted reading such "trash." Also he opposed the wearing of jewelry, for it was both contrary to Scripture and had no practi-cal use.[84] Condemning both the male attraction to tobacco and the female devotion to fashion, he commented, "Men would be better prepared to discern spiritual things, and appreciate the difference between the sacred and profane, if they would stand forth in their godlike manhood, free from the debasing power of appetite; and women would be better prepared to stand by the side of their husbands as counselors, and even to take part with them in political matters, would they disenthrall themselves from the slavery of fashion, which dwarfs and belittles the mind, and leaves them no time to study the weightier matters of life."[85]

Christians who freed themselves of such distractions should take their religion into all aspects of their daily lives. "There is no particular holiness in sloth and inactivity," he wrote. "Carry your religion into your business. Let it make you better in all the relations of life, and shed its hallowed light over all the paths you tread." For Uriah, religion was an all-encompassing way of life, not something relegated to the Sabbath hours or the church building.[86]

CHURCHMAN

Although Smith's main occupations were editing the *Review* and writ-ing his books, in the 1870s he continued to participate in the church organization and helped develop what today we might call a continuing education program for ministers. Every annual General Conference ses-sion appointed him to a variety of positions. In 1871, for example, the delegates elected him secretary of the General Conference, vice president of the publishing association, assistant editor of the *Review*, and secretary of both the Seventh-day Adventist Benevolent Association and the Tract and Missionary Society. In addition, the Michigan Conference elected him its president. Four years later the 1877 General Conference session contin-ued to ask Smith to serve in various capacities. This time around, it elected him secretary pro tem of the publishing association, editor of the *Review*, and secretary pro tem of the Health Reform Institute, in which capacity he was asked to revise the articles and bylaws to strengthen the institute's legal position. At the same time, leadership appointed him to a committee to revise the constitution of the Tract and Missionary Society. Both sessions typify the responsibilities that the denomination called on him to fulfill at each annual meeting. He performed a different kind of function when in 1879 the Tract and Missionary Institute devoted one hour each day to parliamentary procedure, presumably directed by Uriah, who would soon write his own rules of order.[87]

In 1872 Smith published "A Declaration of the Fundamental Principles Taught and Practiced by the Seventh-Day Adventists." The statement does not appear to have had any official endorsement, although the denomination's publishing committee may have approved it. "We have no articles of faith, creed, or discipline, aside from the Bible," Uriah stated. "We do not put forth this as having any authority with our people, nor is it designed to secure uniformity among them, as a system of faith, but is a brief statement of what is, and has been, with great unanimity, held by them." Writing it to provide information for inquirers, he explained that Seventh-day Adventists differed from most other Christians in believing that the dead are unconscious, that the "unrepentant wicked" would be destroyed rather than burn permanently in hell, that the Ten Commandments, including the seventh-day Sabbath, held perpetual authority, and that the Holy Spirit continued to operate within the church, the latter probably a reference to the visions of Ellen White. Distinguishing Seventh-day Adventists from other Adventists of the time, he further stated that they did not set dates for the Second Advent. Following this preamble, he then listed 25 beliefs, the first such statement of Seventh-day Adventist doctrine.[88]

In 1872 the denomination sent Smith as a delegate to the general meeting of the Seventh Day Baptists, who also routinely appointed a delegate to the Seventh-day Adventist General Conference sessions. The two denominations thought that "personal intercourse" between them would promote better understanding. Uriah commented that the two groups "should have no guns to point at each other, but should direct our efforts against the common enemy who seeks to pervert or destroy the law of Jehovah." Although D. M. Canright served as the official delegate in 1875, Smith accompanied him to the meeting.[89]

As editor of the *Review* and officer of the publishing association, Uriah was involved both in deciding what went into the paper and the physical development of the publishing house. Smith frequently explained the purpose of the *Review*. In 1870 he asserted that it "should be the *best religious paper in the world*," stating further that it was the only Adventist periodical presenting "a consistent position on the Advent question." A week later he announced that it would be enlarged to provide about double the amount of reading material.

"We want all this space filled with living, flaming words of truth, something that will arrest the attention of the unthinking, instruct the ignorant, convince skeptics, establish the wavering, stir up the backsliding, comfort believers, strengthen the weak, cheer the desponding, and bring us all nearer to Christ, and more into sympathy with His will, and into the Spirit of His work."

But the editors could not accomplish such lofty goals unless God's Holy Spirit filled the church itself. "And while we try to have a paper worthy of a cause," he said, "we want a cause worthy of the paper. A living cause is worthy of a living paper. But the paper cannot long retain its life, if the cause is in a feeble, languishing condition."[90]

By 1877 Smith seemed to shift the burden for maintaining the pulse of the movement to the magazine itself, stating that "there are truths for this time clearly developed, sharp and well defined, to which the people must be aroused or perish. In such truths as these the *Review* undertakes to deal. It will give the trumpet no uncertain sound." The following year he restated his belief that the *Review* played a significant role in maintaining the cause. The periodical would "endeavor to observe clearly the signs of the times," he announced, "proclaim them faithfully, maintain uncompromisingly its defense of the downtrodden truths of the Bible, and act well its part in preparing a people for the coming of the Lord."[91]

In addition to attempting to fulfill such a large purpose through the content of the *Review*, Smith was also concerned with the physical process of producing the paper. James White announced in 1870 the desire to construct a new building for the publishing association, a project completed in 1872. Then in 1873 Uriah informed his readers that a new cylinder press had been received and was working. Three years later he reported that the publishing house was installing a new boiler and engine from the Jackson Foundry and Machine Works. And in 1878 he told of the addition of another 7,000 square feet to the building, bringing the total space to 20,000 square feet. As the physical facilities developed, the publishing work was clearly expanding, for besides the *Review* and books, it was producing the *Youth's Instructor*, *True Missionary*, and *Health Reformer* plus two foreign language journals, *Advent Tidende* (Danish), and the *Svensk Advent Harold* (Swedish).[92]

About 1867 Ellen G. White wrote a *Testimony* directed toward Smith and others in Battle Creek, noting that he had written *Thoughts on the Revelation* at night after working at the *Review* office all day. "I protest against such suicide," she said. Rather than being confined to their desks, she recommended that such individuals "would be serving the cause of God by attending meetings and taking periods of recreation. They would be preserving physical health and mental strength in the best condition to devote to the work." Uriah apparently heeded her advice, for although he went to camp meetings in Michigan as early as 1869, he soon became a regular on the national camp meeting circuit. An unknown writer, probably an associate, described him as "an argumentive speaker, clear and logical, possessing marked ability and a pleasant address."[93]

Smith reported frequently on such summer and fall camp meeting trips. Often he told of the spiritual renewal that occurred during such conclaves. In 1870 he informed his readers that the Sabbath service during the Charlotte, Michigan, meeting found "sinners pressing forward under the burden of their guilt, expressing with deep feeling their determination to seek and serve the Lord; parents searching up and bringing forward their children; and others, their unconverted friends, with exhortations and tears." At the New York camp meeting in 1876 the speakers enjoyed "great freedom" and the social meetings, in which people gave testimonies of their spiritual situation, experienced "seasons of interest and freedom." That same year the Maine meeting saw more than 60 individuals come forward. "Most of these bore testimony, feelingly, in reference to their condition and the step they had taken. Freedom was enjoyed in the season of prayer that followed." During 1875 Uriah spoke of his pleasure in traveling with James and Ellen White. "In all our long association with them," he wrote, "it has never chanced to be our lot to thus be with them in such a series of consecutive meetings from state to state." He affirmed the value of the Whites' testimony and counsel during the trip.[94]

Although Smith clearly intended his camp meeting reports to encourage

spiritual revival among his readers, his news was not always positive. For
example, in 1871 he spoke of a Saturday night at the New England meeting
being bothered by "sons of Belial" and "howling" around the grounds. He
contrasted such "fanatical spirits" with "the work of present truth [which]
does not consist in noise and yells and excitement and frenzy. It is a deep,
sober, solemn, intelligent work of preparation for the test of the judgment
which we are soon to pass." At other meetings the problem was not fanaticism but a low spiritual state. "During the forepart of the meeting," he reported from Ohio in 1876, "there was an evident lack of the Spirit of God
among the people. This was manifested in such a spirit of gossip, jesting,
and levity among some, as showed that the weight and solemnity of the
message was not felt by all of them." Fortunately testimony by the Whites
changed the atmosphere. Two years later he noted that the leaders at the
Maine camp meeting "have seemingly become too much satisfied with
the theory without a corresponding consecration of the heart and zeal of
action." He observed that "there was not, consequently, that breaking away
and yielding to the melting influence of the Spirit of God, and the coming
in of spiritual triumph and victory in the meeting that was desirable."[95]

But most of his reports were positive, often telling of the large attendance,
although he provided no indication how anyone calculated the figures. The
1870 Charlotte, Michigan, meetings attracted 4,000 people for its Sunday
services. Seven years later the Michigan camp meeting had more than 2,000
attendees. Three thousand people came on Sunday to hear Ellen White
speak on temperance at the 1877 Vermont meeting, while between 7,000
and 8,000 attended the Sunday afternoon sessions at the following year's
New England meeting. Smith frequently referred to non-Adventists attending such sessions, which such numbers would have required. We must remember that at a time when entertainment and other events to break up the
monotony of everyday existence were few, a camp meeting, whatever the
denomination, provided something of potential interest.[96]

In addition to camp meetings, he also participated in the development
of "biblical institutes," which provided instruction for the denomination's
ministers who up to the 1870s had no training other than experience "on
the job." Proposing "to give instruction theoretical and practical in regard
to the presentation of present truth," the first institute took place in Battle Creek in December 1874 and January 1875. In the spring of 1877 a

second institute convened in Oakland, California. Uriah reported in the *Review* that in Oakland he and James White presented the equivalent of 64 lectures, and that at the end of the Institute it ordained two individuals and six received ministerial licenses. A published synopsis of the lectures suggests what might have been presented at the other institutes as well. The Oakland presentations focused on such distinctive Adventist teachings as the prophecies, the Sabbath, and the state of the dead, and appear to have had in mind helping Adventist ministers to meet objections. The lectures gave little attention to more general Christian beliefs, such as the doctrine of Christ. While in California, Smith visited seven churches and what was probably a camp meeting. He reported that "physically [California] is a peculiar and wonderful land. To an eastern man it seems somewhat strange to find the thunder and lightning all underground, and to see the winters exhaust themselves wrestling with the towering summits of the Sierras, so that they never find their way into the valleys below."[97]

A few months later Uriah participated in another biblical institute, this time in South Lancaster, Massachusetts, and organized by Stephen Haskell. It involved two sessions of Bible lessons and most days a third session of "miscellaneous exercises, such as a drill on the pronunciation of Bible names, spelling of uncommon words, construction of sentences, parliamentary practice, etc." Not wanting to leave the impression that attendees were limited to mental activity, Haskell reported that "a good-sized woodpile at the door, and a fence to be built, gives them an excellent opportunity to exercise an hour each morning." Smith, who presumably presented most of the Bible lessons, had, according to Haskell, "much freedom in speaking." Uriah observed that the institute involved "three weeks of constant and earnest study of the truth and communion with God." At the close of the institute the 62 students adopted a resolution, saying "that we hereby manifest our thankfulness to Bro. U. Smith for his patient, earnest efforts in expounding and illustrating the principles of present truth, and that we sympathize with him and bid him Godspeed in his faithful labors to advance the work of the third angel's message."[98]

Upon his return home, Smith gave a series of "Bible lectures" at Battle Creek College, as he had been doing occasionally since its opening in 1874, which some who attended described as better than the biblical institutes. Designed to prepare individuals for the ministry, they dealt with "subjects of the most intense interest to everyone who is in any degree awake to the importance of the time in which we live." Shortly thereafter, in March 1878, Uriah conducted another biblical institute for the Adventist ministers in New York and Pennsylvania. As in New England, it had three one-and-a-half hour meetings each day, two addressing the Bible and one miscellaneous matters. For the 45 attendees, Smith presented 31 of the 35 lectures, with Haskell delivering the other four, and in addition Uriah spoke for church six times and attended 13 meetings "devoted to literary and miscellaneous activities." Another biblical institute took place in Battle Creek in the fall of 1879 with a somewhat broader curriculum than at earlier convocations, for in addition to lectures from Uriah Smith and James White, it included John Harvey Kellogg speaking on scientific and hygienic subjects and a "Professor Hamill" on elocution.[99]

PERSONAL LIFE

Obviously an extremely busy man, Smith probably had relatively little time for his family and personal affairs. Unfortunately, only a few scattered sources record this side of his life and therefore offer few glimpses into his family life. An 1874 letter from Harriet to Ellen White refers to Uriah reading the Bible passage that begins "Remember now thy Creator" and explaining it to his children. His daughter, Annie, was "listening intently till suddenly she sprang from her high chair and came to sit on my lap. I saw she was excited and asked if she need not go to bed. She said no, she wanted to hear all papa read, but whispered in my ear that SHE WAS GROWING OLD and it haunted her till she dropped asleep." A short time later Smith wrote to Ellen White expressing his appreciation for her attention to his children. "Wilton and Leon," he said, "we think are trying to be good Christians and Wilton especially seems inclined to enter upon the Christian life." He went on to explain that "they both unite regularly with us in family worship and Wilton speaks in the district meetings, and has once in the Sabbath afternoon meeting at the meetinghouse. We shall try to do our duty by and for them." During this period the Smiths had added two more sons to their family, Samuel Parker in 1872 and Charles Stevens in 1875. At some point they also took in Alma L. Wolcott, whose father had died in the Andersonville prison during the Civil War, because her mother was unable to care for her.[100]

Uriah's long absences from home that began in the 1870s clearly affected his wife. A letter from Harriet, probably written while he was helping J. N. Andrews in Boston in 1871, indicated that she was going to hire a "colored woman" to help with washing and other household activities. While he was on the camp meeting circuit in 1875 she asked him to write more often to tell her where he was. "You must remember I do not keep track of your wanderings," she stated. "I feel it an increase of care now that you are not at hand to carry your share of the family responsibility, but so far all goes well." Harriet reported that she had visited Sojourner Truth, who lived near Battle Creek and had close relations with the Adventists, which gave her a break from her household duties. But "Parker asks if Papa isn't coming home again, [and] I believe wants to see you as much as any of us." About the same time Wilton told his father that "Parker says he does want to see Pa so much and Ma asked him what he would do when you came and he said he would kiss you and climb up in your lap and get your rule."[101]

In her 1871 testimony to the Battle Creek church Ellen White was quite critical of the Smiths' child-raising practices. She accused Harriet of having "undue affection" for her children, whom she said were "coming up unlovable and unloved" because of a lack of effective discipline. In particular, Annie had "been gratified and indulged, until she is ruler of the house," which would lead to a dire outcome. As with other aspects of this testimony, we have no record of a response by the Smiths. As strongly as Ellen White could criticize the Smiths, she also expressed kindness and concern. In 1881, for instance, she expressed her desire that Uriah could escape the cold Michigan winter that year. "Anytime you will do this my good Healdsburg home shall be at your service free of all expense," she wrote. "I wish that your wife could go with you and would urge this if I thought it of any use, but I know she would not wish to leave her children."[102]

But it was not only Harriet that felt the burden of Uriah's absences. As early as 1870 Smith invited her to join him at the camp meeting for the weekend. Then with his characteristic wry humor he said, "There are other bipeds no better looking than I, who have the privilege of having their wives with them at camp meeting, [and] I would like to have mine here too. . . . I think it would do you good to come [and] that you would enjoy it." Again, while attending the 1877 biblical institute in Oakland, California, he wrote to Harriet, telling her that he would have preferred

being in Battle Creek, where he could use the library for his writing projects, but that if she were with him he would "enjoy himself immensely."
Furthermore, he said that he did not want to attend camp meetings that
year. He expressed his wish that she could "see some of the nice places
here, more especially as regards the surroundings. I have never witnessed
anything to compare with them," concluding that he would like a similar
setting in the new earth. When describing the scenery he had observed
while visiting various churches, Smith revealed an aesthetic appreciation
that seldom appeared in his published writings.

"The Napa Valley is beautiful, a valley from three to six miles wide,
level and smooth as a house floor, covered with immense vineyards, wheat
fields, almond orchards, peach [and] cherry trees, besides the various varieties of ornamental trees, around the nice residences and the whole inter-
spersed with the wide-spreading live oak. The valley is bounded on either
side by a range of mountains from 1000 to 3100 feet high, I should judge,
which are very [picturesque]."

Uriah further described the soda springs in Napa, the sulphur springs
and quicksilver mine near St. Helena, and farmhouses in the mountains.
He told Harriet that he hoped to get back to Battle Creek for their twentieth wedding anniversary, but it would be a "pretty tight squeak."[103]

While in New England that same year, Smith visited his family in West
Wilton, where he witnessed his brother Samuel's baptism, rejoicing with
his other sibling, John, that they were "all in the same faith and hope."
Also he enjoyed a "royal" breakfast prepared by Samuel, including "sweet
potatoes, potatoes, broiled codfish, sweet corn, cucumbers, watermelon,
muskmelon, johnnycake, Graham biscuits, white biscuits." Again reporting to Harriet regarding food on the trip, he said that he had had dinner
at a dining hall in Lowell, Massachusetts, that included corned beef, potatoes, turnips, beets, squash, bread and butter, and shelled green beans. "It
was a splendid dinner," he wrote, "all for 25 [cents]."[104]

Somehow, Smith found time to tinker with his inventions. As early as
1873 he asked his wife if she had heard from the patent office. About two
years later, on May 25, 1875, Smith received a patent for his "folding-seat
for school desks." The application stated that "the object of my invention is
to produce a school-seat that will readily adapt itself to the movement of the
body of the student as he sits down or rises up at his desk." This he accom-

plished, Smith explained, "by so constructing the folding device that the rear edge of the seat shall rise instead of the front, as the seat is folded up, at the same time that the front is carried back from the student, as will appear by reference to the accompanying drawings." Harriet reported in 1875 that the patent had arrived and that a Henry Winslow had visited Battle Creek and in behalf of "school parties" wanted to purchase $3,000 worth.[105]

Obediah Davis and Howell Gardner of Battle Creek began manufacturing the seats in 1877 and sold the business to the Union School Furniture Company in 1880. An advertisement for the desks described them as "unrivaled for Simplicity, Convenience, Beauty, in use in all the leading schools in Michigan. Rapidly Superseding All the Old Style Hinge Seats." A fire in 1891 or 1892 closed the business, however. Meanwhile, funds from the sale of the patent rights enabled Smith to build a large mansard-style home located on present-day University Avenue in Battle Creek. Smith's previous biographer, Eugene Durand, commented that some criticized it as "extravagant," but that Uriah shared it by entertaining and accommodating church employees during General Conference sessions. The house appears to have been a comfortable one, for Harriet later described it as "a pleasant home" and Uriah said that the stove kept the parlor, sitting room, and bedroom warm in winter.[106]

The few glimpses of the private side of Uriah Smith that survive suggest that he had warm relationships with his family despite his dedication to work and his frequent travels and that he maintained contact with his brothers. Although his frequent absences were hard on his wife, they appear to have affected him as well. Furthermore, despite Adventist strictures on diet, he enjoyed food that did not always fit the health reform emphasis. A writer and editor, he also had his practical side, as evidenced by his inventions. Smith was living a full and varied life and appears to have achieved reconciliation with his denominational leadership by the mid-1870s, but new and seemingly unexpected conflicts would tear that peace apart as he entered a new decade.

---

[1] US to JW, Apr. 23, 1869.
[2] US to EGW, Apr. 28, 1869.
[3] US to JW, May 4, 1869.

[4] JW to ?, no date. EFD believes that this letter was written in 1873 (see *Yours*, pp. 273, 274), which is plausible, but I favor an 1869 date because White was a more central character in that year's controversy than he was in the 1873 conflict. There is no definitive way to settle the date, however.

[5] US to EGW, May 22, 1869.

[6] US to JW, Nov. 16, 1869.

[7] Transcript of diary of HS, Jan. 1, 1869. The diary entry appears to be misdated.

[8] *A Record of Some of the Pride and Extravagances of the Battle Creek Church.* Quoted in EFD, in *RH*, Feb. 3, 1983, p. 6. I have been unable to find the original document.

[9] GWA to [?] Abbey, Oct. 12, 1869.

[10] MRH, *Flames*, pp. 60-62; HS to JW and EGW, 1870.

[11] *RH*, Oct. 18, 1870, p. 144; Nov. 1, 1870, p. 160; Dec. 6, 1870, p. 200; Dec. 13, 1870, p. 208.

[12] *RH*, Sept. 26, 1871, p. 116; HS to US, [no month] 19, [1871].

[13] EGW, *Testimony to the Church at Battle Creek* (Battle Creek, Mich.: Steam Press of the Seventh-day Adventist Pub. Assn., 1872), pp. 34, 46.

[14] GIB to JW, Sept. 17, 1872; GIB to JW, Oct. 15, 1872.

[15] GIB to JW, Oct. 15, 1872.

[16] GIB to JW, Oct. 15, 1872 (this is a second letter written on the same day as the one cited in endnote 12); JW to [?] Abbey, May 12, 1873.

[17] Harmon Lindsay to JW and EGW, May 15, 1873.

[18] GWA, diary, May 17 and Sept. 8, 1873; JW to Trustees of the Publishing Association, July 6, 1873; GIB to JW, Oct. 23, 1873.

[19] GWA, diary, Nov. 5, 6, 17, and 18, 1873.

[20] US to HS, July 1 [1873]; HS to US, undated but postmarked Sept. 23, [1873].

[21] *RH*, Dec. 2, 1873, p. 196; Dec. 23, 1873, p. 12; US to JW, Feb. 17, 1874; *RH*, Aug. 18, 1874, p. 68.

[22] US to HS, June 23, 1875; JW to WCW, July 11, 1875; JW to WCW, July 15, 1875; JW to WCW, Sept. 14, 1875; JW to WCW, Apr. 12, 1876.

[23] US, *Thoughts, Critical and Practical, on the Book of Revelation* (Battle Creek, Mich.: Steam Press of the Seventh-day Adventist Pub. Assn., 1865), p. 8.

[24] James R. Nix, *A Collection of Twelve Early Adventist Sermons That Illustrate Advent Preaching* (Silver Spring, Md.: North American Division Office of Education, 1989), p. 75.

[25] US, *Thoughts, Critical and Practical, on the Book of Daniel* (Battle Creek, Mich.: Steam Press of the Seventh-day Adventist Pub. Assn., 1873), p. 125.

[26] EFD, *Yours*, pp. 215, 216.

[27] *Ibid.*, pp. 216, 217; *RH*, Nov. 26, 1872, p. 192; Jan. 21, 1873, p. 48; Mar. 17, 1903, p. 6; Apr. 7, 1903, p. 8.

[28] US, *Daniel*, pp. 37, 49.

[29] *Ibid.*, pp. 123, 129.

[30] *Ibid.*, p. 145.

[31] *Ibid.*, p. 164.

[32] *Ibid.*, p. 196.

[33] *Ibid.*, pp. 232, 233.

[34] *Ibid.*, pp. 235, 236.

[35] *Ibid.*, p. 240.

[36] *Ibid.*, p. 344.

[36] *Ibid.*, p. 371.

[38] US, *Revelation*, p. iv.

[39] *Ibid.*, p. 87.

[40] *Ibid.*, p. 117.

[41] *Ibid.*, p. 127.

[42] *Ibid.*, p. 139.

[43] *Ibid.*, p. 183.

[44] *Ibid.*, p. 207.

[45] *Ibid.*, p. 226.

[46] *Ibid.*, p. 233.

[47] *Ibid.*, pp. 233, 234.

[48] *Ibid.*, pp. 238, 245.

[49] *Ibid.*, p. 247.

[50] *Ibid.*, p. 265.

[51] *Ibid.*, p. 282.

[52] *Ibid.*, p. 283.

[53] *Ibid.*, p. 301.

[54] *Ibid.*, pp. 327, 328.

[55] US, *The United States in the Light of Prophecy; or An Exposition of Rev. 13:11-17* (Battle Creek, Mich.: Steam Press of the Seventh-day Adventist Pub. Assn., 1874), pp. 32, 50.

[56] *Ibid.*, pp. 77, 85-87, 129, 154, 156.

[57] *RH*, May 13, 1875, p. 157; Jan. 20, 1874, p. 44.

[58] *RH*, Dec. 12, 1871, p. 205.

[59] *RH*, Jan. 31, 1871, p. 53; July 16, 1872, p. 36; May 24, 1870, p. 180; Mar. 28, 1871, p. 116; Aug. 4, 1874, p. 60; Jan. 27, 1874, p. 52; July 12, 1877, p. 24.

[60] *RH*, Mar. 24, 1874, p. 120; July 26, 1877, p. 36; Aug. 2, 1877, p. 44; Feb. 27, 1879, p. 68.

[61] *RH*, June 6, 1878, p. 180.

[62] *RH*, Feb. 22, 1877, p. 64; May 9, 1878, p. 148; July 18, 1878, p. 28.

[63] Jim Allison, "The NRA (National Reform Association) and the Christian Amendment," *The Constitutional Principle: Separation of Church and State* (http://candst.tripod.com/nra.htm); Dennis Pettibone, "The Sunday Law Movement," in *The World of Ellen G. White*, ed. Gary Land (Washington, D.C./Hagerstown, Md.: Review and Herald Pub. Assn., 1987), p. 120; *RH*, Mar. 29, 1870, p. 116; Jan. 31, 1871, p. 52; Jan. 16, 1872, p. 36; Mar. 5, 1872, p. 92; Apr. 7, 1874, pp. 132, 133; June 9, 1874, pp. 204, 205; Dec. 2, 1875, p. 172; July 13, 1876, pp. 20, 21; Sept. 18, 1879, p. 100; Oct. 30, 1879, p. 149.

[64] *RH*, Aug. 29, 1871, p. 84; Aug. 20, 1872, p. 80; Mar. 10, 1874, p. 100; Aug. 4, 1874, p. 60; July 24, 1879, p. 36; May 9, 1871, p. 164; Jan. 6, 1874, p. 28.

[65] *RH*, Feb. 24, 1874, pp. 84, 85; Aug. 2, 1877, pp. 44, 45; Nov. 11, 1875, p. 149; Nov. 25, 1875, p. 164; Nov. 21, 1878, p. 164; Dec. 12, 1878, p. 188.

[66] Roger Daniels, *Coming to America: A History of Immigration and Ethnicity in American Life,* 2nd ed. (New York: Harper/Collins, 2002), pp. 135-140.

[67] *RH*, Mar. 14, 1871, p. 100. For a survey of Seventh-day Adventist views of the Catholic Church during this period, see Reinder Bruinsma, *Seventh-day Adventist Attitudes Toward Roman Catholicism, 1844-1965* (Berrien Springs, Mich.: Andrews Univ. Press, 1994), pp. 75-202.

[68] *RH*, Dec. 27, 1870, p. 13; Feb. 10, 1874, p. 69; Feb. 1, 1877, p. 36; Feb. 21, 1878, p. 60; July 4, 1871, p. 21; July 9, 1872, p. 28; Feb. 3, 1874, pp. 60, 61; Feb. 11, 1875, p. 52; June 13, 1878, p. 192.

[69] *RH*, May 2, 1871, p. 156; Sept. 26, 1871, p. 116; June 20, 1871, pp. 4, 5; May 20, 1875, p. 164; Mar. 11, 1875, p. 88; Jan. 13, 1874, p. 36; Jan. 18, 1877, p. 20.

[70] *RH*, Feb. 18, 1875, pp. 60, 61; Feb. 25, 1875, p. 68; June 21, 1877, p. 196; Oct. 13, 1874, p. 124.

71 *RH*, Apr. 2, 1872, p. 124; Apr. 9, 1872, p. 132; Apr. 30, 1872, p. 156; May 14, 1872, p. 172; May 28, 1872, p. 188; Nov. 19, 1872, p. 180; Dec. 3, 1872, p. 196.

72 US, *The Testimony of the Bible on the State of the Dead* (Battle Creek, Mich.: Seventh-day Adventist Pub. Assn., 1873), pp. 3-60.

73 *Ibid.*, pp. 196, 224.

74 *RH*, Apr. 18, 1871, p. 140.

75 *RH*, July 14, 1874, p. 37; Mar. 22, 1877, p. 93; Dec. 8, 1874, pp. 188, 189; Feb. 7, 1878, p. 44; Jan. 15, 1875, p. 24.

76 *RH*, Jan 15, 1875, p. 20; Apr. 21, 1874, p. 149; Apr. 11, 1871, p. 132; Feb. 20, 1879, p. 60.

77 *RH*, Jan. 23, 1879, p. 28.

78 *RH*, May 16, 1878, p. 156; Jan. 10, 1878, p. 12; Dec. 16, 1873, p. 4; Jan. 24, 1878, p. 28; Jan. 3, 1871, p. 20.

79 *RH*, Apr. 18, 1871, p. 140; May 27, 1873, p. 192; Mar. 21, 1871, p. 108; Apr. 19, 1870, p. 140; Feb. 24, 1874, p. 85; Apr. 25, 1871, p. 148.

80 *RH*, Jan. 6, 1876, p. 6.

81 *RH*, June 1, 1876, p. 173; Aug. 17, 1876, p. 60; Aug. 31, 1876, p. 76.

82 *RH*, Mar. 29, 1870, p. 116; June 16, 1874, p. 4; Sept. 9, 1875, p. 80.

83 *RH*, May 15, 1879, p. 156.

84 *RH*, Oct. 3, 1871, p. 124; Oct. 1, 1872, p. 128.

85 *RH*, Oct. 13, 1874, p. 126.

86 *RH*, July 4, 1871, p. 21.

87 *RH*, Feb. 14, 1871, pp. 68, 69; Oct. 4, 1877, pp. 105, 106; Jan 2, 1879, p. 4; US, *Key to Smith's Diagram and Parliamentary Rules, Together With Concise Hints and Directions for Conducting the Business of Deliberative Assemblies* (Battle Creek, Mich.: Review and Herald Pub. Assn., 1881).

88 *A Declaration of the Fundamental Principles Taught and Practiced by the Seventh-day Adventists* (Battle Creek, Mich.: Seventh-day Adventist Pub. Assn., 1872), pp. 3, 4; *RH,* Nov. 24, 1874, p. 171.

89 *RH*, Sept. 10, 1872, p. 104; Sept. 24, 1872, p. 116; Oct. 7, 1875, pp. 108, 109.

90 *RH*, Dec. 13, 1870, p. 204; Dec. 20, 1870, p. 4.

91 *RH*, June 28, 1877, p. 4; Jan. 3, 1878, p. 4.

92 *RH*, June 14, 1870, p. 205; Jan. 16, 1872, p. 36; Dec. 30, 1873, p. 24; Mar. 16, 1876, p. 88; June 27, 1878, p. 4; EFD, *Yours*, p. 73.

93 EGW, *Testimonies*, vol. 1, p. 520; *RH*, June 22, 1869, p. 207; June 29, 1869, p. 8; July 6, 1869, p. 16; July 27, 1869, p. 37; Aug. 24, 1869, p. 72; Aug. 31, 1869, pp. 77, 78; *American Biographical History of Eminent and Self-made Men, Michigan Volume* (Cincinnati: Western Biographical Pub. Co., 1878), p. 92.

94 *RH*, Sept. 20, 1870, p. 108; Sept. 21, 1876, p. 100; Sept. 14, 1876, p. 92; July 15, 1875, p. 20.

95 *RH*, Sept. 12, 1871, p. 100; Aug. 24, 1876, p. 68; Sept. 19, 1878, p. 101.

96 *RH*, Sept. 27, 1870, p. 116; Oct. 4, 1877, p. 108; Sept. 20, 1877, p. 100; Sept. 12, 1878, p. 93.

97 *RH*, Sept 29, 1874, p. 120; Dec. 1, 1874, p. 184; Jan. 8, 1875, p. 12; Mar. 29, 1877, p. 104; May 3, 1877, p. 140; *The Biblical Institute: A Synopsis of Lectures on the Principal Doctrines of Seventh-day Adventists* (Oakland, Calif.: Steam Press of the Pacific S.D.A. Publishing House, 1878); *RH*, June 14, 1877, p. 188.

98 *RH*, Nov. 1, 1877, p. 140; Nov. 8, 1877, p. 148; Oct. 18, 1877, p. 128; Nov. 22, 1877, p. 164.

[99] *RH,* Dec. 2, 1873, p. 200; Mar. 9, 1876, p. 77; Feb. 14, 1878, p. 56; Mar. 28, 1878, p. 104; Apr. 18, 1878, p. 124; Aug. 29, 1878, p. 80.

[100] HS to EGW, Feb. 21, 1874; US to EGW, May 14, 1874; George L. Caviness to Andrews University Heritage Room, Feb. 7, 1988; EFD, *Yours,* p. 33.

[101] HS to US, [1871]; HS to US, [1875]; WS to US, June 12, 1875. Hoare, "Notes," states that Smith conducted a funeral service for Sojourner Truth in 1883, but contemporary evidence suggests that it was not the case.

[102] EGW, *Testimony to the Church at Battle Creek,* pp. 46, 47; EGW to US, [no day or month] 1881.

[103] US to HS, Sept. 27, [1870]; US to HS, Apr. 26, 1877; US to HS, May 14, 1877.

[104] US to HS, Aug. 29, 1877.

[105] US to HS, July 1, [1873]; WS to US, June 12, 1875; HS to US, [1875]; United States Patent Office—Uriah Smith of Battle Creek, Michigan., "Improvement in Folding Seats for School-Desks," Patent No. 163,611, May 25, 1875.

[106] Clipping entitled "Bank Exhibit to Recall Early History of the City," possibly from the Battle Creek *Enquirer and News.* "Uriah Smith's School Seat Found in Church Attic," *Lake Union Herald,* Sept. 9, 1980, pp. 9, 10. EFD, *Yours,* p. 165. The newspaper clipping states that the factory burned in 1892, while Durand gives the date as 1891. Also, Durand states that Battle Creek College used the seats when it opened the 1875 school year. Because the patent was issued in 1875 and manufacture did not begin until 1877, it seems unlikely that the college had the seats in 1875, as Durand states, unless someone else made them. HS to WS, postmarked June 16, 1884; US to WS, Mar. 20, 1884.

CHAPTER VI

A TROUBLED TIME, 1880–1894

Although Uriah Smith had avoided controversy since the early 1870s, new conflicts emerged, opening the 1880s with an administrative issue and closing them with a theological one. Despite the problems, he maintained his faith in the church and its message, continuing to promote, explain, and apply Adventist belief through both the *Review* and his other writings. Also, the denomination found new ways to sell and distribute his commentaries on the biblical books of Daniel and Revelation that established them as classic contributions to Adventist literature and further enhanced his position as the premier Adventist interpreter of prophecy. Nonetheless, Smith had to deal with the fact that Jesus had not yet returned, which since his conversion to Adventism he had expected to occur soon. Also he continued to struggle to reconcile his emphasis on the need to obey God's law as represented in the Ten Commandments with acceptance of the belief that salvation ultimately comes through faith in Christ's righteousness. Although he had good experiences during these years, the 1880s was a particularly troubled time for a man who had held the esteem of his fellow church members for more than 25 years.

THE "COLLEGE TROUBLES"

In January of 1882 George I. Butler, president of the General Conference, wrote an urgent letter to W. C. White, saying, "We have on our hands a terrible crisis in the college, the worst we have ever had." Battle Creek College, which opened in 1874, had recently appointed Alexander Mc-Learn, a new convert to Adventism (but who had not yet officially joined the church), as its president in 1881 after Sidney Brownsberger resigned. Unfortunately, McLearn understood little about the denomination's educational objectives, which included both Bible study and a manual labor program that the denomination still struggled to clarify and implement. From the beginning, conflict between McLearn and Goodloe Harper Bell, a strong disciplinarian who headed the English Department, had filled the 1881-1882 school term. Bell had been involved with the institution from its start and was used to a great deal of autonomy. After an address by Ellen White in December 1881 urging that the college give greater emphasis to the Bible, among other things, the board established a committee that asked Bell and Smith to teach a Bible course. Bell resisted, wanting more control over his courses in exchange.[1]

When the board recommended in response that Bell be given more independence, many of the faculty threatened to resign. As charges flew back and forth, the board under Smith's leadership pursued an investigation involving eight hearings, ultimately resulting in a censure of both Bell and McLearn. Invited to participate, Butler arrived one day after the investigation had begun. He reported to White that two night sessions extending until 1:00 or 2:00 in the morning had already taken place. Apparently the majority of the board was siding with Bell, for Butler said that three or four students were circulating a paper asking that Uriah Smith, who was a member of the board, give a "minority report," explaining why he was differing from the majority. "At first he thought he would not," the GC president stated, "but yesterday he said 'as things were shaping' he might do so." Butler further explained that some were connecting the college controversy with tensions between the *Signs of the Times*, which William C. White was editing in California, and the *Review*, edited by Uriah Smith in Michigan. Exasperated at the situation, he told White, "I have never seen anything like this in Battle Creek. Some of that side seem to me to have a satanic spirit and the positions of all seem most unreasonable. I find a bad, yes, a bitter spirit against [Stephen] Haskell and you for the part you took at the conference. It reaches high up in the office. Such talk as this, I hear that Haskell and you came on from California determined to put out McLearn. Poor Bell is made the starting point of this, and that you wanted to get Uriah shelved up in the college so the *Review* would be deprived of him, and that Haskell wanted to do this so the *Signs* could take the lead.

"I have scouted the conspiracy business but you see how last night Uriah spoke it out in the strongest light before the members of the faculty. I think I will be the most unpopular man in Battle Creek with a class, and a large class."[2]

The Battle Creek *Nightly Moon*, a newspaper inclined to sensationalism, had a field day with the events, frequently reporting them under the title "The College Circus." On January 10, although not naming Bell, it described his behavior as "coarse and overbearing and the result has been prejudicial to the school." Students had held an "indignation meeting" the previous evening, January 9, with 160 of them signing a protest statement expressing their disgust "with the action of the faculty." Reporting on meetings held on January 24 and 25, the paper stated that the denominational and college leaders had pursued a process of "soaping," probably referring to obfuscation and what today we might call "spin." More specifically, it said that the "governing authorities are obdurate, and determined to retain the recalcitrant teacher [Bell]," prompting the students to go home in a "rage." Assessing the situation, the reporter concluded that "as a whole these two meetings have been unproductive of good, for the people are not fools and do not propose to be soft-soaped simply to see how it would feel." With students and members of the Battle Creek Adventist Church urging Smith to present a minority report, the *Nightly Moon* observed a few days later that "Eld. Uriah Smith is the only member of the school board who has remained true to the faculty and school; but when we take into account his fine intellect and his high moral worth, may we not safely regard him as a majority of the board."[3]

Butler, of course, saw things differently. At the end of January he wrote to Haskell, focusing on Uriah's role in the controversy. "Brother Smith is really the biggest chunk we have to deal with," he reported. "He is the recognized head of the opposition to the board. They look to him, quote him, and he counsels with them I am certain, and I feel sure gives the rest of us away by telling them what we say on the board." The GC president further stated that Smith "takes a square stand against us on nearly all points" and "spoils much of the effect of what we do or say." According to Butler, Uriah "alone constitutes the minority," and if he did issue his own report, Butler would produce a rebuttal. When the board asked McLearn and two teachers to resign and they refused, Smith protested the request, Butler said, claiming that "this was a "conspiracy' to get McLearn out, which you and Will [William C. White] started in the conference and this was but a step in the plan. I tell you he was not the quiet Uriah he generally is." As the GC president had suggested in his earlier letter, it is apparent that the controversy was not just about the administration of Battle Creek College but also reflected tensions between the California and Michigan church administrators and publications. Smith seems to have felt that his position as editor of the *Review* and the church's chief spokesman was threatened.[4]

In early February Butler reported to W. C. White that the college controversy had been quiet for a while but that nonetheless the situation remained "terrible." "But our trust is in God, and we are working away faithfully and patiently and, I hope, meekly." By February 20 the denominational president concluded that a large part of the Battle Creek church was against him, which in turn affected who took the pulpit on Sabbaths. Smith had preached the previous two Sabbaths, but Butler did not think that it was a good idea for him to continue. "Of course this begins to pinch our pleasant friend [Smith] a little, and he is beginning to feel that he is in a tight place," he told White. "His thick and thin supporters don't want these 'conspirators' to preach, and they pinch him on one side and it is a little embarrassing to have the members of the Gen. Conf. Comm. sitting down in the body of the house Sabbath after Sabbath. I am just mean enough to enjoy it a little." Butler further told of a confrontation in which McLearn's son, a student at the college, had pushed Bell down the stairs and had been subsequently expelled. The GC president said that Smith had opposed the action and "seemed inclined to censure Bell." But because of Smith's influence at the *Review* office, college, and church, "my hands are perfectly tied." Nonetheless, Butler was going to stay in place rather than leave. "I have had enough to break any ordinary man down, whose backbone is not made of cast steel. But when I think I am right I am not crushed so very easily, as probably these people will find out." Now the situation had become a clash of wills.[5]

Two days later Butler again wrote to White, reporting on a meeting with 75 to 100 prominent members of the Battle Creek church (during this and other controversies it appears that the congregation played an unofficial but powerful role in influencing denominational decisions), held either that day or the previous one. The GC president talked for about two hours reviewing and explaining the situation. Some in the audience protested that Smith had not been allowed to give a minority report. At some point Uriah spoke, saying that despite having a petition with 200 to 300 signatures urging him to give a minority report, he was not yet willing to do so. He explained that he did not want to "crush Bell," but also desired to keep McLearn "from being crushed." Butler commented that "the impression left upon my heart and many others [was] that the meeting was very sad. The spirit is as stiff as ever. They seem blinded by the cunning Uriah, among the rest." To complicate things, Butler reported that a controversy also surrounded Smith's leadership at the Review and Herald publishing house. "The show is decidedly a hard one," he said.[6]

On March 14 Uriah wrote to Ellen G. White, the first surviving document that directly gives his point of view. He told her that the problems had begun within three days of the beginning of the school term in August 1881, when Bell had concluded that McLearn was infringing on his rights. The investigation that took place in January 1882, according to Smith, did not support Bell's claim and did not involve disciplinary issues, something added later to the complaints against McLearn. "My position has been that whatever faults were discovered in the course of the policy of Prof. McLearn," Smith stated, "the board should go to him like men and Christians, and give him a chance to correct them, before displacing him without any such chance." Uriah further stated that he believed McLearn was willing to be instructed, was interested in the spiritual welfare of the young people at the college, and was a Christian gentleman "whom we had better not lose if we can help it." Referring to the February meeting reported on by Butler, Smith seemed to agree that with the church leaders on one side and many members of the Battle Creek church on the other, he was caught "between two fires."[7]

Several weeks later Butler wrote to Ellen White, referring to her letters to Smith. Although Uriah had shared them with the GC president, they had not talked about their contents and nothing had been said about Smith reading them to the church, something that White had apparently requested. Also Butler did not like an article that Smith had written about the college for the *Review* in which Uriah had obliquely referred to the recent problems and expressed a hope that there would be no "material change" in the faculty during the coming months. "It has been a bitter experience to me, I tell you," Butler said, "to have Brother Smith do as he has. His confidence has been given to Gage, McLearn, Miller, and a lot more whom I feel sure are not in the light and school matters with us have been a forbidden theme for a long time." On the other hand, he reported that apart from these issues, he and Smith got along fine and "have no unpleasant words." But, he concluded, "here is Dear Brother Smith with all his precious talents—so kind and so good I feel that I am no body beside him in many respects. Yet it seems to me he is in a great fog bank so far as seeing the evil tendencies of the times in some respects. In this school matter he seems to me perfectly blind. We are not in REAL union." As he looked forward to the camp meeting season, Butler could not see how they could work together.[8]

On March 28 Ellen White sent a Testimony to Smith but addressed to the Battle Creek church, which suggested that he was to present it to the congregation. She told Uriah that he was "on the wrong side" of the college controversy and that his "course is unjustified and unchristian." When she learned that Smith had not read the Testimony to the church, she wrote on June 20 another one, stating that "Eld. Smith questioned the propriety of bringing the testimony before the church at all. Thus he takes responsibility of standing between God's word of reproof and the people." Even more strongly than in her first communication, she said that Smith was "again working on the side of the enemy."[9]

In mid-July 1882 Butler expressed himself in stronger terms. "Uriah's course seems to us unaccountable only on the supposition of the influence of relatives and friends," he wrote to Ellen White. "I have tried very hard to treat him kindly and show love and interest for him, and we have not had a word of trouble only on the college matter. But there is a great gulf between us, really, as much as I wish otherwise." After the board had dismissed McLearn, the GC president reported to Ellen White that Smith and others had raised $50 for him and at a meeting at which they had presented him with a bouquet had expressed their admiration and sympathies. "They had, I should judge," Butler commented, "a genuine mutual admiration society." Then he noted that the next day the college board had been served with papers notifying that McLearn was suing it for $2,000.[10]

The following August, Smith wrote to Ellen White, telling her that he had "never had any controversy with the Testimonies, or with your work;

and I do not intend to have." He said that he had not regarded her spring letter to him as a testimony because he "had always supposed that a testimony was based on a vision, and I did not understand that you had had any vision since the recent trouble in the college commenced." Further he stated that he had no "intention of withholding it from the church, or of belittling or casting any slight upon it." If he had done anything wrong, he said that he was sorry and "shall try to see and make it right."[11]

Much to Butler's satisfaction, Smith left Battle Creek later that month. The GC president was hopeful that Ellen White could help him, now that he was away from the bad influences of the Adventist community. "He is such a nice man, so kind and pleasant," Butler stated. "I never had anything cut me up worse than this lack of union between us. To feel that we could not be in harmony, it made me feel exceedingly bad. I told him so several times. But I saw no other way I could do."[12]

In December Smith wrote a long defense of his actions to Ellen White, telling her that "you certainly have been misinformed, and are mistaken in regard to these things." Although he rejected reports that he had attempted to blacken Bell's character, he continued to believe that the man's charges against McLearn had not been sustained. "And I know that in all this trouble," he said, "I have acted in the integrity of my heart, as I felt assured that justice and right demanded." Expressing a good deal of emotion, he concluded, saying, "I have a conscience void of offense in this thing. I have nothing to take back till facts can be changed, or it can be shown that I have mistaken them. What kind of a person do you think I am? Do you think after my experience of thirty years in this work, that I shut my eyes and plunge recklessly around, not knowing what I am about, and then suddenly get my eyes open and see that I have been wantonly outraging every principle of right and justice and truth and honor? . . . I intend to know before I take a position that there is good ground for it, and to be careful where I step, and act conscientiously in the fear of God. This I have tried to do. And when I thus stake a position, I do not intend to be driven from it, till I see at least just as good reason for changing it, as I had for taking it."[13]

By February 1883 Butler was reporting to Ellen White that because Smith had not liked her most recent Testimony to the Battle Creek church he had refused to serve as an elder. Furthermore, he had heard that Uriah was not attending many church meetings, probably referring to Sabbath services.[14]

THE AUTHORITY OF ELLEN WHITE

The testimonies that Ellen White had written to Smith during the college "troubles" placed him in a difficult position. In 1881 James White had died, and Smith, despite his frequent conflicts with the man, had written appreciatively of his contributions to the denomination in the *Review*. But more recently he had seemingly ignored Ellen White's counsel, and the *Sabbath Advocate*, apparently a local independent publication, was spreading the news that he had rejected the Testimonies. In June 1883 Butler wrote to Ellen White to tell her that he had seen Uriah while visiting Battle Creek. "He was pleasant," the GC president reported, "but according to all accounts he is as firm as ever in his views, and from the positions he takes in a quiet way it would not seem that he had any great practical faith in the Testimonies."[15] Smith was aware of this perception, but felt that he was caught in a situation with no easy way out. "I still hold that Sister White has been shown things in vision, and that is a manifestation of Spiritual Gifts," he wrote to minister D. M. Canright in August, "but they do not stand on a level with the Scriptures, and should not be made a test of fellowship." Furthermore, he said that he was "aware that what I have written will not materially help my case in regard to the testimonies; for it brings me into direct antagonism with what Sister White has last published about me."

Referring directly to the dilemma in which he found himself, Smith said that "logically my case cannot be let alone till I have acknowledged what [Sister White] wrote in our school troubles, which I have no evidence was or is vision, and as I wrote to [Brother White]. I now have to discriminate between 'testimony' and 'vision.' Well, I think I know myself as well as [Sister White] knows me, and I leave all these things in the hands of God, determined to seek to do His will here, and find a place in His kingdom hereafter."[16]

But the issue was not only Smith's response to White during the college "troubles." Canright had previously written to Smith regarding omissions, particularly with regard to the "shut door" belief, in Ellen White's tract "A Word to the Little Flock" when republished in *Experience and Views*.

Smith said that he had not been aware of the discrepancy. "It seems to me
that the Testimonies, practically, have come into that shape, that it is not
of any use to try to defend the erroneous claims that are now put forth for
them," he commented. "At least, after the unjust treatment I have received
the past year, I feel no burden in that direction."[17]

Asking Canright to contribute an article to the *Review*, Smith explained
at length his position regarding the Testimonies: "I do not take the discon-
solate view of our experience that you seem to, for if the visions should
drop out entirely, it would not affect my faith in our biblical theories at all;
hence I should not consider my experience worthless, nor my life thrown
away; for I am rooted and grounded on our doctrines. I believe the system
of prophetic interpretations we present is sound, and that so far as we
have been instrumental in presenting it to the world, we have done a good
work. I didn't learn any of these things from the visions, and they don't
stand on their authority. You ask if there is any way out. I do not know,
or rather, while there must be some way through present difficulties (for
God will carry on and bring through His own work), I do not now see
what that way is. The idea has been studiously instilled in the minds of
the people that to question the visions in the least is to become at once
a hopeless apostate and rebel, and too many, I am sorry to say, have not
strength of character enough to shake off such a conception, hence the
moment anything is done to shake them on the visions they lose faith in
everything and go to destruction. I believe this state of things never would
have occurred had the position of our people on this manifestation of the
gifts been correct. If our people would come together and calmly, candidly,
kindly, and freely deliberate upon this matter, I believe, as I have said to
you and others, that a consistent position could be found, which would
free the subject from difficulties, meet and satisfy the scrutiny of an intelligent public, and not rob the gift of a whit of the good it was intended
to do. But there are many too doggedly bigoted and stubborn to offer any
very flattering outlook in this direction. If the matter could be got along
without any violent disruption anywhere, it would be better. This is what
I dislike, and fought against in our college troubles."[18]

After White had criticized him in her Testimony to the Battle Creek
Church, saying that he had rejected the Testimonies, Smith told Canright
in July that "if I say that I haven't rejected them, I thereby show that I

Uriah Smith in the early 1860s. This photograph is part of a collection of pictures of early SDAs prepared by J. Warren Bacheller, longtime friend and coworker of Uriah Smith.

This ambrotype is the earliest known picture of either Uriah or Harriet Smith. It was taken in the late 1850s, likely as a wedding photo in 1857.

Uriah Smith in the mid-1870s, about age 43.

Harriet Smith in the mid-1870s, about age 44.

Smith family in the early 1890s. Left to right: Uriah Wilton, Charles Stevens, Harriet Newall, Annie Arabelle, Uriah, Leon Alberti, and Samuel Parker.

Birthplace and childhood home of Uriah Smith in West Wilton, New Hampshire. This mid-1800s picture shows a porch that was likely added after the Smiths occupied the home.

The second home owned by the Smiths in Battle Creek. Uriah and Harriet Smith are pictured here with friends and family.

Contemporaries of Uriah Smith. Top left, James and Ellen White. Top right, George I. Butler. Bottom left, A. T. Jones. Bottom right, E. J. Waggoner.

Standing, from left: George Amadon, Uriah Smith, Myron Cornell. Sitting, from left: Martha Amadon, Harriet Smith, Cornelia Cornell, and Lucinda Hall. This picture was taken in June 1865 shortly after the death of Lucinda's husband, William Hall.

Uriah Smith performed numerous weddings during his lifetime. This picture was taken on December 31, 1891, at the wedding of George Wells and Myrtle Gerould.

Uriah Smioth was a very ingenious and resourceful person. Here are some of his creations. Top left: An engraving of West Wilton in 1847. Top right: A drawing of Virginia's Natural Bridge in 1850. Bottom, from left: his prosthetic leg patent, his design patent for automobiles, and a copy of his well-known Daniel and the Revelation.

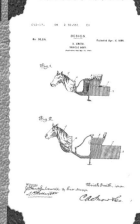

Four lifelong friends and coworkers at the *Review* office. From left, George Amadon, Oswald Stowell, Warren Bacheller, and Uriah Smith.

The *Review and Herald* office, c. 1868. Uriah and Harriet Smith lived with the Dodge family in the house to the left of the office shortly after their marriage.

Above, left: the first issue of the *Review* to list Uriah Smith as resident editor. Above, right: instructions for the postmaster in Rochester, New York, which lists all members of the "Rochester family." This card was made between the fall of 1853 and the fall of 1854 and kept by Harriet Smith.

Uriah Smith, with muttonchops, near the end of his life. c. 1900.

have, for I contradict this one." He continued to express his frustration regarding his situation. "Her attack upon me seems to be most uncalled for and unjust," he complained. "She has forced me, without cause, into a very embarrassing position, because if I say nothing, of course it will be taken as a virtual acknowledgment of the correctness of the charge. But if I do say anything, I must speak my convictions, which will not be at all satisfactory to them."[19]

In October he told Canright and his son Wilton that he and Harriett had met with White and that many of his perplexities, "which have been a trial to me," had been relieved, again repeating the pattern of resistance followed by submission that he had followed in previous controversies. "Now I would much rather a person would be radical on the testimonies, even if they are not all what they claim to be, than to give up on the present truth," he said, "for this latter I believe to be vital to our future well-being." Although he does not seem to have changed his mind regarding the Testimonies, he was willing to keep his views to himself for the good of the church. "So the best light I see for myself is to cast my influence in so far as it will go with the body, and wait further developments. [Sister] White is doing a work which no other person seems fitted for doing, and which is of great value to the cause. So I will get along with my private trials and hold them in abeyance for the general good."[20]

Despite his private reservations, Smith subsequently came to the defense of Ellen White on several occasions. The first occurred when A. T. Jones and others began promoting the prophetic visions of Anna Garmire, a young woman in the Battle Creek area. Ellen White condemned Garmire and her teachings at the 1884 Jackson camp meeting, saying that there "would be no definite time message given of God since 1844." In a written statement dated August 7, 1885, she urged Adventists to "give not one word of sympathy or support" to the Garmire movement. Smith and Butler wrote an undated pamphlet entitled "An Exposure of Fanaticism and Wickedness" that may have appeared after White's statement, for they referred to her condemnations of Garmire both private and public. Citing an 1884 tract, "Another Angel Come Down From Heaven," which included accounts of Garmire's visions at age 14, they observed that they had "never read a more trivial, illogical, weak, and silly production upon any religious topic." Garmire's father, who was pushing to have his daughter recognized as a prophet, had written to both George Amadon and Smith in June and July asserting that the Second Coming would occur before the corn had matured. "We know from the Bible and the Testimonies," they wrote, "that Anna and Mr. Garmire must be mistaken in these statements."[21]

Two years later he was again defending Ellen White, now against criticisms put forward by D. M. Canright, his erstwhile correspondent who had recently left Adventism. Although not naming Canright, in two June 1887 editorials he wondered why people opposed the visions. "People who accept the visions," he wrote, "constitute the largest *united* body of Sabbathkeepers or Adventists to be found in the world." A month later he addressed the issue about which he and Canright had corresponded, arguing that White's visions had not taught the "shut door" and that there had been no suppression of her early views in later reprintings. In December he published a *Review and Herald Extra* responding to Canright's criticisms of Adventism. He accused the former Adventist minister of exaggerating his importance among Seventh-day Adventists and said that he misrepresented Adventist positions.[22]

Finally, in 1891 Smith preached a sermon in the Battle Creek church, apparently on behalf of a "Spirit of Prophecy Committee." Pointing out that Paul had taught that the spiritual gifts had been given to the church and that they were to continue to the last days, Uriah asked how Adventists should respond to Ellen White's gift. "Our relation to it is our relation to something which arose with this work," he stated, "which has gone right forward with it, side by side, which has interwoven itself into and through it and all about it, from the day this message began until this present hour." The gift of prophecy had counseled, admonished, and instructed Seventh-day Adventists from their beginning and should be "accepted, cherished, and obeyed." Although Smith does not seem to have ever abandoned his reservations regarding the Testimonies and their use, as he had told Canright in 1883 he kept his views private and worked for the good of the whole.[23]

ORGANIZATIONAL MATTERS

Despite his involvement in the controversy at Battle Creek College, Smith remained an active church member. Throughout the 1880s the denomination continued to elect him to numerous offices at its annual

General Conference sessions. A few examples will suffice. In addition to being reelected editor of the *Review*, Smith was appointed secretary of the 1880 session, as well as being put on the publication committee. In 1883 he served on the Resolutions Committee. The following year he was appointed to a committee to examine publication issues related to *The Sentinel*, the denomination's religious liberty magazine, and another committee that was "to consider any theological questions which may be brought before it." Then in 1885 he became a member of the Board of Trustees of the Seventh-day Adventist Educational Society. With Adventists coming into conflict with Sunday laws, in 1885 he served on a committee to look into their arrests for working on Sunday, while two years later he was appointed to a committee to help those who needed a legal defense. Also in 1887 he served on a committee to implement a new fiscal year for the General Conference, extending from October 1 to September 30.[24]

Besides such appointments, the General Conference sessions frequently gave him specific tasks to perform. In 1882 leadership asked him to revise *The Biblical Institute* "and prepare it for a question book to meet the wants of those just embracing the truth." The next session requested him to revise J. N. Andrews' pamphlet "Order of Events in the Judgment" and appointed him to a committee to review R. S. Owen's view of the seven trumpets of Revelation. The 1886 General Conference session invited him to edit a biweekly publication to use in "ship and city missions." Under the title *Gospel Sickle*, it continued for only one year, after which administration consolidated it with the *Temperance Outlook and Sabbath Vindicator*. Finally in 1889 the church asked him to prepare a Week of Prayer reading entitled "The Rise and Progress of the Message, and What It Is Destined to Accomplish."

Smith also frequently preached at the Battle Creek church, although former General Conference president John Byington had mixed reactions to the sermons. In a May 1881 diary entry Byington commented that "[Brother] Smith is sound in theory but lacks in energy." Again in February 1884 he said that Uriah had sound doctrine but more energy was wanted. Entries in January and November 1886 indicate that Byington thought that Smith should give more attention to the emotional side of religion. Other times, however, he assigned Smith good marks; his comments in June, July, and August 1884 included "a good discourse," "a very good discourse," and "a good sermon." Moreover, each year Uriah presented a series of doctrinal lectures at Battle Creek College, reporting in 1885, for instance, that he had a regular attendance of 95. Many years later an individual who had attended Battle Creek College in 1892 remembered Smith walking "to his office in [the Review and Herald building], waiting momentarily for that wooden leg to swing into place." But somewhat similar to Byington, he commented that Smith was "a fine writer but no speaker." Whatever his limitations, between his duties as *Review* editor, organizational activities, special assignments, preaching in Battle Creek, and lecturing at the college, he was a very busy man.[25]

During the summer and early fall, Smith continued to attend camp meetings, his itinerary varying from year to year. His brief reports occasionally mentioned traveling companions: Ellen White and George I. Butler in 1884, William Farnsworth and Stephen Haskell in 1886, and, possibly, Ellen White and Farnsworth in 1887. It is not always clear whether Smith went with his fellow speakers on a camp meeting circuit or whether they simply came together at particular places from different directions. Sometimes the subjects of his sermons are also mentioned: the second coming of Jesus and the mark of the beast at Spring Arbor, Michigan, in 1881, the need to improve one's talents at the 1881 Iowa meeting, the "Eastern question" at the 1884 New York meeting, and "Christ standing at the door, ready to enter if we only open to Him" at an 1889 meeting in Kalamazoo, Michigan. Although Smith's sermon subjects are identified only a few times, it is apparent that while he probably most often spoke on prophecy, he occasionally touched on other areas of the Christian faith. As before, Smith also sometimes reported camp meeting attendance: 2,000 on Sunday at the 1880 Alma, Michigan, meeting; 1,000 the following year in Spring Arbor, Michigan; 1,800 "Sabbathkeepers" at Jackson, Michigan; some 6,000 at a Sunday meeting in New York in 1884; and 2,600 in Michigan in 1886. He reported some 300 in attendance at the 1888 Indiana camp meeting, saying that people seemed to lack urgency and that many arrived late and left early. When weather interfered with proceedings, Smith took note. At the 1881 Iowa camp meeting a storm one afternoon brought one and a half inches of rain and hail the size of almonds. A hard rain in Vermont in 1886 forced the conference business meeting to move quickly. (Uriah seemed to appreciate the fact that discussion was short.)[26]

At times Smith also reported unique aspects of such meetings. Regarding the 1884 New York camp meeting, he stated that the newspapers "make prominent the fact that we do not seek to excite wild and boisterous demonstrations, but to convince the judgment by calm and earnest reasoning." The 1885 Pennsylvania camp meeting took place on the shores of Chautauqua Lake, where the steamship company offered free excursions that provided the opportunity to visit the Chautauqua Assembly Grounds. Then in 1886 he told his readers that the local street railway had put up "two large electric lamps to light the premises" at the meeting in New Bedford, Massachusetts. "This is somewhat of a novelty so far as our camp meetings are concerned," he commented, "but it proves eminently successful." That same year the tents arrived at the New York camp meeting after it had begun. Surprisingly, at the Kalamazoo, Michigan, convocation in 1889 "outsiders" complained that it had no sermons on distinctive elements of the Adventist faith. Uriah recommended that future camp meetings "devote a certain portion of time to such doctrinal points as might be thought important for them to hear." Several years earlier, after observing that the Michigan Ministerial Association had a program of scheduled speakers in 1882, Smith recommended that the church's camp meetings adopt a similar practice, something that they apparently were not doing.[27]

Traveling the camp meeting circuit was not an easy task, despite the value of being able to meet with Adventist adherents far from Battle Creek. In 1882 Smith summarized his recent itinerary: "Thus in the space of sixteen days we had traveled twenty-seven hundred and fifty-nine miles, been up six entire nights on the cars, and spoken twelve times. Under this somewhat taxing experience, we feel measurably worn, but otherwise in excellent health."[28] Such trips were not always burdensome, however. Uriah reported his attendance in 1882 at a quarterly meeting in Camden, Michigan, which probably did not require as much of him as did the camp meetings:

"We greatly enjoyed this visit to Camden, and the hospitable home which we found with one of the oldest families in the place. The dedication at Hazelton, the Ministerial Association at Otsego, and this occasion at Camden have been seasons of rare spiritual enjoyment; and the relaxation thus afforded from office duties has, we think, been of physical benefit also. We hope to be able to enjoy more such the coming summer."[29]

Although Smith had written his commentaries on Daniel and Revelation in the 1860s and 1870s, the 1880s were the period in which they became major sellers beyond the denomination. He prepared a new edition of the books, with about 50 added pages, which came out in 1881. But the following year, at the suggestion of literature evangelist George A. King, the publishing house combined them into a single volume to sell door to door. George Butler announced the new publication, saying that denominational books intended for the general public must be put into a form that "will suit the popular taste." He further explained the evangelistic value of the works: "These volumes contain the very pith and marrow of present truth, the very foundation on which it stands. If the truths contained in these volumes are accepted, the other truths believed by us are inevitable."[30]

The church then started a major campaign, urging the sale of "thousands upon thousands" of copies. "This is no mere moneymaking scheme, no speculation," Butler declared. "With us it assumes the proportion of a religious duty to get the light before the world on the glorious subject of prophecy." By August 1882, 2,000 books had sold, showing that the denomination could present its literature to the public if prepared properly. The publishing house therefore prepared a new larger, more attractive edition. Publishing leaders hoped to sell 10,000 volumes by the end of the year. "This book is calculated to reach the most intelligent class of minds," the General Conference president again commented. "It is best adapted to the wants of thinking people." As 1884 drew to a close, Butler announced that thus far colporteurs had sold nearly 25,000 copies. Such success had prompted the Review and Herald publishing house to begin setting type in October for a German edition, for sale to immigrants from that country.[31]

By the next year, however, sales had slowed, for colporteurs had discovered that they could make more money selling the magazines *Signs of the Times* and *Sunshine*. Butler protested that they were not justified in dropping the book, for it "constantly appeals to the facts of history." He especially saw *Daniel and Revelation*, as it became popularly known, as a means of reaching a more educated and intellectual class of people than Adventism had appealed to previously. "It will accomplish more with this class of people than with those who are ignorant. The subjects of the sanctuary, prophetic time, and many others, require a fair degree of intelligence, thought, and reflection, for their understanding. It is just the book for such persons to read." By midsummer he was urging the conferences and their tract societies to push the literature evangelism program more strongly, noting that "we are nearing the end. We must make every effort to disseminate the light of truth. *Thoughts on Daniel and the Revelation* is a most important means by which to accomplish this. Brethren and sisters, *use it; use it faithfully*, and thus save precious souls for the Master." Such pleas apparently had a positive effect, for the *Review* reported in October that large quantities of the book were being shipped, although it supplied no statistics.[32]

APPLYING DOCTRINE AND PROPHECY

Smith's main job, of course, was editing the *Review*, through which he continued to guide the denomination's doctrinal thinking. The prophetic perspective shaped his outlook, although in the 1880s he did not spend as much time explaining the biblical prophecies, and spiritualism did not attract as much of his attention, for its popularity had faded somewhat as the experiences of the Civil War became more distant in time.[33] But the Sunday law movement, which continued to gain momentum, and the increase in immigration (which brought in more Roman Catholics), as well as events abroad, gave him plenty of opportunity to apply his prophetic understanding to current events.

As before, Smith's premillennial prophetic interpretation led him to believe that the world was moving on a downward path, a belief that he found confirmed by the events of every passing year. In 1882 he noted such things as the corrupting influence of money on politics, tidal waves, military conflict, and the growing disregard of law, though he gave no specific examples. Two years later he stated that floods and droughts are the "preliminary fulfillment of the predictions concerning the shaking of the powers of the heavens, just as the decline of the Turkish empire and the present workings of spiritualism are preliminary fulfillments of Rev. 16:12 and 13."[34] A visit to New York City in 1884 confirmed to him personally that American society was deteriorating quickly. "The sights and sounds of a great metropolis in these days contain an impressive lesson for the student of prophecy. How like the description given us of the days of Noah and Lot, when, representing how it would be in the last days, worldliness was the irresistible tide and fleshly gratification the all-absorbing passion. What chance is there for the truth in such a scathing caldron of mammon and pleasure?"[35]

In 1885 he stated that infidelity, intemperance, and Mormon polygamy, none of which he approved, would drive religious activists to further endanger liberty. That same year he listed three "questions"—Eastern (i.e., Turkey), labor, and Sunday—as inevitable conflicts. In even more general terms, the following year he wrote that "we need no better evidence that we are drawing near the close of our work, than the manifestations we now have of the wrath of the enemy [Satan] against us. He is a good student of prophecy. He doubtless has a better idea than we can have of this world's future history, especially the events that are immediately in store for it." Smith argued against the concept of progress in an 1887 editorial and repeated the same idea in 1888. When he stated that the basic question is whether the world would get better or worse, unsurprisingly he said it was getting worse. Again in general terms, he claimed that "verily Christ's true kingdom must be at hand, or so much driftwood would not show itself upon the current, and so many counterfeits spring into existence. Meanwhile, the flood of evil and iniquity, perplexity, and distress, swells apace in all the world." And at the beginning of 1889, looking toward the new year, he outlined three reasons he believed that the end was near: "the growth of the third angel's message," the Papacy's attempt to "subvert liberty of conscience in our land" and its effort to achieve national recognition, and a European war that was "inevitable in the near future."[36]

Smith applied his general outlook when analyzing particular issues that he believed Adventists should be particularly concerned about. He continued to hold strong anti-Catholic views, saying in 1880 that Catholicism "has always been but a mass of superstition and iniquity" and arguing in 1889 that it opposed private judgment, freedom of conscience, and religious liberty. Furthermore, it was willing to lie to pursue its ends. But not only was Catholicism a corrupt system, it was also plotting to take over the country. One means was through establishing parochial schools wherever it could. "Thus is Rome's opposition to American institutions, and the liberty which they foster, becoming more and more outspoken," he wrote in 1888, "—a sure evidence of the growth of her power, and of the confidence which she feels in her ability to become mistress of the situation." That same year he described Catholic opposition to public schools in Georgia and its efforts to obtain state support for its own schools as part of a "Romish plan" to colonize the state so extensively that it would come under church control. Also he claimed that the Jesuits were out to break the entire system of public education.[37]

In 1883 Smith noted that Italy had become prosperous after Victor Emmanuel II had "kicked the crown of civil power off the pope's iniquitous head" 13 years previously. "Is there any connection between this remarkable change, and the fact that the pope's civil power has been taken away, and that Italy has become virtually the most Protestant country on the continent of Europe?" he asked. "Let the world look at these facts and curse into oblivion that system of spiritual tyranny, priestcraft and superstition, which buries beneath the mildew of death all countries where it is fostered, and reduces its subjects to superstitious pigmies." Whatever he might have meant by calling Italy a "Protestant country," it is clear that he saw Catholicism's potential influence in the United States as dangerous to the American economy and society as well as religion.[38]

Even more nefarious in his mind than Catholicism's grasp for power was the willingness of Protestants to join with their apparent archenemy to support Sunday legislation. In 1880 he criticized the editor of the *Christian World* for praising the Roman Catholic bishop of Buffalo, New York, who had written a circular denouncing the profanation of Sunday. "Protestants and [Catholics] combined could speedily secure such legal enactments as would make a Sunday-Sabbath law binding throughout all the land. When a Catholic bishop issues such a circular as the one herein referred to, and a Protestant editor hails it with undisguised glee, it is strong evidence that such a consummation as regards the Sunday institution is not far distant."[39]

Eight years later Smith criticized United States president Grover Cleveland for sending a present to the pope on the occasion of his jubilee, saying that "no true Protestant can reflect without indignation on the shameful sycophancy of [the president's action]," which Uriah interpreted "as a bid for the Roman Catholic vote of this country." In 1889 he applauded the publication of *The American*, an anti-Catholic paper in Marlboro, Massachusetts, and criticized "recreant Protestants" who were joining Catholics to change the "government into a religious despotism."[40] As if it was not enough to believe that Catholics and Protestants were working together, as early as 1883 he claimed to see both Mormons and Catholics seeking separately the same goal: "The control of this nation is fiercely and persistently sought by two implacable enemies. The Romish hierarchy, on the one hand, seek to subject the nation to their power; and the Mormons, on the other, are exerting all their energies to accomplish the same end. We believe the world is too near the end of its history to allow time for either project to be accomplished, but not so near that great evil and trouble may not arise from the workings of these organizations before the end."[41]

Clearly, for Smith the nation's liberty was under threat from all sides. Interestingly, however, when he traveled to California for the 1887 General Conference session, he stopped off at Salt Lake City, where he reported to his readers on the impressive acoustics of the Mormon Tabernacle. He further expressed admiration for what the Mormons had accomplished, but criticized their religious views and practices.[42]

Uriah also identified and criticized many weaknesses that he found in contemporary Christianity. When Dwight L. Moody and Ira Sankey republished a hymnbook to use in their popular evangelistic meetings, Smith in 1880 saw it only as a moneymaking scheme for the "traveling revivalists." He believed that the "so-called revivals" did not represent "genuine Christian reform," because "there must be more of the law of God, and less of the merely sensational." Somewhat similarly, in 1885 he questioned the emerging Holiness movement, which emphasized the need for Christians to experience the perfecting influence of the Holy Spirit. Adventists, Smith believed, must show them their errors and introduce them to the truth. If they rejected such "light," then Adventists should not affiliate with them. "Their shouts must be to him [the Sabbathkeeper] as hollow as sounding brass," he commented, and "their high professions, the climax of blind presumption." When Holiness ideas began influencing Adventism in the 1890s, he must not have liked it, especially when one of its advocates, A. T. Jones, became editor of the *Review*, but he managed to keep his silence.[43]

Writing in 1880 about the widely accepted belief in natural immortality and hell, which he called "unscriptural doctrines" that had been "foisted into the Christian system," he held those who promoted them as responsible for "the skepticism of the present day." Christian churches that used plays and other entertainments to raise money also drew his ire in 1882.[44] The following year he objected to theologians who abandoned or adjusted

Christian beliefs to bring them into accord with the findings of modern science.

"We had always supposed that Christianity did possess some fundamental principles; that among these were a belief in the authenticity and credibility of the Scripture of the Old and New Testaments, a recognition of the fact that man by sin has fallen and must depend on a Redeemer for his future well-being, and that Christ has provided the requisite atonement for all who will accept of it."[45]

Moreover, even as he extended Christmas greetings to his readers in 1886, Smith reminded them of the season's pagan origins. "Not that we have faith in the old pagan festival of the 25th of December, baptized into a sanctified falsehood by an error-besotted, self-styled Christian Church, and called Christmas, nor any particular respect for that ancient and unnatural arrangement that divides the year in the dead of winter, as it divides the day in the dead of night."[46]

As Smith looked at such religious trends, he concluded that the division between Adventism and other Christians was becoming more and more clear. "Our controversy with prevailing religious beliefs is narrowing down rapidly," he wrote in 1887. "It is not to be so much a question as to whether there is any Sabbath or not, but only as to which day is the Sabbath; not so much as to whether there is to be any second coming of Christ or not, but as to what constitutes that second coming."[47]

Uriah's prophetic interpretation that the United States government would collude with ecclesiastical power events seemed to be confirmed during the 1880s as several states passed laws outlawing work on Sundays and eliminated exemptions in existing laws for those who observed Saturday as the Sabbath. Historian Dennis Pettibone writes that between 1885 and 1896 more than 100 Adventists were arrested for breaking Sunday laws. While most were in the Southern and border states, particularly Tennessee and Arkansas, they also extended as far as Texas, Pennsylvania, Rhode Island, and California. Many Seventh Day Baptists as well as Jews also found themselves the targets of such laws.[48]

In addition to the state efforts, the National Reform Association (NRA) in 1879 began a campaign to establish a national Sunday law. The Woman's Christian Temperance Union (WCTU) and the newly formed American Sabbath Union soon joined the NRA in bringing petitions to Congress demanding such an ordinance, claiming that they represented 14 million Americans. "All but a handful of these petitions came from ministers, churches, other ecclesiastical bodies, and religiously oriented temperance organizations," Pettibone writes. "The chief petitioners, aside from the WCTU, were Presbyterian, Methodist, and Congregational groups. Most major Protestant denominations participated in the petitioning." Responding to their efforts, Senator H. W. Blair of New Hampshire introduced a Senate bill in 1888 that would outlaw most secular work and recreation on Sundays in areas exclusively subject to federal jurisdiction as well as shut down both the movement of mail and the railroads. When Blair's bill failed to pass Congress, Sunday law advocates unsuccessfully sought a law for the District of Columbia, which was under congressional authority, but did push Congress to pass one closing on Sundays the 1893 Chicago World's Fair, which received government funding. Congress, however, provided no means of enforcement, and the fair opened on Sundays anyway.[49]

Smith viewed such developments with alarm. Commenting on the Republican argument in California that a Sunday law was only a "police regulation," he said in 1882 that "they cannot forbear revealing the fact at almost every turn that it is as a religious institution, after all, that they want it enforced." Later that same year he again argued that the Sunday law plank in the California Republican platform was a purely religious thing that had no connection with temperance, despite the fact that it proposed to close saloons on Sunday. Efforts to link Sunday legislation with prohibition posed problems for Adventists, who supported restrictions on the sale of alcoholic beverages while opposing legal protection of the Sunday Sabbath. Perhaps such conflicting desires led Uriah in 1887 to soften his argument a bit as he called for exemptions from "indiscriminate Sunday legislation."[50]

Meanwhile, he spent more space editorializing against the NRA than he did against state laws. Seeing NRA actions as confirming Adventist interpretation of prophecy, Smith argued in 1880 that "if the view we take of the prophecy is correct, the movement is as sure to come as the earth is to make one revolution on its axis during the next twenty-four hours; and if it comes, the more improbable it has appeared, the more striking will be the fulfillment. So we put on record such remarks as the movement draws out, pro and con, and await the issue."

Again emphasizing the religious aspect of Sunday legislation, three years later he asked whether anyone would deny that the NRA was seeking the "enforcement of theological institutions by civil penalties." In December 1883 he attended an NRA convention in Ohio, reporting that "they intend to reach and control the masses when the time comes to strike" and predicted that a great crisis was looming. A few weeks later he commented that ultimately America would subordinate civil authority to religious power.[51]

Despite the ascendancy of the NRA, Smith recognized that society was becoming more secularized, but he also understood that secularization itself prompted religious leaders into action. Writing in 1880, he stated, "The increasing demands of infidelity are sure to create a counter-action among religionists. This is inevitable. And perhaps more will join in the movement for the religious amendment from fear that the infidels will secure their ends, than from any other cause. Let the agitation proceed. We are not sorry for the sign." In 1885 he again called attention to increasing secularization but said that the NRA and other organizations were fulfilling prophecy.[52]

With the nomination of Democrat Grover Cleveland for United States president in 1884, Uriah apparently thought that the Democrats would win the upcoming election. Consequently, he believed, the Sunday issue would come to the front in 1888 as religious forces solidified in reaction. "We believe the hand of Providence is now specially interposing in all national affairs," he wrote, "to hasten the fulfillment of prophecy for this time." During 1887, as the WCTU moved to support Sunday laws, Smith described it as "being roped into connection with the National Reform Association." As Sunday law advocates began arguing that such laws would protect workers, particularly those in stores and barbershops who often had to labor seven days a week, Smith denied such a benefit. Their only hope, he believed, would come "from the creation of a bond of union and sympathy between capital and labor."[53]

When Blair introduced his Sunday bill in 1888, he seemed to fulfill Smith's prediction four years earlier that the issue would climax in a presidential election year, and Uriah commented that the bill was an "indication of what is soon coming upon us." By early 1889, however, he seemed to draw back, stating that he did not expect the bill to pass, but even if

it did, it would not be a fulfillment of Revelation 13 but simply a breach
in the first line of defense against religious despotism. He also believed
that the reported millions of petitions to Congress supporting Blair's bill
were greatly exaggerated. Nonetheless, while perhaps not immediate, the
movement subordinating the state to the church was advancing. "But in
this land of many creeds and many churches," he wrote in 1889, "it is
necessary that a sufficient degree of union should be secured between the
denominations to lead to a concert of action, before the image to the beast
can be formed. That union is fast coming, and the image is not a great way
off."[54]

The effort to force Sunday closing on the upcoming World's Fair in Chicago also caught his attention. In an 1891 editorial he argued strongly
for the separation of church and state. "But we would like to know why
Christians should consider it stepping on their toes, if the managers of the
exposition do see fit to keep it open on Sunday? When was the world put
into their hands to regulate as to what days they should rest and labor?
When and by what authority were they raised to that pinnacle of moral
impudence where they could dictate to the nations as to their religious
duties and bring everyone to the standard of their own prejudices and
intolerances? Let us give them a prescription which will save them from
getting into such a pit: it is this: Let them not thrust their ecclesiastical toes
out into the path of civil and religious liberty to try to trip up those who
are walking therein, but withdraw them to the proper place, and then they
will not get trodden upon."[55]

While Smith was primarily concerned with the specter of a national
Sunday law, he also disliked several other aspects of a rapidly changing
American society. The years between the Civil War's end in 1865 and the
beginning of the twentieth century saw the industrialization of the United
States, which greatly expanded the wealth of entrepreneurs and offered
job opportunities for mostly unskilled workers. Immigrants from eastern and southern Europe, often from peasant backgrounds and Catholic,
Orthodox, or Jewish in religion, now outnumbered those from northern
Europe as they flocked into the country to take advantage of work opportunities. Because the factory jobs were often unsafe, required long hours,
and paid low wages, labor conflict soon emerged.[56]

As early as 1880, Smith noticed the accumulation of wealth by such people as the Astor family, Cornelius Vanderbilt, and Jay Gould. At the same time he also recognized that labor unions and communism were continuing to expand their efforts to limit and even destroy such monopolies of capital. In words that Karl Marx could almost have written, Uriah saw a coming conflagration between the adversaries. "The wages of the laborers have been kept back by fraud. The gold and silver, instead of being circulated and doing good, has rusted in idleness in the coffers of the rich," he said. "But the day is at hand in which the lofty looks of men shall be humbled, and the haughtiness of men shall be bowed down, and the gold and silver, hoarded with so much covetousness and care, shall be thrown to the moles and bats, as the worthless trash that it is."

In contrast to Marx, though, Smith took a biblical perspective. The prophets had predicted such economic and social developments, and they were, therefore, seemingly inevitable. Although he supported the aims of those who opposed financial monopolies, he said that the concentrations of wealth fulfilled James 5:1-6. Despite his criticism of the wealthy, he had little sympathy with the attempts of labor to organize unions. When he arrived in Oakland for the 1887 General Conference session, for example, he reported that the local Adventist church was unfinished "owing to the tyranny of the labor union in forbidding men to work, if any of the conditions do not suit them."

While he did not usually believe in political solutions to the nation's problems, Uriah nonetheless in 1883 called for the government to establish and operate a telegraph service. "Let the country be released from the remorseless clutch of the monopolists in every way possible," he urged. Commenting in that same year on efforts to clean up government corruption, he stated his belief that the nation was caught between anarchy and the necessary but unlikely prospect of civil service reform. "How rapidly are the signs fulfilling about us!" he concluded.[57]

As he had earlier criticized Irish immigrants, Smith now condemned the wave of other newcomers to America. "The worst classes are swarming in, the ignorant, diseased, depraved, and vicious classes," he declared in 1888, "who care nothing for anything that is precious to the true American citizen; and this influx is changing for the worse the moral condition of society, especially in the cities." In his comment Smith reflected an anti-immigrant viewpoint common among Americans, particularly those of English descent. A New Englander by origin, Smith retained his old geographical and ethnic loyalties and prejudices. Referring to reports in 1889 of farmers struggling with drought in the West, he called on them to return to New England, where he believed they could do better. "For our part," he wrote, "we would rejoice to see the tide turn, and to see New England filling up with a good class of American citizens, rather than that undesirable alien class who are coming in as fast as possible, and who make their boast that they will yet capture that portion of the country to their alien ideas and the Romish religion."[58]

In perhaps his strongest statement on the connections between immigration and the power of the Roman Catholic Church, in 1894 he criticized a Presbyterian pastor who opposed the anti-immigrant American Protective Association. "Probably another Jesuit in disguise in the pulpit of a Protestant church. The man belongs in the Romish church; and why does he not go there? All Protestants who claim that the papal church is the church of Christ are logically bound to acknowledge her claim that she is the only infallible teacher, and go back into her communion. If the time ever comes for which he prays, when there will be only one church, that church will be Roman Catholic."[59]

In 1885 Smith summarized his views on the contemporary condition of his country in *The Marvel of Nations*, an update of his previous work, *The United States in Prophecy*. Although published about two years before H. W. Blair introduced his Sunday bill, the work incorporated virtually all of the themes of Smith's editorials during the decade of the 1880s regarding the United States. He began the book with the observation that America had attracted the attention and admiration of the world. "As the student of prophecy, in common with all mankind, looks with wonder upon the unparalleled rise and progress of this nation," he stated, "he cannot repress the conviction that the hand of Providence has been at work in this quiet but mighty revolution." Then he supported his assertion with numerous quotations from newspapers and magazines commenting on the material, geographic, political, and religious progress of the nation.[60]

The central part of the book repeated his interpretation that the two-horned beast of Revelation 13 represented the United States, with the horns symbolizing civil and religious liberty but pointing toward a future that would undermine those principles. As Uriah looked at the country, he saw it racing downhill. Wealth was leading to luxury, luxury to corruption, and corruption pervading all parties. Popery had emerged to prominence on American shores, while the Protestant church was apostate, having failed to purify itself of false doctrines. Furthermore, movements such as spiritualism, trade unionism, socialism, free love, and communism were spreading throughout the population. He saw the repression of liberty on the horizon. "God is no respecter of persons nor of churches," he wrote. "And if the Protestant churches apostatize from Him, will they not be just as efficient agents in the hand of the enemy as ever pagans or papists have been? Will they not then be ready for any desperate measure of bigotry and oppression in which he may wish to enlist them?"[61]

Smith pointed to the activity of the National Reform Association and other organizations seeking the legal establishment of Sunday observance, which to him was the key issue, the "mark of the beast." "Then what shall we have? The church sitting in judgment on men's religious opinions, the church defining heresy, and the state waiting at its beck to carry out whatever sentence shall be affixed to a deviation from what the church shall declare to be 'Christian laws and institutions.' But was not this exactly the situation in the darkest reign of Roman Catholicism? And would not its production here be a very 'image to the beast'? Yea, verily."[62]

Indeed, he thought that American Protestants might surrender themselves to Catholicism, which would receive them "back into her bosom as erring, repentant children." Such a development would be dangerous, however, for "the Catholic Church is the same today in its intolerant and bloodthirsty instincts that it always has been. It makes its boast that it never changes. Once let it gain supreme control in this country, and how soon would every Protestant place of worship in the land be sealed up as silent as the tomb, and every Bible be banished, not from the school alone, but from the homes and hands of the people, and rigid conformity to the Catholic ritual alone be enforced by flood and flame, dagger and dungeon."[63]

As he had stated in the previous version of his book, he did not expect a union of church and state in the medieval sense, but rather an "image" in which the "ecclesiastical establishment [is] empowered by the state to enforce its own decrees by civil penalties; which, in all its practical bearings, will amount to exactly the same thing."[64]

The denomination used *Marvel of Nations* to promote its new religious liberty journal, *American Sentinel*. "As the book speaks of the work to be done in our government, and is very salable," George I. Butler wrote in 1886, "we believe that our brethren generally can obtain many subscriptions for them both among the most intelligent class of people." The following year Smith assigned both *Daniel and Revelation* and *Marvel of Nations* in his college lecture course.[65]

Outside the United States, the situation of Turkey, what many called the "Eastern question," caught his attention, because he believed that the prophecy in Revelation 9 foretold that country's fate. In 1882 he said that although the Papacy, the United States, and Turkey constituted "the three great objective points of prophetic interest," the Eastern question attracted special attention because "matters may come to a crisis there sooner than elsewhere." A short time later he thought that Russia and Austria were moving toward war, a conflict that would bring about the destruction of Turkey. Even if that did not happen right away, he believed, "whatever move is made the result is that Turkey comes still nearer her manifest doom without power to recede." Interpreting European affairs in light of his beliefs about Turkey, in 1883 he referred to a European conference that dealt with regulation of navigation on the Danube River. "Russia is slowly gaining back the prestige she needs to enable her to strike again toward the object of her ambition," he stated, "—the possession of Constantinople." With no crisis coming to a head that year, in September he explained the delay as the inability of the European nations to decide how to divide the Turkish territory. Nonetheless, he asserted, "the peace of Europe hangs upon a very slender thread."[66]

As 1885 closed, Smith saw events in the United States and Europe forming a pattern that suggested world history was drawing to an end. "Why may not even now a new era be opening in this work? What is to hinder? Outside of our own field but little remains to be done. A few more moves in the East, which may rapidly transpire, will complete the prophecy there. A little more advancement in our own country in the direction of a union of church and state, and the prophecy is fulfilled here. The greatest work yet remaining seems to be the warning that is to go through this message to all the world."[67]

The following year things seemed to be heating up once more in the

East. Smith quoted from a London cable dispatch in September 1886, concluding that the European states were coming to an agreement regarding the disposition of Turkey.[68] A few months later he expected a "speedy trial in war." Commenting at length on the situation, he said, "[Russia, Austria, Germany, and France] must either sit still and be crushed under self-imposed burdens, without any compensation of foreign spoils, territorial acquisitions, or satisfied national glory, till the nation collapses in bankruptcy, anarchy, and ruin, or they must assume a still greater burden and make a more desperate effort, in order to try the chances for victory in a conflict of arms. There is no alternative. And so the world centers all its eyes on the inevitable field of conflict to catch sight of the first puff of battle smoke, and opens all its ears to hear the echoes of the first guns of a war the end of which no man can foresee."[69]

Again, in January 1887 he stated his expectation of an "explosion" in Europe, but admitted that he did not know when it might occur. Some two months later he predicted that Turkey would soon fall and thereby usher in the final events of earth's history. "Thus the downfall of Turkey, which every intelligent person will not hesitate to admit is inevitable in the very near future," he wrote, "becomes the signal for the beginning of the reign of Christ, His advent in the clouds of heaven, the time of trouble, the resurrection of the dead, and the end of all things."[70]

In October 1890 he seemed to be exasperated that the "Eastern question" still remained unsettled. "Let her [Turkey] go out, retire, vanish, disappear, or as the prophecy (Dan. 11:45) expresses it, let that power come to its end with none to help it. And then let the next step immediately follow: 'And at that time shall Michael [Christ] stand up, the great prince which standeth for the children of thy people' (Dan. 12:1)."[71]

As much as Smith believed that the biblical prophecies laid out the world's future, his confidence that humanity was living in the last days was based on the Adventist doctrine of the heavenly sanctuary, about which he had written extensively. "The time might have been given to the taking away of papal supremacy, or the rise of the United States, or the commencement of spiritualism; but these are all utterly indefinite as compared with that closing work of Christ in the heavenly sanctuary which constitutes its cleansing, which begins at a definite point of time

[1844] and continues till probation ends, till every case has passed this investigative judgment, and all the saints are sealed preparatory to the coming of Christ, and delivered from the further power of oppression and evil."[72]

In 1889 Uriah wrote a four-part series entitled "Bible Reading on the Sanctuary." He explained that rather than referring to the earth, Canaan, or the church, as others had argued, the sanctuary in Daniel 8:14 was located in heaven. Israel's earthly sanctuary was patterned after the heavenly, but the only element that the two held in common was that they had two compartments, the holy and Most Holy places. Not missing any chance to argue for the seventh-day Sabbath, Smith noted that according to Revelation 11 the law of God is located in the ark in the heavenly sanctuary. "The force of this tremendous fact," he concluded, "forever pulverizes every argument which is brought forward to prove that the law has been abolished, or in the slightest degree changed."[73]

The "cleansing" that occurred on the "Day of Atonement" in the earthly sanctuary, when the priest went into the Most Holy Place, removed or pardoned the sins of the Israelites that had accumulated during the previous year, but it did not destroy them. "Pardon is simply the removal of sin from the sinner," he explained, "so that it no longer stands to his account." Because some other party must extinguish the sins, the priests transferred them to the scapegoat, which they sent into the wilderness to die, a process that would eradicate the sins placed upon it. Interpreting the ceremonies in the earthly sanctuary as the "type" prefiguring the "antitype" of the heavenly, Smith understood that the actions of the priests foretold those of Christ.[74]

After His crucifixion, Christ returned to heaven and began His ministry in the holy place, or first apartment, of the heavenly sanctuary, which now superseded that of the earthly priests, and entered the Most Holy Place, or second apartment, on October 22, 1844, to begin the final phase of His work. In a lengthy paragraph Smith summarized the parallels between the services in the earthly and heavenly sanctuaries:

"So far as human services can represent the work of the Savior, so in every essential particular He performs a work answering to that of the priests on earth, in connection with the earthly sanctuary. He receives confession from the penitent sinner; He pleads for him His blood; He transfers his sin to the sanctuary on high; and He carries on His work till finally He enters the Most Holy Place, makes the atonement, and cleanses the sanctuary of which He is minister above, as the priests cleansed the sanctuary here on earth. Then the work of salvation being done, He will take His position as king, and establish that kingdom of which there shall be no end."[75]

HEALTH, INVENTIONS, AND FAMILY

In today's terms Smith was what we would call a "workaholic," a characteristic of many early Adventist leaders driven by their belief that they must warn the world that Christ would soon return, bringing earthly history to a close. It was also probably a characteristic of Uriah's personality. In 1880 he editorialized: "A book notice in one of our exchanges [papers and magazines] commences thus: 'A pleasant little book with which to idle away a summer afternoon is' so and so. Yes, but who has summer afternoons which he can afford to idle away? In view of the needs and responsibilities of the present, and the destiny of the future, how such words sound! Better let such books and idleness go together, and in a world in which life and its possibilities is so serious a matter, fill up the time with earnest work. Instead of having summer afternoons to idle away, we would be glad if someone could devise means whereby two or three extra ones for labor could be thrown into each week."[76]

Two ministers who knew Smith later in his career recalled seeing items that reinforced, if somewhat humorously, his emphasis on work. J. O. Corliss remembered a "striking sketch [apparently drawn by Smith], fastened to the wall near his office chair. It represented a dead person lying in a coffin, with a statement beneath in a bold hand, 'This man was talked to death.' It proved sufficient to curtail intended common conversation in his office during business hours." A future president of the General Conference, W. A. Spicer, recalled that "there was a notice on [his] door, in dark purple-colored ink and in large letters:

"'Editors' Room
Busy? Yes, always.
If you have any business,
Attend to your business,
And let us attend to our business.'"[77]

Responding to a questioner who asked whether it was appropriate to

play the card game Authors, Smith responded by saying that such activities as croquet, Authors, and ball were not in themselves demoralizing but
were a waste of time, fruitless, and unprofitable. He further explained, "If
we are in the last days, and the end of all things is at hand, how can we
afford to spend a moment in such a foolish manner? We have none too
much time to seek the necessary preparation for the coming crisis, to cul-
tivate our minds, develop character, discharge our duty to those around
us, aid in advancing the cause of truth, and in every way act like sensible
men and women who believe what we profess, and who realize what both
common sense and the Scriptures teach us, namely, that in such a time as
this, it is worse than folly to squander precious moments in any manner
which does not contribute directly toward our eternal interests."[78]

Uriah also strongly opposed attendance at theaters and circuses, stating
that "true pleasure is found only in a spiritual life."[79]

Given his constant activity in church affairs, editing, and writing, it is
not surprising that he experienced frequent illness, particularly in the
early to mid-1880s. In March 1881 George Butler wrote to Ellen White,
telling her that Smith's Bible lectures at Battle Creek College had become
too much of a burden after D. M. Canright, who was to provide assistance,
"got off the track."

The combination of full responsibility for the lectures and Smith's other
work "had pretty much near used him up. His head was in such a condition that he could not sleep nights, and he had the chills return upon him.
So he had to give them [the lectures] up some days and has been poorly
ever since. Brother Smith felt that he was not well used, and I felt so too.
But what could we do? But we have felt that it is too much to make Brother
Smith go through that constant pull of five months every winter with all
his other cares. At his age he begins to feel the effects of wear, like some of
the rest of us."[80]

In June of the following year Smith reported that he had an attack of
ague (malaria) that began on a Sabbath and continued through the week.
Although the chills had stopped, he would be unable to attend meetings
in Saginaw and probably miss a church dedication in Edenville. Harriet
wrote to their son Wilton in May 1883 that his father was having head-
aches. "This afternoon (Sab.) he is lying upon the carpet in the sun with
a wet bandage about his head. I am hoping if he goes to camp meetings

this season that the change will help him. So much brain labor is killing him."[81]

A short time later Uriah himself described his condition to Ellen White in more detail. "The trouble has seemed to be mostly in my head. Ever since about the first of January, I have had almost a constant pain across my forehead, and it has been so that if I coughed or sneezed, or stooped down, or jarred my head in any way, it seemed as if it would fly to pieces. The doctors at the sanitarium tell me that the blood vessels of the brain have been so charged with blood by constant use that they have lost the power to control and drive the blood away, and that unless I can give up all mental labor for a while and give the brain a chance to recuperate, the difficulty will become disease [and] be hard to cure."[82]

Harriet also suffered ill health, for in August she complained to Wilton of light-headedness. She said that Dr. Kellogg called it a "softening of the brain" resulting from a lack of blood and had recommended that she take a trip, which she did, joining her husband at the New York and Maine camp meetings. They also took a side trip, for in a letter written to her "brothers and sisters" after her return she spoke of visiting relatives at her birthplace in Paris, Maine, and Uriah's relatives in West Wilton, New Hampshire. Presumably, the trip provided much-needed relaxation to the couple.[83]

The next year he seemed to be doing better, telling Ellen White that he had "endured the winter remarkably well. The most trouble I have had was with the slippery going." But he then outlined a series of editorial and writing tasks he hoped to complete before summer. Seemingly unable to slow down, he rejoiced "in the prosperity of the work, and the prospect of its speedy triumph, and I want to do what I can do to the best advantage, and all I can do, to help it forward."[84]

In March 1885, however, Butler reported to W. C. White that Smith was not doing well. "Brother Smith's health has also been very poor. I have been alarmed about him. He looked real bad in his face. He could sleep but little, and he had such a pain in his head he could do very little. I tried to have him take a trip away with Harriet. I was really afraid he would have something serious. We were in a close place. The teachers have been sick considerably this year, which has been a hindrance to the school. It seemed too bad to take away Brother Lewis from Brother Smith, but in talking with him we became satisfied he would [as] soon as . . . have his son Leon to help him as Charles, and the latter really rather teach than to work in the office. . . . We thought Leon, who desires to give himself to the Lord's work, could work in to good advantage. We sent for him, and Brother Lewis went to teach part of the classes. Brother Smith had to drop his lectures at the college on account of his health. He is rather better. He has been able to give but few lectures in the Tabernacle."[85]

About the same time, Uriah reported in the *Review* that he had given 74 lectures at the college, but had cut the course short. "Our own state of health admonished us that we must relax a little the strain of labor we have been under some months past."[86] A little later he further explained his health condition and what he thought the remedy might be in a letter to Wilton. "My head has been in such a condition that it seemed almost impossible to think, and I knew I could not try to do that kind of work to my advantage. . . . If I could change work a while, letting up on literary labor and spending a portion of my time in mechanical work, developing my new artificial leg, pentecycle, parallel ruler, domestic elevator, reclining chair, and steamboat wheel, all of which exist in my mind in embryo like the golden eggs in the goose of Aesop's Fables, this would be the best recreation I could have, and I think that under such treatment my brain would recover its usual tone in a short time."[87]

Smith also told his *Review* readers that he would attend the Pennsylvania camp meeting in June but not any others, for he had too much work at the office and "my condition of health is such that it would be imprudent to undertake a series of continuous camp meetings, with the fatigue of travel, loss of rest, and other unfavorable circumstances connected with them." In October 1886 he informed Wilton that his health was much better than during the past two years. It is the last extant report of Smith's health for the remainder of the 1880s and early 1890s.[88]

We have no evidence that he received time off to work on his "mechanical" projects, but brief references in letters and other sources indicate that he continued with some of them despite the fact that none of the inventions appear to have come to commercial production. In 1886 he told Wilton that he had developed a new shorthand system. "I call it 'Tonography' from the Greek. 'Tonas' a tone or sound and 'graphic' to write. I have the system all fitly framed [and] compacted together, but I want to test it as to its speed before making it public." He also said that he had in mind a machine "to demonstrate the doctrine of definite days on a round world, and the change of days at the day line, which I wish I had time to make." Nothing seems to have come of the idea.[89]

In 1887 he asked Wilton, who was working in California, to investigate a John Dixon of the Pacific Patent Agency, for Uriah had invented "an improved car seat," apparently for trains. He reported that agents in the East had warned him against Dixon. "If he is a man who can do anything for me, of course I would like to have him, but I do not want to give him a chance to swindle me out of the Pacific Slope." Smith's surviving correspondence contains no additional references to the car seat. In a letter to his brother Wilton written perhaps in 1888, Parker Smith appears to refer to the "pentecycle" his father had mentioned. "I do not have a [bicycle]," he told Wilton, "but Pa has a machine down [in the] cellar, that he made, that I can ride, and I guess it gives about as much exercise as riding a [bicycle]." Battle Creek historian Berenice Lowe describes another unique invention. "Because he tired waiting for a streetcar, he had a cane that had an attachment to open as a stool." Uriah was also "a skilled cabinetmaker," recalled Ernest Lloyd, a writer and editor who knew him late in life. Eugene F. Durand further noted that Smith had a workshop in the backyard of his second home, where "he would relax a few hours when editorial duties allowed, perhaps two afternoons a week, by working with his tools."[90]

Both Uriah and Harriet appear to have taken a deep interest in their children. In 1883 she wrote to Wilton describing Parker as "real good about the chores, quite an improvement upon my first edition of boys." Three years later she called Parker "just a splendid boy" and told Wilton that the youngest son Charles was "a great reader [and] good scholar [and] a good boy generally." However, Uriah was concerned with Wilton's apparent indifference to religious matters. In May 1883 he wrote to Ellen White, telling her that Wilton was going to Oakland to work at the Pacific Press. "He could have been a help to me here in writing, but I thought it would be better for him spiritually to go there," Smith said. "He will not have the opportunity there to excuse himself from religious duties in the church and Sabbath school that he would here." A few months later Uriah contrasted Wilton's actions with those of daughter Annie and second-oldest son Leon. Reporting that Annie was to be baptized the next Sabbath, he said that "she takes the step deliberately and I think understandingly."

He described Leon as "quite faithful in his religious duties in the church, the [Sabbath school], the [Tract and Missionary] society, and the family." But he expressed sorrow that Wilton "did not even kneel at family prayers when you first reached California. . . . Remember, the vows of a religious profession are upon you."[91]

Wilton seems to have stayed in Oakland, where he was learning the bindery business, until the spring of 1887, at which time Uriah planned on him working for the Review and Herald Publishing Association upon his return to Michigan. In April 1887 Smith wrote to him, saying, "I am glad you have the disposition expressed in your letter to be faithful in your work, and leave everything in the best possible shape there when you leave. But just as soon as you can get through there, and leave everything right and straight, we shall be glad to see you. I asked Bert [probably a foreman at the press] yesterday when he would be ready for you; and he said, 'This afternoon!'" Several years later Uriah apparently again told Ellen White of his concerns regarding Wilton, for she wrote that "her soul longs to have Wilton take his place under the bloodstained banner of Prince Immanuel."[92]

The family also had to deal with occasional illnesses. Parker reported to Wilton in February 1884 that "Charlie has been having a slight attack of scarlet fever, and I have had the stiff neck. We can't go out in the dining room at all. They put a sign up on the house that said scarlet fever on it. I [couldn't] go to school Friday afternoon because Ma was afraid I would carry it over there." Apparently wanting to allay any concerns that Wilton might have had, Uriah told him a few weeks later that "Charlie had no sickness worth mentioning." Two years later Harriet expressed worry about Annie's health, not saying anything specific but telling Wilton that his sister had left school. Annie could not have been too ill, however, for Harriet also said that she was taking music lessons.[93]

Parker kept a diary for a few months in 1884 and for a full year in 1887 that gives additional brief glimpses into his family life. In April 1887 he reported planting peas with Uriah and the next month said that he and his father had put poles in the ground for the bean plants. He also occasionally recorded items for family meals, buying chicken and oysters on January 4, 1884, and chicken for dinner a few days later on January 9. During 1887 he reported having oysters for dinner on January 2, buckwheats (presumably pancakes) for breakfast on January 6, maple sugar and pancakes for breakfast on March 28, and turkey for dinner on November 24. Also he reported buying pressed beef for his mother on August 1 and getting a roast from the meat market on September 9. Such information gives only incidental elements of the family diet, but they do further indicate that the Smiths did not adopt the vegetarianism advocated by Dr. John Harvey Kellogg and Ellen G. White.[94]

Despite his advocacy of nearly constant work and the lack of any evidence that he engaged in recreational activity other than gardening, working with his inventions, and occasional visits with relatives, Uriah does not seem to have objected to his family's pursuit of other kinds of pleasure. Returning from a camp meeting trip in 1884, Uriah brought the family a kazoo, hardly a serious musical instrument. As a teenager Parker was actively involved in informal baseball and football games, and at one point his father bought him a baseball. In addition to playing, Parker was also an enthusiastic spectator at more formally organized "match games," recording on June 9, 1887, that he had watched a baseball game between the *Review* office and the Advance Shops and Foundry, a local business, and on June 13 one between the sanitarium and the college. On August 2 he went to city park to view a game between teams from Battle Creek and Charlotte.

During October 1884 Parker traveled to Chicago, probably with his mother and younger brother, where he saw panoramas depicting the Battle of Gettysburg and the siege of Paris. He also visited Lincoln Park Zoo and went to a fair. In August of that same year Harriet reported to Wilton that with the "dusky portion of our community" she had attended a parade marking the fiftieth anniversary of the British emancipation of slavery in the West Indies (known as Emancipation Day), at which Frederick Douglass made a speech. She called the occasion a "grand success."[95]

Annie also engaged in a bit of fun. In 1886 she wrote to Wilton describing a double wedding that her father had conducted at their house. "Pa occupied about 15 or 20 minutes in reading Scripture," she told her brother, "to the effect that it was not good for man to be alone, and that a man should leave all [and] cleave unto his wife, etc. Also that the husband is head of the wife (hissing by the ladies)." She also noted that "of course the young folks must get into mischief, so we emptied some of them [little

baskets on the cake], and filled them with shriveled apples and onions."
Furthermore, she exhibited some independence when she expressed a
desire to attend public school rather than Battle Creek College, for she
thought that she would learn more. Despite Uriah's advocacy of Adventist
separation from the "world," he apparently did not stand in her way, for
she graduated in the Battle Creek High School class of 1889.[96]

Smith himself could engage in a bit of lightheartedness as well. After
Alma Wolcott, who had lived in the Smith home for several years and
was teaching at an Adventist school in Michigan, married fellow teacher
George Caviness in 1882 while Uriah was in Oakland, California, Uriah
wrote them a letter addressed to "My Dear Naughty Children." He told
them that "it was very, very, naughty of you to take the time when *pater
familias* was away off out of reach to do as you have done. But I suppose
I shall have to let you off this time on 'suspended sentence,' the condition
being that you will never do so again!"[97]

Despite his dismissal of Christmas as a pagan holiday in his *Review* editorials, the Smith home seems to have given it at least limited recognition. In a January 1886 letter Harriet thanked Wilton for sending gifts
that brightened a Christmas otherwise without presents. Perhaps because
Thanksgiving did not have pagan connections, the family seems to have
given it more attention, for later that year Uriah wrote to Wilton on the
holiday, saying that the "bird is slowly dizzling [sic] in the oven." He further reported that another family was coming to dinner and that he had
wanted to go ice skating with Leon but the ice was too rough. Although
not connected with Thanksgiving but also giving another indication that
Uriah's activities extended beyond the church, he referred to "Our chau-
tauguan [sic] Circle" being active.[98]

---

[1] For discussion of the Battle Creek College controversy, see Emmett K. VandeVere, *The Wisdom Seekers* (Nashville: Southern Pub. Assn., 1972), pp. 42-45, and Meredith Jones-Gray, *As We Set Forth: Battle Creek College and Emmanuel Missionary College* (Berrien Springs, Mich.: Andrews Univ., 2002), pp. 7-15.
[2] GIB to WCW, Jan. 19, 1882.
[3] Battle Creek *Nightly Moon*, Jan. 10, 25, 26, and Feb. 1, 1882. The paper also pub-lished responses defending Bell and the college administrators. See Jan. 30 and Feb. 7, 1882.
[4] GIB to SNH, Jan. 30, 1882.

⁵ GIB to WCW, Feb. 20, 1882.

⁶ GIB to WCW, Feb. 22, 1882.

⁷ US to EGW, Mar. 14, 1882.

⁸ GIB to EGW, Apr. 26, 1882; *RH*, Apr. 18, 1882, p. 248.

⁹ EGW, *Testimony for the Battle Creek Church* (Oakland: Pacific Press Pub. House, 1882), pp. 20, 28, 42, 47.

¹⁰ GIB to EGW, July 16, 1882.

¹¹ US to EGW, Aug. 10, 1882.

¹² GIB to EGW, Aug. 24, 1882.

¹³ US to EGW, Dec. 1, 1882.

¹⁴ GIB to EGW, Feb. 18, 1883.

¹⁵ *RH*, Aug. 9, 1881, p. 104; Aug. 16, 1881, p. 120; GIB to EGW, June 17, 1883.

¹⁶ US to DMC, Aug. 7, 1883.

¹⁷ US to DMC, Mar. 22, 1883. Canright quoted from Smith's letter in his *Life of Mrs. E. G. White, Seventh-day Adventist Prophet; Her False Claims Refuted* (Cincinnati: Standard Pub. Co., 1919), p. 158.

¹⁸ US to DMC, Apr. 6, 1883.

¹⁹ US to DMC, July 31, 1883.

²⁰ US to DMC, Oct. 2, 1883; US to WS, Oct. 2, 1883.

²¹ "Written Statement From Sister White," Aug. 7, 1885; GIB and US, "An Exposure of Fanaticism and Wickedness" (np., nd.), pp. 5, 7, 8.

²² *RH*, June 7, 1887, p. 361; *RH*, June 14, 1887, p. 376; July 19, 1887, pp. 456, 457; *Advent Review Extra*, December 1887, pp. 3, 4.

²³ "The Spirit of Prophecy and Our Relation to It," sermon by US, Mar. 14, 1891, in *GC Daily Bulletin*, Mar. 18, 1891, pp. 146-153.

²⁴ *RH*, Oct. 14, 1880, p. 252; Dec. 12, 1882, p. 776; Nov. 4, 1884, pp. 700, 701; Nov. 24, 1885, pp. 728, 729; Jan. 11, 1887, p. 28; Nov. 29, 1887, pp. 744, 745.

²⁵ *RH*, Jan. 7, 1882, pp. 10, 11; Nov. 20, 1883, pp. 732, 733; *The Gospel Sickle*, Feb. 1, 1886, p. 4; Dec. 22, 1886, p. 192; *RH*, Nov. 5, 1889, pp. 596, 597; JB, diary, 1881, 1884, 1886; US to EGW, June 30, 1885; R. A. Lovell to [E. K.] VandeVere, Feb. 7, 1958.

²⁶ *RH*, May 24, 1881, p. 328; Oct. 14, 1884, p. 648; Oct. 21, 1884, p. 664; Aug. 17, 1886, p. 518; Aug. 24, 1886, p. 536; Oct. 5, 1886, p. 616; Aug. 30, 1887, p. 552; June 7, 1881, p. 360; June 21, 1881, p. 393; Sept. 2, 1884, pp. 568, 569; Sept. 3, 1889, pp. 552, 553; Aug. 19, 1880, p. 136; Oct. 7, 1884, p. 632; Sept. 25, 1888, p. 616.

²⁷ *RH*, Sept. 2, 1884, p. 568; June 16, 1885, p. 376; Aug. 31, 1886, p. 552; Oct. 5, 1886, p. 616; Aug. 27, 1889, p. 536; Apr. 25, 1882, p. 264.

²⁸ *RH*, Dec. 5, 1882, p. 760.

²⁹ *RH*, Apr. 18, 1882, p. 248.

³⁰ *RH*, July 12, 1881, p. 48; Mar. 28, 1882, p. 208.

³¹ *RH*, Apr. 11, 1882, p. 240; Aug. 15, 1882, pp. 520, 521; Dec. 9, 1884, p. 778; Nov. 4, 1884, p. 704.

³² *RH*, Apr. 21, 1885, p. 256; Apr. 28, 1885, p. 267; July 21, 1885, p. 456; Oct. 27, 1885, p. 672.

³³ For examples of Smith's occasional comments on spiritualism during this period, see *RH*, Jan. 22, 1880, p. 56; Feb. 12, 1884, p. 104; Feb. 19, 1884, p. 120.

³⁴ *RH*, May 2, 1882, p. 280; May 30, 1882, p. 344; May 6, 1884, p. 296.

³⁵ *RH*, Oct. 28, 1884, p. 680.

³⁶ *RH*, Jan. 13, 1885, pp. 24, 25; May 12, 1885, p. 296; Apr. 13, 1886, pp. 233, 334; May 31, 1887, p. 344; Sept. 4, 1888, p. 568; Nov. 27, 1888, p. 744; Jan. 1, 1889, p. 8.

[37] *RH*, June 10, 1880, p. 376; Nov. 26, 1889, p. 744; Sept. 18, 1888, p. 608; Sept. 4, 1888, p. 568; June 12, 1888, p. 376.

[38] *RH*, Mar. 6, 1883, p. 152.

[39] *RH*, Sept. 2, 1880, p. 168.

[40] *RH*, Sept. 11, 1888, p. 584; Jan. 1, 1889, p. 8.

[41] *RH*, Mar. 13, 1883, p. 184.

[42] *RH*, Nov. 22, 1887, p. 728.

[43] *RH*, Jan. 8, 1880, p. 25; Aug. 4, 1885, p. 488.

[44] *RH*, May 13, 1880, pp. 312, 313; June 13, 1882, p. 376.

[45] *RH*, Oct. 23, 1883, p. 664.

[46] *RH*, Dec. 21, 1886, p. 792.

[47] *RH*, Nov. 29, 1887, p. 744.

[48] Dennis Pettibone, "The Sunday Law Movement," in *The World of Ellen G. White*, ed. Gary Land (Washington, D.C./Hagerstown, Md.: Review and Herald Pub. Assn., 1987), pp. 113-119.

[49] *Ibid.*, pp. 120-123.

[50] *RH*, Mar. 21, 1882, p. 184; Sept. 12, 1882, p. 584; Jan. 18, 1887, p. 40; Pettibone, pp. 123, 124.

[51] *RH*, Dec. 16, 1880, pp. 392, 393; Mar. 27, 1883, p. 200; Dec. 18, 1883, p. 792; Jan. 1, 1884, p. 8.

[52] *RH*, Nov. 25, 1880, p. 352; Jan. 13, 1885, p. 24.

[53] *RH*, Nov. 18, 1884, p. 736; July 19, 1887, p. 456; Dec. 18, 1888, p. 792; July 23, 1889, p. 472; Pettibone, p. 124.

[54] *RH*, May 29, 1888, p. 344; Feb. 12, 1889, pp. 104, 112; Feb. 26, 1889, p. 144; Oct. 22, 1889, p. 664.

[55] *RH*, Dec. 8, 1891, p. 760. See also Ben McArthur, "The 1893 Chicago World's Fair: An Early Test for Adventist Religious Liberty," *AH* 2, no. 2 (1975): 11-21.

[56] Among other groups, Roger Daniels notes that 400,000 Poles arrived in the nineteenth century and 4.1 million Italians came between 1880 and 1900, both largely Catholic. Meanwhile, the number of Jews increased from 1.5 million to 7 million between 1880 and 1900. See *Coming to America: A History of Immigration and Ethnicity in American Life* (New York: Harper/Collins, 1990), pp. 180, 219, 223. About the same time, membership in the Knights of Labor grew from 19,000 in 1881 to 700,000 in 1886, with numerous strikes, mostly involving railroads, in 1884. The Knights died out after the failure of strikes in the 1890s. The American Federation of Labor was founded in 1886, but did not achieve prominence until the twentieth century. See Henry Pelling, *American Labor* (Chicago: Univ. of Chicago Press, 1960), pp. 63-73.

[57] *RH*, Aug. 19, 1880, p. 136; Feb. 22, 1881, pp. 120, 121; Nov. 22, 1887, p. 728; Sept. 25, 1883, p. 616; Jan. 30, 1883, p. 72.

[58] *RH*, Feb. 28, 1888, p. 136; Nov. 12, 1889, pp. 713, 714.

[59] *RH*, Mar. 27, 1894, p. 208.

[60] US, *The Marvel of Nations: Our Country: Its Past, Present, and Future, and What the Scriptures Say of It* (Battle Creek, Mich.: Review and Herald Pub. Assn., 1885), pp. 19, 22-88.

[61] *Ibid.*, pp. 16, 91-145, 165, 166.

[62] *Ibid.*, pp. 189-208.

[63] *Ibid.*, p. 243.

[64] *Ibid.*, p. 263.

[65] *RH*, Feb. 9, 1886, p. 88; Jan. 5, 1886, p. 16; Apr. 19, 1887, p. 256.

[66] *RH*, Jan. 31, 1882, p. 72; Mar. 28, 1882, p. 200; Feb. 27, 1883, p. 136; Sept. 11,

1883, p. 584; Sept. 25, 1883, p. 616. For the historical background of the "Eastern question," see J.A.R. Marriot, *The Eastern Question: An Historical Study in European Diplomacy* (Oxford, Eng.: Clarendon Press, 1940); R. W. Seton-Watson, *Disraeli, Gladstone, and the Eastern Question* (London: F. Cass, 1972); and Richard Millman, *Britain and the Eastern Question: 1875-1878* (Oxford, Eng.: Clarendon Press, 1979).

[67] *RH*, Dec. 22, 1885, p. 792.

[68] *RH*, Sept. 21, 1886, p. 600.

[69] *RH*, Jan. 11, 1887, p. 24.

[70] *RH*, Mar. 29, 1887, pp. 200, 201.

[71] *RH*, Oct. 7, 1890, p. 616.

[72] *RH*, Jan. 5, 1886, p. 8.

[73] *RH*, July 23, 1889, p. 472; July 30, 1889, pp. 488, 489.

[74] *RH*, Aug. 6, 1889, pp. 504, 505; Aug. 27, 1889, pp. 536, 537.

[75] *RH*, Aug. 27, 1889, p. 537.

[76] *RH*, July 29, 1880, p. 96.

[77] *RH*, Sept. 20, 1923, p. 5; June 6, 1940, p. 10.

[78] *RH*, Jan. 18, 1881, p. 40.

[79] *RH*, June 6, 1882, p. 360.

[80] GIB to EGW, Mar. 31, 1881.

[81] *RH*, June 20, 1882, p. 400; HS to WS, May 5, 1893.

[82] US to EGW, May 15, 1883.

[83] HS to WS, Aug. 12, 1884; HS to "Dear brothers and sisters," Oct. 3, 1884. Uriah Smith also visited West Wilton, New Hampshire, between the Maine and New York camp meetings in 1886. See *RH*, Sept. 21, 1886, p. 608.

[84] US to EGW, Mar. 28, 1884.

[85] GIB to WCW, Mar. 21, 1885. Leon Smith first appeared on the masthead as assistant editor in the Feb 1, 1887, issue.

[86] *RH*, Mar. 17, 1885, p. 176 (wrongly printed as 166).

[87] US to WS, Apr. 1, 1885.

[88] *RH*, May 26, 1885, p. 336; US to WS, Oct. 1, 1886.

[89] US to WS, Oct. 1, 1886.

[90] US to WS, Apr. 17, 1887; PS to WS, postmarked Sept. 27, [1888?]; Berenice Bryant Lowe, *Tales of Battle Creek* (n.p.: Albert L. and Louise B. Miller Foundation, 1976), p. 242; *RH*, Sept. 6, 1962, p. 13; EFD, *Yours*, pp. 165, 166.

[91] HS to WS, May 5, 1883; HS to WS, Jan. 2, 1886; HS to WS, Jan. 1, 1886, on the back of Charles Smith's letter to Wilton; US to EGW, May 15, 1883; US to WS, Oct. 2, 1883; US to WS, Apr. 1, 1885.

[92] US to WS, Apr. 5, 1887; AS to WS, May 5, 1887; EGW to US and HS, Aug. 10, 1893.

[93] PS to WS, Feb. 23, 1884; US to WS, Mar. 20, 1884; HS to WS, Jan. 2, 1886.

[94] PS, diary, 1884; PS, diary, 1887.

[95] PS, diary, 1884 and 1887; HS to WS, Aug. 2, 1884. See also Gary Land, "One Boy and Baseball: The 1884 and 1887 Diaries of S. Parker Smith," *Base Ball: A Journal of the Early Game* 4, no. 2 (Fall 2010): 72-78.

[96] AS to WS, Dec. 17, 1886; HS to WS, Aug. 2, 1884; list of Battle Creek High School graduating class, 1889.

[97] US to G. W. and Alma Caviness, Oct. 26, 1882.

[98] HS to WS, Jan. 2, 1886; US to WS, Nov. 25, 1886.

CHAPTER VII

CONFLICT RETURNS, 1885-1894

During the course of some 25 years Smith had become *the* Adventist authority on the interpretation of prophecy. Thus he did not respond well when A. T. Jones wrote to him questioning an aspect of his interpretation. In doing so, Jones not only was challenging Uriah's role in forming the church's theology, but also was implicitly criticizing his presupposition, drawn from the Scottish commonsense philosophy, that the Bible needed no interpretation, for it explained itself. Furthermore, from Smith's perspective, Jones was a young upstart. Formerly a member of the United States Army, Jones had converted to Seventh-day Adventism in 1874 at the age of 23. Twelve years later he became an assistant editor of *Signs of the Times*, and in 1886 became coeditor with E. J. Waggoner. Waggoner was the son of pioneer Adventist minister Joseph H. Waggoner. In addition to editing *Signs*, beginning about 1885 Jones and E. J. Waggoner also taught Bible courses at Healdsburg College, founded two years previously in northern California.

THE 10 KINGDOMS

In May 1885 Jones wrote to Smith, stating that based on his research he was having trouble including the Huns as one of the 10 kingdoms of Daniel. Drawing from Edward Gibbon's *History of the Decline and Fall of the Roman Empire* and the *Encyclopaedia Britannica*, he thought that the Alemanni fit "the bill [the listing of the 10 kingdoms] about a thousand times better than the Huns. They stand about parallel with the Burgundians, more plainly than the Suevi, and will meet every demand of the case historically and scripturally." Uriah responded to Jones on May 28, but unfortunately the letter no longer exists. The younger man wrote again in June, explaining in more detail why the Alemanni should replace the Huns. "It is the truth that we want in this," he wrote, "as well as in the Sabbath or any other part of the Word." Even for those who continue to adopt the historicist approach to the prophecies of Daniel and Revelation, it may be difficult to understand why the issue should have been so important to the two men, but they were concerned to have the *truth* on every matter of belief, including a correct listing of Daniel's 10 kingdoms. Jones closed his letter by saying, "Oh! I wish we could be where we could talk this over instead of having to write it at 2,000 miles distance." He said that he was writing a long letter rather than publishing his views, for he did not want to differ publicly from Smith.[1]

Then in August Jones wrote to Smith again, asking for his help in sorting out the 10 kingdoms and stating more forcefully the contradictions he saw in Uriah's interpretation. "In treating of the ten divisions of the Roman Empire we apply them all to Western Rome because that *territory* only was Rome proper, and it was *Rome* that was divided," he stated. "But when we come to the *four* divisions of the kingdom of Grecia, they are divisions of the *whole Empire* instead of the territory of Grecia proper. What is the best reason to give for this?" he asked. "If we have the ten divisions in the territory of Rome proper, why not the *four* divisions in the territory of Grecia proper? Or if the *four* divisions for the whole empire of Grecia, why shall not the *ten* divisions be of the whole empire of Rome?"[2]

In December Jones sent still another letter, declaring now that the difference between him and Smith revolved around whether Bishop Edward Chandler's list of the 10 kingdoms in his *A Defence of Christianity From the Prophecies of the Old Testament* (1725) is "absolutely correct and that all your efforts are directed to the point of making the prophecy, the history, and everything else, to fit the list." Jones explained that his "sole aim has been and *is* to find out whether Bishop Chandler is right, to find out whether his list is the correct one, and to find out whether that list fits the prophecies."[3]

Meanwhile, Jones began publishing the results of his research in weekly articles in *Signs of the Times*, starting on August 6, 1885, and extending to January 6, 1887, and sent copies of at least some of them to Smith. In

November 1886 Uriah acknowledged receipt of the articles but expressed frustration that Jones had taken the issue into the public realm. Having done so, however, Smith said that he would have to answer it through the pages of the *Review*. Furthermore, he saw no reason to change "a point which has been considered as well established" and which would "unsettle minds upon all points, [and] create confusion which it would be next to impossible to allay." Returning to the issue of publication of the controversy, he told Jones that he regretted "exceedingly to have anything come up which will give an appearance of antagonism between the two papers, and I hope no trouble will grow out of it; but if it does, it cannot be said that the *Review* has precipitated it."[4]

Early in December Jones wrote to Uriah saying that other than a brief reply to his first letter he had received no response to his two subsequent letters. He told him that he had begun studying the issue at the request of the 1884 General Conference session, which had asked him "to get ready to write a series of articles gathered from history on points that showed the fulfillment of prophecy, and put it in the form of *quotations from history* so that our brethren could have the words of the history itself, and not mine, on the subject." Furthermore, he explained, he was concerned that Adventist preachers must be able to respond to their critics, as Protestants and Catholics were coming together in the National Reform Association in support of a national Sunday law. "We shall have to show what the ten kingdoms were. We shall have to give the history for it. We shall have to show the plucking up of the three. We shall have to show the establishment of the Papacy. We shall have to show the kingdoms that remain after the plucking up of the three," he said with growing apocalyptic fervor.

"This, we shall have to do by the words of history itself. And to put into the hands of all our people *the words of history* on these things so that they may know where these words are, and that they may know where to tell others to find them, it is for this cause that I have endeavored to bring [out] these things in the *Signs,* as I was appointed to do."

By "words of history," Jones seems to have meant quotations from recognized historians such as Gibbon, for neither he nor other Adventists were researching original sources.[5]

Jones wrote Smith a more heated letter in late December, protesting that Uriah was attempting to make "the prophecy, the history, and everything else" fit the list of the 10 kingdoms put together by Bishop Chandler. He quoted Smith's letter in May 1885 accusing him of "ransacking" history to make his point but not acknowledging that Jones had said he had no fixed opinion on the issue of the 10 kingdoms. "My 'ranscking [sic] of history' was to find something in favor of the Huns, and I have never found it, and you have not shown it to me," Jones stated. "Of course I am a stranger to you, but even at that I *do* think that instead of thinking what you state, there ought to have been enough charity with you to allow that I was telling the truth."[6]

Smith's four articles entitled "The Ten Kingdoms" appeared in the *Review* during the month of January 1887. Although he did not mention the dispute with Jones, anyone reading both papers could easily see what was going on behind the scenes. In any case, the publication of Uriah's articles prompted Jones to move the argument to a new level in February 1887 when he responded in a printed open letter, apparently distributed to interested parties. After reviewing the historical data, Jones commented that he had "not pointed out all your mistakes, only a part. And as in all these cases you say one thing, while authoritative history says the opposite, I hope you will pardon me if I choose to accept the words and facts of history, instead of your words and theories." The reference to Smith's "theories" as opposed to facts probably hit a raw nerve, for as one who worked in the commonsense tradition he had always emphasized that his ideas were factually based. Finally, Jones closed his letter with another allusion to the significance of facts. "Yet whether they were read by many or by few, I do not count this a matter that at all affects any doctrine. It is only a matter of *fact*, and history must give the facts."[7]

THE LAW IN GALATIANS

Smith may not have deigned to reply to Jones, for we have no record of any further correspondence between the two men. But about the same time that the younger editor was bringing up the matter of the 10 kingdoms, he and his colleague Waggoner challenged Smith over another of his favorite topics, the law and righteousness. Jones and Waggoner began publishing articles in *Signs of the Times* in 1884 arguing that the "added law" of Galatians 3 refers to the Ten Commandments. Following a debate over the issue in 1856, most Adventist leaders had taken the view that the "added law" was the ceremonial system put in place because of transgression of the Ten Commandments and that pointed to Christ.[8]

In June 1886 George Butler wrote to Ellen White, who at the time was in Europe, confessing that it did not please him that Healdsburg College and the *Signs* were promulgating a minority view. He believed that while debate about the issue had been an undercurrent in the church since its beginning, "the time has come for this question to be settled if possible." Although he wanted to write an article providing what he believed was the dominant view on the subject, he desired to take "a reasonable, judicious course" and said to White that if she had "light to help me move carefully, I shall be very glad." He went on to say that it "would be a most bitter pill to many of our leading brethren to be compelled to see the idea taught generally, that the law which was added was the moral law itself."[9]

Butler first published a long *Review* article and next an 85-page book, *The Law in Galatians* (1886), that attacked Waggoner's interpretation, and then arranged for republication of D. M. Canright's *Two Laws*, originally published in 1876, with an expanded section on Galatians. Each of the delegates to the 1886 General Conference session received a copy of Butler's book. At the session he established a nine-member theological committee, which included Smith, Canright, Waggoner, and Butler, to examine and settle the issues related to both the 10 kingdoms and law in Galatians. After the committee split five to four in favor of the traditional views rather than providing the strong support he had hoped for, Butler obtained a conference resolution telling school boards, Sabbath school leaders, and editors to "exercise great care not to permit doctrinal views not held by a fair majority of our people to be made part of the public instruction of said schools, or to be published in our denominational papers, as if they were the established doctrine of the people, before they are examined and approved by the leading brethren of experience."[10]

In 1887 Ellen White wrote to both Butler and Smith, telling them that she could not remember what she had been shown with regard to the two laws. Referring to earlier letters that she had apparently written to the two men, she told them that she did not want them used in a way that "you will take it for granted that your ideas are all correct and Dr. Waggoner's and Elder Jones's are all wrong." She expressed pain that a *Review* article had been too sharp with Waggoner. "The principles that you refer to are right, but how this can harmonize with your pointed remarks to Dr. Waggoner, I cannot see. . . . I have had some impressive dreams that have led me to feel that you are not altogether in the light."[11]

1888 GENERAL CONFERENCE SESSION

White, who at this time was primarily concerned with the manner in which church leaders were treating one another rather than their theology, urged that Waggoner should be allowed to respond to Butler, which he did in a letter that soon became a book, *The Gospel in the Book of Galatians.* Published in 1888, he had the book distributed to the delegates at that year's General Conference session in Minneapolis. Waggoner also had the opportunity to speak to the conference that took place in the newly constructed Adventist church on the corner of Lake Street and Fourth Avenue South. At the same time, the opposition to Waggoner and Jones, led by J. H. Morrison, president of the Iowa Conference (Butler was unable to attend), was prepared to resist the new teachings.[12]

An institute for the education of ministers, similar to the biblical institutes that Smith had helped present for several years, preceded the conference session and took place in the church basement, running from October 10 through 16. This time, however, it was Jones rather than Smith who addressed the subject of the 10 kingdoms, basically repeating the arguments that had appeared in his previous articles and letters. Although Smith's supporters tried to force a vote on the issue, Waggoner blocked the maneuver by arguing that the subject needed more study. Stephen N. Haskell reported in the *Review* that the sentiment of the delegates was overwhelmingly for the old view but that the General Conference session itself would continue to discuss the issue.[13]

On the first day of the General Conference session, which began on October 17 and continued through November 4 and in the church sanctuary, Smith spoke on the topic of the 10 kingdoms, arguing for inclusion of the Huns. But Waggoner's nine lectures, which called upon Adventists to move their emphasis from God's law to Christ's righteousness as the means of salvation, proved to be the highlight of the session. In his *Review* report Smith downplayed the controversy revolving around Waggoner, saying that while everyone agreed with the "foundation principles" of his presentations, "there are some differences in regard to the interpretation of several passages. The lectures have tended to a more thorough investigation of the truth, and it is hoped that the unity of faith will be reached on this important question." Uriah, however, gave no indication that he, Morrison, and others who opposed Waggoner's teaching wanted to achieve unity through coercion, as they had with Jones's teaching regarding the 10 kingdoms. They sought, in the words of historian George Knight, "to establish a creedal statement by majority vote without impartial and thorough Bible study." But Ellen White, who had criticized the 1886 resolution restricting presentation of minority theological views, opposed the new effort to settle theological dispute, and it failed.[14]

Despite the tension between Smith on one side and Jones and Waggoner on the other, the session chose Uriah to serve as its secretary (although soon replaced by Dan T. Jones), and also elected him to serve on the Executive Committee, Book Committee, and the General Conference Association. Following the meetings, Ellen White traveled the camp meeting circuit, attended ministerial institutes, and spoke at churches in the Midwest and East with Jones and Waggoner, appearing to support their view in what was becoming a very hostile environment.[15]

Smith, of course, from the beginning of his career in Adventism had strongly emphasized the necessity of keeping the law and had long struggled to reconcile that concept with the doctrine of righteousness by faith. Although he made no explicit reference to Jones's and Waggoner's role in the 1888 General Conference session, the following year he published comments in the *Review* that seemed to challenge the issue. In April 1889 he argued that Christ made it possible for us to keep the law by giving us a new nature. "When the Lord now tells us to keep it, and we promise to do so, it is with this condition always understood," he stated.[16] The following month he reasserted his longstanding belief in the central position of the law and our responsibility to observe it: "The fact is, the law of God holds a position of essential pre-eminence in connection with all God's dealing with the human family under every condition and in every age. It is the expression of God's will, the rule of life, the standard of judgment. Obedience to it is the sole condition of everlasting life in every age and dispensation, the present no less than all the past."

But, he argued, such a position did not conflict with the idea that we achieve righteousness through Christ. "A true view of this subject does not detract either from the law or Christ, but exalts them both. While it shows that the path of obedience is the only path back to life . . . and that the keeping of the commandments is the one sole and only condition of eternal life . . . , it also shows Christ taking His stand by the law, magnifying and making it honorable, dying to meet its claims, offering us freely of His blood to cancel past transgressions, giving us grace to keep it that we may have life, and thus crowned with honor and glory as a Savior and Redeemer."[17]

In June he followed up with another article that attempted to explain how Christ's sacrifice enabled us to keep the law. "If neither Adam and Eve nor any of their posterity had ever broken the law, the human family would have developed righteousness by the law alone. But because of sin, God must place a new nature within us. . . . Christ comes in and closes up the gulf between us and God by providing a sacrifice to cancel past sin, and gives us a new spiritual nature, through which He proposes to dwell in us to bring us back into harmony with the law, lead us to love and delight in it, and walk in all its precepts."[18]

Finally, in July he wrote that "any view which does not present the Lord of life and the law of righteousness in equal prominence before the mind is an imperfect and incomplete view of the subject."[19]

Meanwhile, the General Conference leaders were trying hard to develop a working relationship between Smith, Jones, and Waggoner. All three men participated in a minister's institute held in Battle Creek that took place from November 5, 1889, to March 25, 1890. About 50 students attended it. But tensions soon emerged after Smith cautioned against new doctrinal views being circulated, and Waggoner, perhaps in response, announced that he would address the covenants, which necessarily included discussion of the law in Galatians. After several meetings to discuss the issue, Waggoner announced that because some individuals had objected to him speaking on the covenants he would not use his assigned hour. Taking his place, Smith lectured on the sanctuary doctrine. A. T. Jones reported that "there has been quite a feeling in the class since." During February conflict intensified when Waggoner insisted on dealing with the covenant question despite Dan T. Jones's efforts to convince him otherwise. Controversy also swirled around the Sabbath school lessons published in the *Review* that dealt with the covenants. "I did not wish to get

Bro. Smith into hot water any deeper than necessary," Jones told George I. Butler, but Smith had published a note on the lessons that had stirred up a "hornet's nest." Although he did not explicitly identify the note, Jones may have been referring to a statement published in the February 11 issue that said that "it is absurd to suppose that God will judge the family of Adam, moral agents, by different moral standards."[20]

In mid-February the church leaders, with Smith, Waggoner, D. T. Bourdeau, and R. C. Porter making presentations, began a "public investigation" of the covenant question, devoting two hours a day for 10 days to the subject. Dan T. Jones observed that "the arguments were presented strong on both sides of the question, and it was left at that without any expression [apparently referring to a vote] being taken." Informing Stephen Haskell of the meetings, Jones said that "the question has now been dropped, and the school is going on with its regular work."[21] A short time later Dan Jones wrote to Robert M. Kilgore, stating that he thought the issue was the "spirit" expressed in the controversy, not the doctrines themselves.

"But if I have been mistaken in the matter I am glad to be corrected. I have thought all the time that Sister White did not mean to say that Dr. Waggoner was correct in his position on the covenant question as far as doctrine was concerned; because it was so manifestly wrong that I could not at all be reconciled to the idea that she would give it her unqualified approval. I think we have been consuming time and labor on points that are not of the most importance at the present time, and have been striving about these [doctrines] when we ought to have been putting our shoulders to the burden and pushing along the car of truth."[22]

But discussions continued, as "explanation" meetings took place in March attended by about 20 individuals, including Ellen White, Uriah Smith, and E. J. Waggoner. Dan Jones reported that "Sister White and Dr. Waggoner said they did not care what we believed on the law in Galatians or on the covenants; what they wanted to see was that we might all accept the doctrine of righteousness by faith, that we may get the benefit of it ourselves and teach it to others. With this I am perfectly in harmony. I believe in the doctrine of justification by faith, and am also willing to concede that it has not been given the prominence in the past that its importance demands."[23]

Reporting on the same meetings to others, Jones referred to the "strain" and strong "tension" in Battle Creek over the issues and the creation of a "party spirit." "Really things seemed to be in a very bad shape," he told R. A. Underwood, "as we were all wearied to think of the position we were getting into." In the end, however, he reported to Eugene Farnsworth that "the meetings proved a great blessing, and have taken out of the way largely the difficulties that have been causing all the trouble here for several weeks in the past." He further commented, "There has been no concession made with reference to the points of doctrine, or the interpretation of the Scripture, but only the spirit that was shown and the way in which the work was done." Jones concluded by saying that he "was surprised to see some things that looked inexplicable vanish away into thin air when a few explanations were made."[24]

Despite his favorable report, a few days later Jones told R. C. Porter that Uriah Smith "does not feel as he should. He cannot understand why some things should be as they are, why Sister White spoke at one time positively against a certain thing, as she did against the law in Galatians, to [Elder] Waggoner several years ago, then turn around and practically give her support to the same thing when it comes up in a little different way, with some different associations. I think that he will be able, however, to see things different by and by."[25] A month later Jones again wrote to Porter saying that he hoped that "this matter of the covenant question and the Minneapolis matter rest for a while until it dies out in the minds of the people."[26]

The following August the General Conference Committee recommended that Smith, Waggoner, and A. T. Jones teach at the minister's school planned for Battle Creek in the fall. W. W. Prescott later replaced Jones. After Waggoner said he would teach only if allowed complete freedom to present what he pleased, it was decided to assign topics. Dan T. Jones reported that Waggoner agreed to this arrangement and seemed to want to work in harmony with the church leadership. "[Brother] Smith is taking hold of it in good earnest this year," he stated, "and I think will feel more at home than he did last year." After the institute got under way, opening with about 60 students on October 31 and extending to February 27, 1891, Dan Jones said that it was "proving a great success." He asserted that Smith, Waggoner, and Prescott "are all taking hold well. They are working together splendidly this year. [Brother] Smith is taking more interest in the school than he has ever taken in the past."[27] In January 1891, however, Jones said that while "taking hold well," Smith had some failings as a teacher. "He does not control his classes, but lets them lead him away from his subject, and they waste much time in the discussion of unimportant points. At least that is the general verdict. I believe I have been sorry for this, and have sometimes thought that I would speak to [Brother] Smith about it, but have not gathered up the courage to do so."[28]

But, in general, Dan Jones could report more positively about Smith than he had a year previously. He said that Uriah had been talking with those over whom he had personal relationships, attempting to "counteract the influence that he has exerted in the past."[29]

ELLEN WHITE AND URIAH SMITH

Meanwhile, Ellen White was concerned about Smith's recalcitrance. She wrote to him in June 1889, saying that she had awakened at midnight "with a heavy burden on my soul from you." Reporting her dream, she stated, "I saw you walked upon a path that almost imperceptibly diverged from the right way. A noble personage stood beside me and said, 'Uriah Smith is not on the brink of a precipice, but he is in the path that will shortly bring him to the brink, and if he is not warned now it will soon be too late. He can now retrace his steps. He is walking like a blind man into the prepared net of the enemy, but he feels no danger because light is becoming darkness to him and darkness light. His only hope is in being undeceived.'"

She further commented that she had read his recent *Review* article. "Now, there was no call whatever for you to write as you did. You place Elder [A. T.] Jones in a false position just [as] Elder Morrison and Nicola and yourself and others placed him in at [sic] Minneapolis."[30]

A few months later she wrote in even stronger terms that "God will have His light come to the people, and you cannot prevent it. You may misrepresent it, you may misinterpret it, you may interpose yourself as you have done between God's working and the people," she stated, "but your efforts, every one that you have made to resist light and the impressions of the Spirit of God, have been an extra step farther and farther from the light and from the Lord." She asked whether he could bear the responsibility for leading "poor, deluded souls" to conclude that the message of righteousness by faith, which she called a "message for this time," "must be error and delusion."[31]

In February 1890 Smith responded to her with a long defense of his opinions and actions, expressing his conservative approach to doctrinal change. "It is not my wish that anyone should allow my position on any question to decide his belief on that subject. . . . Of course, it has always been my purpose to move carefully and cautiously, and not take a position till I felt satisfied that it was from every point of view a tenable one. And then when everything looks plain and clear, I take my position firmly, and do not know how I could consistently do otherwise. And then I cannot be moved from that position till I can see some reasons which seem to me clearer and stronger than those that led me to take it. And then if others profess to see the matter in the same light, I cannot feel to blame them for that."

Uriah went on to explain that he believed that the denomination had settled the issue of the law in Galatians back in 1856, but Waggoner's articles in the *Signs* had now broken the unity and thrown many into confusion. He thought that Waggoner's position was contrary to both Scripture and what Ellen White had previously seen in vision. As for the 1888 General Conference session, he had learned only a few days before it began that the "California brethren" had planned to introduce the topic.

"The real point at issue at that conference was the law in Galatians, but [Brother] Waggoner's six preliminary discourses on righteousness we could all agree to, and I should have enjoyed them first rate, had I not known that all the while that he designed them to pave the way for his position on Galatians, which I deem so erroneous. . . . And when you apparently [endorsed] his position as a whole, though without [committing] yourself on any particular point, it was a great surprise to many. And when they asked me what that meant, and how I could account for it, really, Sister White, I did not know what to say, and I do not know what yet."

He believed that Waggoner and Jones were pursuing a "settled plan" to push doctrinal changes onto the people. If the church accepted Jones's questioning of prophetic interpretation and Waggoner's new position regarding the law in Galatians, "then how are we going to explain the past?" he asked. "How can I believe that the Lord is leading [Brother] Jones in such teaching as that? I cannot, so long as I believe . . . such men as James White, J. N. Andrews, and J. H. Waggoner during the many years they wrote, preached, and published on these prophetic themes. As between the old and the new, my heart is with my former companions in labor.

"It is these things that trouble me. These are the things that I am opposing, and all that I am opposing as far as I know my position. I desire to be in the fullest union with you. I am never happier than when I feel that such is the case, and it is no agreeable situation to me when it is otherwise.

"I believe I am willing to receive light at any time from anybody. But what claims to be light must, for me, show itself to be according to the Scriptures and based on good solid reasons which convinces the judgment, before it appears light to me. And when anyone presents something which I have long known and believed, it is impossible for me to call that new light."[32]

The following March of 1890 Ellen White again wrote to Smith, this time accusing him of refusing her testimonies and thereby undermining her authority within the church, which was being "charged against you in the books of heaven." She connected his actions and attitudes with the earlier confrontation with Bell at Battle Creek College and said that he was strengthening the "hands and minds" of other church leaders against the righteousness by faith message. "And the enemy of righteousness looks on pleased," she commented. In her view the problem was more spiritual than theological. "You have turned from plain light because you were afraid that the law question in Galatians would have to be accepted." Although she had no burden about the law in Galatians, none of those involved in the controversy would ever be "prepared to receive light, either to establish or refute their position, until every one of you are men truly converted before God."[33]

In November she again sent a letter to Smith, raising the issue of her authority by asserting that he had virtually said that he had no "'confidence in the message Sister White bears.' . . . No confession has come from your lips, and I have been compelled to meet your influence in Minneapolis and since that time, everywhere I have been; and now the year 1890 is nearly closed." She accused him of being a "stumbling stone" to others who did not know her or her work, leading them into infidelity. "Will you fall on the Rock and be broken?" she asked. "Will you evade the point as you have done?" Ellen White explained that he would not confess his wrongs to help the church, because "the bewitching power of unbelief and stubbornness has held you."[34]

At the end of December she told him that "a gulf separates us." Once more she brought up the conflict with Bell at Battle Creek College. "I look back and see how you gathered darkness to your soul in the time of the college difficulties," she said. "Have you come out clean in that matter?" She explained that his failure to correct past wrongs was separating his soul from God and was making her own labors of "none account," for people were following his example in doubting her testimonies. "Where is your preparation to be obtained that you may stand in the day of the Lord?" she asked. "Nowhere but low at the foot of the cross. O, it is not too late for wrongs to be righted. Do not confer with flesh and blood," she advised. "Do not say, There are some things I do not understand. Of course there are. Your mind is clouded; but take one step that you do see, then you can see another."[35]

Smith held a private conversation with Ellen White in Battle Creek on January 5, 1891. The following day she wrote to him, saying that she was mystified by his claim that he held no antagonism toward Jones and Waggoner. "The feeling cherished by yourself and Elder Butler," she asserted, "were not only despising the message, but the messengers." Then she condemned Uriah in very strong language. "You have been exceedingly stubborn, and this stubbornness has been as described in the Word of God. 'For rebellion is as the sin of witchcraft, and stubbornness is as iniquity and idolatry.' . . . This stubbornness, my dear brother, can be brought under control only by your falling upon the Rock and being broken. It is a terrible snare to you. It makes you unwilling to confess your wrongs, and every wrong passed over without humble confession will [leave] you and . . . every soul who pursues the same course in blindness of mind and hardness of heart."[36]

Presumably Uriah received this letter before arranging for a second meeting with her that took place in her room on January 7, to which he also invited several individuals, including O. A. Olsen, Goodloe Harper Bell, W. C. White, and others. Once again, Smith exhibited the familiar pattern of submitting to Ellen White's criticisms after a long period of resisting them. According to Dan T. Jones, who was present at the meeting, Smith "confessed that he had taken a wrong course" during the Battle Creek College controversy, and while he had not said anything harsh with regard to Bell at the time, "he had consented to what others said, and thus became a party to the injustice that was done." Uriah then asked Bell's forgiveness for his actions and also acknowledged that he had "taken a wrong course . . . in some respects" at Minneapolis. Dan Jones described Uriah as "very mild in his remarks, but very pointed." Ellen White then spoke briefly and "took [Brother] Smith by the hand and told him that he had said all that she could ask him to say, that God would bless him in the course he had taken." After a few others had expressed their reaction, the hour-and-a-half meeting ended. "All seemed to be impressed with the sacredness of the work in which we are engaged," Jones commented, "and the danger of taking a course that would mar the work, or turn aside any of God's people from the right paths." A short time later, on January 10, Smith made a confession before the Battle Creek church regarding his actions in the "college troubles" and his response to A. T. Jones and Waggoner at Minneapolis and after, followed by another confession before the ministerial institute on January 17. "I think this will entirely relieve the tension that has existed so long in reference to the Minneapolis trouble," Dan Jones stated. Ellen White, seemingly satisfied with Uriah's response, wrote that "[Brother] Smith has fallen on the Rock, and is broken, and the Lord Jesus will now work with him."[37]

But things were not settled, for Uriah Smith still did not accept Jones's and Waggoner's teaching regarding the law in Galatians. Reading between the lines, so to speak, it seems that when he met with Ellen White he had confessed to having a wrong attitude but not to holding an incorrect biblical interpretation or theology. It is significant that in reporting the January 7 meeting Dan Jones referred to Smith's statement that he had reacted wrongly "in some respects" to the Minneapolis meeting, which appears to have left him room for reservations. Responding in September 1892 to a letter from A. T. Robinson that had criticized both him and the *Review*, Uriah expressed his unchanging views of Jones's and Waggoner's position regarding the law in Galatians. Smith asserted that the two men had broken the unity of Seventh-day Adventists "contrary to what has been considered the settled view of the body, according to the Scriptures, confirmed by the Spirit of Prophecy, as long ago as 1856." Division and confusion had come into the church as a result of the new teachings. If the views that Smith had defended in the *Review* were incorrect, "then we have been wrong for the past thirty years, and Seventh-day Adventism has been developed and built up on error. But this I am not prepared to admit. I am not yet prepared to renounce Seventh-day Adventism." He regarded the questions regarding the law as "fundamental and vital to the existence of our faith," but rejected the charge of legalism. "The idea is ridiculous. I consider that charge an insult to the whole denomination." Referring to prophetic interpretation, he also found A. T. Jones's view of the 10 kingdoms "a grave and dangerous error." Once again he explained his conservative approach to doctrinal issues and not so subtly took a swipe at the emerging younger leaders of the church. "Having by long study, and years of observation in the work, become settled on certain principles, I am not prepared to flop over at the suggestion of every novice, [and] I certainly should not think it proper to commit the *Review* to such a course."[38]

Ellen White, who doubtless continued to observe Smith from afar and heard from others about his views, was still concerned with the state of his soul. Shortly before Uriah wrote his letter to Robinson, she told him that he was in danger, "and your only safety lies in walking humbly with your God." She reported that "in Salamanca, N. Y., I was shown again that a great and good God would pardon your transgressions and forgive your sins, if you would humble your heart before God, and come to Him in the meekness of a little child." Reaffirming that Jones and Waggoner had preached a "message of God to the Laodicean church" in 1888 and after, she clearly declared that Smith had rejected it.

"Elder Smith, had you been unprejudiced, had not reports affected you, and led you to bar your heart against the entrance of what these men presented; had you, like the noble Bereans, searched the Scriptures to see if their testimony agreed with its instruction, you would have stood upon vantage ground, and been far advanced in Christian experience. If you had received the truth into a good and honest heart, you would have become a living channel of light, with clear perception, and sanctified imagination. Your conceptions of truth would have been exalted, and your heart made joyful in God. God would have given you a testimony clear, powerful and convincing. But the first position you took in regard to the message and the messenger has been a continual snare to you and a stumbling block."

Not only had Uriah rejected the message, White believed, but in doing so he had negatively affected the church. "The many and confused ideas in regard to Christ's righteousness and justification by faith," she concluded, "are the result of the position you have taken toward the [men] and the message sent of God."[39]

Despite her efforts and those of church administrators, the conflict that emerged in 1888 continued to fester. In June 1893 General Conference president O. A. Olsen wrote to Ellen White, now in Australia. "You ask me to tell you something about Elder Smith," he said. "But what shall I say? He goes along about in the old way. He is not in the light as he ought to be. I feel distressed over his case, but I feel powerless to do anything. It burdens me exceedingly. During the General Conference he utterly refused doing anything. That is, he would not permit nor have any part in giving Bible instruction. I talked with him and tried to reason with him, urging him to move out and take his part, but he would not do it. While I am very glad for the advancement that has been made, still my soul is in deep sorrow over many that are still in great darkness."[40]

Apparently in response to Olsen's letter, Ellen White sent a letter to Smith in August, stating that she was sorry that he did not place himself "in the channel of light. We want you [to] stand up strong, and firmly pressing forward and upward, bearing aloft the banner of truth."[41]

A GENERAL CONFERENCE DECISION

Encouraged by General Conference officers, who were trying to defuse the debate over righteousness by faith by dispersing the leaders in the controversy, White had moved to Australia in 1891. Four years later the denomination sent A. T. Jones on a tour of Europe and the Near East and W. W. Prescott, president of both Battle Creek and Walla Walla colleges, on a world tour.[42] Meanwhile, the administrators, obviously dissatisfied with Smith's attitude and his performance as editor of the *Review*, decided to use a similar approach with him. In early April 1894 Stephen N. Haskell wrote to Ellen White telling her that in addition to the General Conference Committee sending him and Smith to a meeting in New England, it was also being contemplated that Smith, "if they can bring it about," go with him to Europe. Commenting on the possibility, he added, "But it does seem to me, Sister White, if some of these old hands who have had an experience in the early part of the message could only be brought more to the front and counseled with, it would not only encourage them, but it would equalize the work more. Those bearing responsibility at the present time have not had the experience in the early part of the message that some have had, and if they the old ones do appear to be a little slow and behind the advance of the work, it appears to me that it would be a help to them if they were committed a little more, and be made to feel as though their testimony was not altogether out of date. I have particular reference to [Brother] Smith. I have felt deeply for him; visited his house a number of times, and had a number of talks with him, and I am in hope that our visit together in New England will be a blessing to him. There are various things that appear to me like light, which I think he can get hold of, and if he does get hold of them and bring them out in the paper, he can work wonders with his pen."[43]

Near the end of the month the Foreign Mission Board voted to send Smith and Haskell to attend the general meetings in Europe. Olsen wrote to William C. White, giving details that did not appear in the *Review* report. He told White that Uriah "takes kindly to the idea of going to Europe." Smith had requested that his son Wilton accompany him, with Wilton's traveling expenses but not wages paid by the denomination. The General Conference officers readily agreed, recognizing that the trip might be difficult for Smith because of his artificial leg. Therefore, they "were trying in every way to make it as pleasant for him as possible."

Olsen further explained why the church leaders were so willing to accommodate Smith's desires. "It will be a very good thing for Elder Smith to get out and see the work in other parts of the world. It will help to broaden his mind, and being with Haskell I am certain that [Brother] Smith will get hold of ideas and experiences in the work that he could not get hold of at Battle Creek. In this way he will also be taken away from surroundings that are not the most favorable in every respect. . . .

"We have not circumscribed Elder Smith's trip to Europe. He has a desire to visit Rome, and would like to go to Jerusalem; and the Review and Herald board as well as the Foreign Mission Board are willing that he should take just as extended a trip as he may feel pleased to do; for I believe that the longer trip he can take the more good will be accomplished in every way. His editorials written from the standpoint of visiting different parts of the world will certainly be very interesting reading; and then if we look after some other matters quite carefully, I believe that the *Review* can be much improved."

Referring to this last point, Olsen also stated that they had selected G. C. Tenney, who had been serving as editor of the *Bible Echo* in Australia, to be first assistant editor of the *Review*, in which capacity he would be in charge of the paper while Smith was away. Further explaining his desire for Smith's departure, Olsen said that "while this will not accomplish everything that I could desire for the *Review*, yet I think it will be a beginning, and that the providence of God will help us in the future to make that paper more what it is meant to be."[44]

---

[1] ATJ to US, May 18, 1885.

[2] ATJ to US, Aug. 24, 1885.

[3] ATJ to US, Dec. 27, 1885.

[4] US to ATJ, Nov. 8, 1886.

[5] ATJ to US, Dec. 3, 1886; On the significance of the Sunday law movement to this debate over the 10 kingdoms, see WWW, *E. J. Waggoner: From the Physician of Good News to Agent of Division* (Hagerstown, Md.: Review and Herald Pub. Assn., 2008), p. 96.

[6] ATJ to US, Dec. 26, 1886. Jones's reference to Smith's letter as written on June 3 appears mistaken. Instead, he seems to be referring to a letter written on May 28, to which Jones had responded on June 3.

[7] *RH*, Jan. 4, 1887, pp. 9, 10; Jan. 11, 1887, pp. 24, 25; Jan. 18, 1887, pp. 40, 41; Jan. 25, 1887, pp. 56, 57; ATJ to US, Feb. 3, 1887.

[8] See GRK, *A. T. Jones: Point Man on Adventism's Charismatic Frontier* (Hagerstown, Md.: Review and Herald Pub. Assn., 2011), pp. 26, 27, and WWW, p. 100.

[9] GIB to EGW, June 20, 1886.

[10] *RH*, Dec. 14, 1886, p. 779; Mar. 22, 1887, pp. 182, 183; WWW, pp. 101, 102.

[11] EGW to GIB and US, Apr. 5, 1887.

[12] WWW, pp. 103, 125; GRK, *A. T. Jones*, p. 41.

[13] A. O. Tate notes, A. T. Jones, Bible Study, Wed., Oct. 11, 1888, 10:30 a.m.; *RH*, Oct. 16, 1888, p. 648; Oct. 23, 1888, p. 664; WWW, p. 126.

[14] WWW, pp. 129-134; GRK, *A. T. Jones*, pp. 40-44; *General Conference Daily Bulletin*, 2, no. 7 (Oct. 26, 1888), 3.

[15] *RH*, Oct. 23, 1888, p. 664; Nov. 6, 1888, p. 698; Nov. 13, 1888, p. 712; *General Conference Daily Bulletin* 2, no. 1 (Oct. 19, 1888): 1, 2; GRK, *A. T. Jones*, p. 52; WWW, p. 125.

[16] *RH*, Apr. 23, 1889, p. 264.

[17] *RH*, May 21, 1889, pp. 328, 339.

[18] *RH*, June 11, 1889, pp. 376, 377.

[19] *RH*, July 2, 1889, p. 424.

[20] ATJ to R. A. Underwood, Jan. 20, 1890; DTJ to GIB, Feb. 13, 1890; *RH*, Feb. 11, 1890, p. 94; GRK, *A. T. Jones*, p. 53; WWW, p. 161.

[21] DTJ to J. O. Corliss, Feb. 16, 1890; DTJ to J. O. Corliss, Feb. 28, 1890; DTJ to SNH, Feb. 28, 1890.

[22] DTJ to R. M. Kilgore, Mar. 16, 1890.

[23] DTJ to J. H. Morrison, Mar. 17, 1890.

[24] DTJ to R. A. Underwood, Mar. 21, 1890, DTJ to E. W. Farnsworth, Mar. 21,

1890. See also DTJ to WCW, Mar. 18, 1890, and DTJ to GIB, Mar. 27, 1890.

[25] DTJ to R. C. Porter, Apr. 1, 1890.

[26] DTJ to R. C. Porter, May 5, 1890.

[27] DTJ to W. W. Prescott, Aug. 27, 1890; DTJ to J. B. Thayer, Sept. 3, 1890; DTJ to R. M. Kilgore, Sept. 4, 1890; DTJ to R. C. Porter, Oct. 23, 1890; DTJ to R. A. Underwood, Nov. 24, 1890; *RH*, Sept. 30, 1890, p. 602; Nov. 4, 1890, p. 688; Mar. 3, 1891, p. 144.

[28] DTJ to GIB, Jan. 1, 1891.

[29] DTJ to GIB, Jan. 26, 1891.

[30] EGW to US, June 14, 1889. White may have been referring to an editorial appearing in *RH*, June 11, 1889, pp. 376, 377.

[31] EGW to US, September 1889.

[32] US to EGW, Feb. 17, 1890.

[33] EGW to US, Mar. 8, 1890.

[34] EGW to US, Nov. 25, 1890.

[35] EGW to US, Dec. 31, 1890.

[36] EGW to US, Jan. 6, 1891.

[37] DTJ to R. M. Kilgore, Jan. 9, 1891; DTJ to R. H. Underwood, Jan. 10, 1891; DTJ to C. H. Jones, Jan. 16, 1891; EGW to "Brother and Sister [J. S.] Washburn," Jan. 8, 1891.

[38] US to A. T. Robinson, Sept. 21, 1892.

[39] EGW to US, Sept. 19, 1892.

[40] OAO to EGW, June 13, 1893.

[41] EGW to US and HS, Aug. 10, 1893.

[42] GRK, *A. T. Jones*, pp. 185-187.

[43] SNH to EGW, Apr. 20, 1894; 14th Meeting, General Conference Committee, Spring Session, Apr. 13, 1894, 3:30 p.m., General Conference Committee Minutes.

[44] *RH*, May 15, 1894, p. 312; OAO to WCW, Apr. 27, 1894.

CHAPTER VIII
"THE GREAT GLOBETROTTING TRIP"
MAY 1894-JANUARY 1895

On May 1, 1894, Uriah and his son Wilton left Battle Creek by the Michigan Central Railroad at 7:08 p.m. on what Wilton called "the great globetrotting trip to Europe and Palestine." The following day they toured the Niagara Falls area and then went on to West Wilton, New Hampshire, Uriah's boyhood home, where his brother Samuel and Abner Holt, probably a family friend, met them. After several days of visiting relatives, on Wednesday, May 9, Uriah went to South Lancaster, Massachusetts, to attend the last five days of conference meetings, at which both he and Stephen Haskell spoke. Wilton, meanwhile, traveled to Boston for a short tour that included attendance at a professional baseball game, rejoining his father in South Lancaster on Friday. On May 14, together with Haskell, they traveled to New York City, from where the three men would leave for England.[1]

Two days later, on Wednesday, May 16, they almost did not make their boat. T. A. Kilgore, who had their tickets for the White Star steamer *Majestic* in the *Sentinel* office safe, forgot to bring them when they went to the port and had to run back after them. Wilton reported that they waited on the dock while the crew pulled in one gangplank and were about to hoist the second one "when Kilgore came rushing up, so we just barely made it." The Adventist travelers were the last ones to board the ship.[2]

The passage to England was uneventful. Uriah told his wife that their second-class cabin was comfortable "when you get used to the cramped room." He reported that the ship had 180 second-class passengers and 190 in first class and steerage. After smooth sailing the first two days, they ran into some rough weather near Newfoundland, which resulted in both Uriah and Haskell experiencing seasickness. "Friday morning," Smith wrote, "I was able to get down about half a breakfast, which I surrendered before noon, and skipped my dinner, but was ready for supper." But by the next day the sea had become much smoother. Uriah told Harriett that he slept well at night and had napped during the day as well. "As to fare," he wrote his wife, "if one likes pork in its various forms of sausage, ham, bacon, Irish stew, etc., we would have no lack of that. But we have had besides, broiled steak, roast mutton, roast beef, chicken, and fish, which has all been good. But the drink—ugh! The coffee is about the most execrable decoction I ever tasted. I tried a cup of tea, and it made me sick. Then I fell back on hot water, but that tasted as if it had had salt mackerel boiled in it. So nothing was left but cold water, minus the 'cold.' It tasted well enough, but was lukewarm."[3]

Wilton, always alert to the foibles of vegetarians, described Haskell attempting to "pick out a vegetable diet from their bill of fare" and ending up with bread and butter and cheese. "But one day they had some corned beef and that was too much of a temptation. In spite of all the articles he has lately been putting through the *Review,* and the prospect of his soon writing a book against meat eating, he could not resist that corned beef, but put into it as though he hadn't had anything to eat for a week. Once or twice after that I believe they had the same, and he never refused."[4]

After a trip of six days, five hours, and 30 minutes, the *Majestic* arrived at Queenstown and then took another 13 hours to get to Liverpool, where the travelers disembarked. George R. Drew, a pioneer of Adventist ship ministries in England, met them and assisted them through customs, after which he took the visitors to his home for the night. "His wife prepared us some supper," Wilton told his sister, "—an egg apiece, bread, butter, bran coffee and sauce. We made out very well, but Pa looked hungry when we got through." The following day Haskell remained in Liverpool while the Smiths took the 11:00 a.m. train for London, traveling through "a more romantic and picturesque portion of country than I was anticipating," Uriah told Harriet. The hills, valleys, fields, grazing cattle, and church steeples "reminded me constantly of New England." Uriah and Wilton arrived at London's St. Pancras station about 4:30 p.m., where Uriah's son Leon Smith and Leon's wife, Meda, met them. The couple had recently moved to

London, where Leon served as an editor for denominational publications. Elder Robinson and Henry Simkin also greeted them. That night Uriah and Wilton stayed in Leon's apartment.[5]

On Friday Uriah and his two sons toured the British Museum, which Wilton reported as "a place well worth the visit." On Sabbath Uriah preached in the morning to the Adventist group at their chapel on Duncombe Road, while Haskell, who had rejoined them, spoke in the afternoon. Sunday morning Uriah and Wilton went to St. Margaret's Church, next to Westminster Abbey, to hear Archdeacon Farrar, whose sermon Uriah liked quite well, and that evening Uriah preached again in the Adventist chapel. On Monday they resumed their sightseeing, visiting the Tower of London, the Natural History Museum, and Madame Tussaud's wax museum, which disappointed Wilton "perhaps because I had heard them [the figures] cracked up so highly." Although noting that they "could just take a glance at a whole forest of objects of interest, which we could not stop to study," Uriah enjoyed the sites very much, stating that "if I should see nothing more, it has well repaid me for the trip." That evening W. M. Jones, a Seventh Day Baptist minister who had lived in Palestine for several years, and his wife visited and gave them "many points in reference to both country and people" in anticipation of their visit. On Tuesday they repacked their things and in the evening, together with Haskell, took a train to Harwich and boarded a small steamer crossing to the Hook of Holland. Although they had second-class tickets, Wilton led them directly to the first-class cabins, where they went immediately to bed, thinking that if they were asleep it was less likely that they would get "routed out." No one bothered them, however, and the next morning they paid an extra six shillings. "The better accommodations for a good night's rest," Wilton told his mother, "were well worth the difference in price." About 7:00 a.m. they reached the Hook, where they boarded a train for Hamburg.[6]

SCANDINAVIA

Traveling through Holland, Wilton observed the freshness of the vegetation, the well-cultivated gardens, "old-fashioned Dutch windmills," and large herds of cattle. The latter, he noted, were "all black and white. It was very seldom I saw one of the reddish-brown color so common in America." Reaching Hamburg shortly after 10:00 p.m., they met Louis R. Conradi, chief administrator of the church in Germany and Russia, who took them to his home at the Adventist mission. About 3:00 p.m. the next day they took a train for an hour-and-a-half trip to Lubeck, where they immediately boarded a steamer for Copenhagen. This time they actually had first-class tickets. They arrived at Copenhagen about 7:00 the next morning, June 2, and M. M. Olsen took them to his home.[7] For the next two months, beginning with Copenhagen, they organized their travel plans around the meetings of the various European conferences, which provided them with lodging and board. Mixing pleasure with business, Uriah and Wilton included as much sightseeing as they could.

Work began the very next day as both Haskell and Uriah presented Bible lessons in the morning and the afternoon. Sometime into the meetings Wilton observed that his father had "spoken several times, once in the evening, which is rather tiresome for him; and he cannot sleep well after it. They had him on to talk this evening, but he told them he wished they would get somebody else, and so they have." Reflecting more broadly regarding the impact the trip was having on Uriah, Wilton stated that "this is certainly a change for Pa. It breaks up his old rut, and I believe will do him good. He don't have any office to go to at just such a time every day, has to take his meals when he can get them, and cannot get off into his private office and read and [write] all the evening, but has to sit around with the brethren and talk." He also noted that his father was nervous about traveling in a foreign country, where few people spoke English, and worried about what they would do if someone failed to meet them as planned or if they missed the train. Of course, it was in part to help in situations such as these that he had brought Wilton along. Meanwhile, Uriah told Harriet that he was becoming more comfortable speaking through an interpreter.[8]

But they were able to get away from the meetings at times to visit Copenhagen's National Museum, where Uriah was particularly impressed with the ethnography department's exhibits depicting various cultures around the world, as well as the Natural History Museum, the Thorvaldsen sculpture museum, and Christiansborg Palace, among other places. Observing Danish culture, Uriah told his *Review* readers that "it seems to be the universal idea that whatever is drunk must come out of a bottle; and if one were to ask for water except for bathing purposes, it would hardly be known what was wanted. Of course there are mild and temperate drinks, but the most that is used is of the stronger kind. Good water can be had, but many of the people are apparently total strangers to a good draught from nature's own brewery."

He also observed the secular character of the country, pointing out that people used Sunday primarily for business and pleasure rather than religion. Nonetheless, he believed that Satan would find a way even in such a society to persecute Sabbathkeepers.[9]

Their Danish Conference meetings over, together with several others who had attended, on June 11 at 2:00 p.m. the Smiths and Haskell left by boat for Christiania (Oslo), Norway, arriving there some 17 hours later. The conference had arranged rooms for them just across the street from the mission, which Uriah noted was located between a Roman Catholic church and the state church. "Thus our work is sandwiched in between the old mother of apostasy," he told readers of the *Review*, "and the oldest daughter, which, being only partially reformed and stopping there, might as well not be reformed at all." That evening they ate a salmon and omelet dinner at a hillside restaurant that gave them an excellent view of the city and harbor. The salmon prompted Uriah to observe to his wife that Denmark and Norway were a paradise for good fish, which "are brought in alive, [and] so kept till the customer takes. So we can be sure of having them fresh. Flounders are excellent. I had two of that kind at a restaurant in Copenhagen, fried; they were excellent and are cheap too. But our people are being made to believe that they must not eat fish!"[10]

The meetings began the next morning, Wednesday, June 13, with Uriah speaking twice daily. On Sunday he and Wilton were able to get away to visit a museum and art gallery, a castle built by King Oscar I, a Catholic church from the eleventh or twelfth century, and an early Norwegian house. The following day the church members rode in carriages to hold a meeting on the mountainside of Hollen Kollen. "The city with its pleasant suburbs, the bay with its many islands, and the more distant ocean lay spread out as a panorama at our feet," Uriah wrote, "and the subjects which naturally suggested themselves to the different speakers were the beauties of nature and the power of God as manifested in His works, together with what awaits the people of God in that rest that remains for them."[11] After the meeting, most of the church members walked to the top of the mountain to view the country from an observation tower. Wilton wrote in his diary that "the mountains were mostly covered with pine trees. Little mountain streams were dashing along here and there and picturesque little lakes nestled in the valleys. Beneath us to the south lay Christiania, with its green cultivated fields around it and the fjord beyond, dotted with islands and covered with sailboats and steamers. Clouds were flitting across the sky, which gave the landscape that checkered appearance of sunshine and shadow, which only enhanced its beauty."[12]

On June 21 a businessman who supplied the Adventist publishing house with paper treated the American visitors and the mission staff to a dinner at a restaurant in St. Anne's Park. "It was a splendid affair," Uriah wrote Harriet, "got up in such a style as 'Ole Moses,' never engaged in before. The table was beautified with flowers, [and] the dishes came . . . decorated in the most ornate manner." Although Uriah told his *Review* readers "that respect was had to our well-known principles on the subject of proper articles of food, so that during its nine courses nothing could be accounted as offensive to those principles was urged upon either sight or palate," it was hardly a meal of which Dr. John Harvey Kellogg would have approved.

"The first course was boiled salmon, with new potatoes in cream; second course mutton chop, with green peas; third course, young chickens served in halves; fourth course, roast veal, with Saratoga chips; fifth course, lettuce [and] egg salad; sixth course, a pudding, like a corn starch pudding, with some kind of a red dressing, the nature of which in my verdancy I did not know, but the more initiated afterward said that it was a rum pudding. Whew! But it was good all the same. Seventh course, fruit, strawberries, pineapple, melons [and] cherries; eighth course, nuts of all kinds, with cream dressed cookies; ninth course, ice cream, which *was* cream. For drink we had raspberry juice in water, and raspberry and apricot soda water. When we got through we felt as if we had had a genteel sufficiency."[13]

Wilton commented that he had never attended "a more elaborate banquet or one where the food was better cooked or tasted nicer. It was an occasion long to be remembered." Of course, he could not refrain from observing that "the vegetarians all went back on their colors except [Elder] Haskell." Afterward the group went for a carriage excursion of about three hours to a park on the opposite side of the city from what they had previously visited. Uriah commented that "this was also a most enjoyable ride."[14]

Meanwhile, Uriah had been reading the railroad guides and decided that "it was essential that he should spend the Sabbath where the sun does not set, and thus demonstrate positively that it can be kept there." The conference leaders were not much impressed by his argument and were concerned about the expense, but shortly thereafter, Wilton reported to his sister, "they went down and procured us first-class tickets on a first-class steamer." The following Sunday, June 24, together with a "brother Olsen," Uriah and Wilton left Copenhagen at 1:55 p.m. to take the train to Throndhjem, where they arrived at about 7:00 the next morning and were met by several church members. They visited St. Olaf's Cathedral that afternoon, and Uriah spoke at the Adventist church in the evening before they boarded the excursion steamer, which left the dock at 10:00 p.m.[15]

The eight-day round trip began smoothly, although they encountered some rough water on the night of June 24, Uriah saying that the boat "bobbed like a popinjay [and] I could not keep my feet at all." Despite his seasickness, the scenery impressed Uriah. "And so it goes day by day (for there is no night)," he wrote Harriet, "more mountains, more fjords, mountains higher, fjords deeper, mountains larger, fjords broader, mountains multiplying, fjords multiplying, till it seems there is no end of them." About 10:00 p.m. on June 25 they crossed the Arctic Circle near Hestmando Island, the event celebrated by the firing of a "bomb."[16] Uriah wrote in the *Review* that "the sun hung low in the northern sky, and apparently two hours high, not dropping down to the horizon in a nearly perpendicular line, as it would appear in a more southern latitude, but slowly approaching the horizon directly north, at a very acute angle. The sky and a bevy of fleecy clouds that hovered around were tinged with all the gorgeous coloring of an evening sunset. A few rocky islets lifted their heads slightly above the water in the far distance, and cast their long, dark shadows toward us over a sea of fire. It was a scene not calculated soon to fade from memory. The hour of midnight at length came, and the sun shone with a full disk on the horizon directly from the north."[17]

Wilton, who seems to have prepared Uriah's reports for submission to the church paper, thought that his father had engaged in some literary license, telling his sister that he spoke "about some islands that I didn't know anything about, 'casting their long dark shadows toward us over a sea of fire.'" They were "about as [fiery] as Goguac [the lake near Battle Creek] would be perhaps half an hour before sunset when it is a little cloudy."[18]

The excursion next crossed the Vestfjord to the Lofoten Islands, arriving at Tromso on June 27, where they visited a Lap encampment and viewed a recently caught whale at a whaling station. "The smell all around the place was terrific," Wilton commented, "and it was quite amusing to see the ladies and some of the men standing around holding their noses." The following day they arrived at Hammerfest, one of the northernmost towns in the world. After they left Hammerfest, rough weather threatened to force them back. "We got the full benefit of the 'Washoe zephur' [sic] that was careering around in that locality at the time," Wilton wrote Annie.

"The boat stood first on one end and then on the other and rolled over on her side and dipped her rail under water. Pa was in his bunk but got pitched out onto the floor, and my typewriter also went smash off the table onto the floor. I [stayed] up on deck and really enjoyed seeing the boat pitch around. There was a fascination and a charm for me in seeing the great billows roll up and break in seething whitecaps. The boat seemed to rush at the waves like an angry animal and get tossed about in playful scorn. It was grand to see the water churned to foam, boil and whirl, and break over our bow as we dashed through it."[19]

Uriah, meanwhile, was seasick much of the time, telling Harriet that he had skipped a number of meals. Nonetheless, "I was glad to have some bad weather," he remarked, "because I wanted to see all sorts; but of course we could have got along with a little less than we had."[20]

On June 29 they sailed to the North Cape. Wilton "climbed to the top of the cape in a drizzling and driving rain with the wind blowing about 40 knots an hour," while his father stayed on deck and viewed the cliff through his glass. Thoroughly soaked, on returning to the ship Wilton and Mr. Hutchinson, a passenger from San Francisco, got a bottle of beer for one of the stokers, who allowed them to sit by the furnace door until they dried out. Uriah, of course, was especially interested in the midnight sun and its implications for Sabbath observance. He told Harriet that he imagined he "could detect the transition from evening twilight to morning twilight as the new day began. But Wilton thinks that is a great stretch of the imagination." After another stop at Tromso, on July 1 the boat arrived at the Svartisen glacier. Wilton went out on the glacier and "found it very difficult and dangerous walking, the surface being a succession of steep ridges and deep fissures and gorges at the bottom of some of which there was water—no knowing how deep. Had it not been for the little dirt on the ice it would have been impossible to get over it at all, prepared as we were." Afterward Wilton took a boat ride on Spring Lake, at the foot of the glacier, which took him close to the edge of the ice. Again, Uriah could not go out on the glacier but reported to Harriet that "the sight of a great valley between high mountains filled with solid ice, [and] running back [and] rising higher [and] higher till it was lost in the clouds, was a grand sight."[21]

On July 3, their excursion trip over, they arrived at Throndhjem. While Uriah spent part of the day writing, Wilton walked around the city with Mr. Peterson, a furniture manufacturer from Chicago, and later in the day visited Lefossen Falls, about five miles outside the city. "It was a warm and dusty but pleasant drive," he wrote in his diary. "It was just haying time and in many fields they were cutting and hanging it up on racks to dry. The falls are well worth a visit." That evening Uriah and Wilton left by train about 7:00 p.m. for Christiania, accompanied by "quite a number of our tourist friends from the 'Sigurd Jarl.'" "We pulled the seats together for a bed," Wilton wrote, "and made ourselves quite comfortable for the night."[22]

Arriving in Christiania on July 4, Wilton took his typewriter to a repair shop, but unsuccessfully looked for a flag and fireworks to celebrate the American Independence Day and had to "content myself with drinking pop and eating nuts for a celebration." With John Lorntz, presumably a local Adventist, who accompanied them to help with the language and travel connections, they left Christiania to attend the last three days of the Swedish meetings in Grythyttehed. After arriving on Friday, Uriah spoke five times during those three days. When the meetings closed, they spent the following Monday in Stockholm, where they visited the king's library, which contained a copy of the "Devil's Bible." Once again Uriah wrote for his *Review* readers from a stern Protestant perspective. "It is called the Devil's Bible from the full-page portraiture which it contains," he said, "of what was supposed to be his infernal deformity, devised with all the grotesque, ridiculous, and horrible features which the unbalanced brain of a superstitious monk in the gloomiest cloister of the Dark Ages could invent." After an hour's carriage ride around the city, they caught the train for Göttenborg, reaching it the following morning about 7:00 a.m., and then took a steamer to Frederikshavn, Denmark, where they thought they were going to meet the Danish ministers. Once there, however, they received a message from the ministers telling them to go immediately to Hamburg, Germany. They left about 5:00 that evening and arrived in Hamburg at 8:30 the next morning, July 11.[23]

THE CONTINENT

After spending the day in Hamburg writing and examining routes for future trips, the two men left that night for Switzerland, reaching Cologne the next morning. Following a visit to the cathedral they took a train to Bonn, where they then boarded a steamboat for a voyage up the Rhine. Uriah reported to his *Review* readers the contrast between the ancient ruined castles and the river and the modern manufacturing plants. At Mainz they transferred to a train, which left at 11:30 that night for Basel. First touring the Imprimerie Polyglotte, the Adventist publishing house, which Wilton found "kind of dark and dingy and uncomfortable," they visited the graves of John Nevins Andrews and J. H. Waggoner. That evening they boarded an 11:30 train for Colombier, the site of a camp meeting. Unfortunately, no one met them at the station, and it was beginning to rain. Although Uriah "kicked a little about walking," they had no choice but to walk to the encampment, getting there in time for supper.[24]

For the next week they were involved in the Swiss camp meeting, held outdoors in tents, an American phenomenon that the Europeans found curious. On Monday, July 23, they boarded the train for the return trip to Hamburg. Uriah commented that the government-operated railways made it easy to take a different return route on their round-trip ticket. They visited Bern and Lucerne, where they crossed Lake Vierwaldstetter. First viewing the Alps, Wilton reported to his mother, Uriah exclaimed, " 'Those ain't mountains; no mountains ever got so high as that. Those are clouds.' " Of course, they were mountains, and soon the Smiths boarded the incline train to ascend the Rigi. Uriah reported the view in the *Review:* ". . . with all its variety of cities and villages, churches and farm buildings, roads and rivers, lakes and lawns, fields and forests, fruit trees and vineyards, was a most impressive view from such a height, where one seemed almost to be suspended in midheaven." They then spent a short time in Zurich, where they visited the armory and saw the armor that Ulrich Zwingli wore at the time of his death. On July 25 they visited the Rhine Falls. Haskell, who was traveling with them, declined to go to the falls, saying that "all we could see would be some water falling over some rocks," but Uriah judged the falls "beautiful but not as grand and magnificent as those in America."[25]

The following day they visited the castle in Heidelberg and then went on to Frankfurt, where Haskell left them as they traveled to Eisenach. On July 27 the Smiths visited the Wartburg, where they viewed the room in which Martin Luther hid and in which he translated the New Testament into German. Nearly out of money, in Hanover they stayed in a beer hall located in a back alley, where they had a surprisingly comfortable stay. One evening they "took in a typical German beer garden," Wilton told his mother. "The place was brilliantly lighted, a large band discoursed fine music, and thousands, from the best families apparently, sat around in groups chatting, laughing, and drinking beer or tea and coffee. Everything was quiet and courteous, nothing boisterous or rough. We sat at a table and listened to the music with the rest, only we drank soda water instead of beer. I had hard work to tear Pa away when I thought it was time to go." Sunday they visited the grave of an atheist who had vowed that it would never be opened, but the roots of a plant had worked their way into cracks and broke the stone apart.[26]

Monday they took the train for Hamburg, where Uriah would be attending meetings. While staying at the Hamburg mission, both men complained about the food. "They are running this mission here on the vegetarian system," Uriah wrote Harriet. "Nothing is too inviting. For supper last night, for instance, we had graham bread, of the coarse sawdusty kind, and a little bitter at that, and a saucer of sauce composed of currants, plums, cherries, and gooseberries, four of the sourest things under heaven, and nothing more. . . . I cannot get enough of that kind of fodder to hurt me. But I think the extremes to which the matter is carried in some quarters will lead to a reaction, and cause them to take liberties they would not, if a more liberal course were pursued. . . . But I confess that the very name 'hygienic,' as practically defined by our people, has come to be a terror to me."[27]

Wilton commented that the "grub we get here . . . *is* right down on the backbone of the health reform—no meat whatever, the grahamest kind of graham bread with only now and then a little butter, potatoes without gravy, and vegetables cooked in the plainest kind of style, almost without seasoning. But still they generally have plenty of it, and I am getting so I like some of the dishes quite well, although I thought at first that if there was ever a case where homicide would be justifiable, it would be to kill the compounder of some of these conglomerations."[28]

Meanwhile, Haskell returned to London on August 8, preparatory for leaving for South Africa, and Uriah was busy with meetings that ran through August 16. The stay in Hamburg brought the first phase of the Smiths' trip to an end. Uriah told Harriet that Wilton had been "just the help on the journey that I need, looking after the luggage, getting checks, tickets, etc. I could not get along without him." Furthermore, "he is very popular wherever he goes, getting acquainted with people on the boats, [and] so learning much from them. It is amusing to see him wrestle with the German, but he generally makes them understand what he is driving at." Although Uriah did not mention it, one of Wilton's jobs was to procure his father's "indispensable" bottle of soda. "When we are traveling," Wilton wrote to his brother Charlie, "especially if it is warm and dusty, my first duty when the train stops is to rush out and get Pa a bottle of pop; and he is ready for one at about every station." From this point on in the journey, without church people to meet them and make arrangements for travel and lodging, Wilton would become even more indispensable.[29]

While in Hamburg Uriah and Wilton formulated their plans for the remainder of their trip, including a 30-day tour of the Middle East conducted by the Thomas Cook Company. On Sunday, August 19, they left for Berlin accompanied by some Adventists from that city. During their stay in Berlin, Uriah spoke once to the church of 13 members, and they visited the Museum of Art and the palaces of Wilhelm I and Frederick the Great. Regarding the relics at the palace of Wilhelm I, Uriah told his *Review* readers that "it satisfies one's curiosity at least to know that he is looking upon the best that this world can produce, and which he can easily persuade himself represents the limit of human conception and achievement." But, he concluded, such things do not compare with heaven and the things of God.[30]

On August 26 Wilton and Uriah left for Wittenberg, where they viewed the statues of Luther and Melanchthon and the Schlosskirche, where Luther had nailed his 95 theses to a side door. In his *Review* report Uriah commented on allegorical paintings by Cranach the Younger that contrasted "popery and the gospel of Christ." In a negative understanding of allegory, he further commented that Germany, because of its pursuit of higher criticism, "is giving up the Bible by turning it into allegory." Told about a spring whose water Luther prized, the two men took a carriage about 20 minutes outside of the city only to find a beer parlor built over the spot and the spring "turned into a slop basin for the rinsing of beer bottles and the emptying of its malodorous dregs."[31]

On August 27 Wilton and Uriah took a train to Leipzig, arriving about 5:30 in the evening. The city was a book-publishing center. With an introduction from Conradi to one of the business leaders, they received a guided tour through some of the largest printing and binding establishments. They left for Dresden on August 30, where they visited the Picture Gallery and the Zoological Gardens before going on to Prague on Sunday, September 2.[32]

Uriah reported in the *Review* that "the road threads its way along the winding course of the [Elbe] river, passageway being often hewn out of the solid rock, and thrust by tunnels through projecting mountain spurs. The scenery is romantic and charming. Interesting villages and cities are located at frequent intervals at the foot of the bluffs along the river, and at several points the ruins of ancient castles crown the [heights]."[33]

At Prague, Uriah was disappointed to find "no statue of Huss or Jerome," but appreciated that the city had the best fruit they had yet encountered in Europe, something that along with good vegetables he missed greatly. After visiting the Imperial Palace, the "Burg," the following day they traveled to Vienna, where they toured the imperial library, the royal stables, and St. Stephen's Church, as well as the palaces of Franz Joseph and Lichtenstein, among other sites.[34]

Now that he and Wilton were on their own, Uriah reported that they did "not go to the grand mogul establishments, nor to the third-rate places, but take those of medium grade, where we find more reasonable prices, [and] our accommodations and fare that are good enough." He further explained that they had thus "far found excellent beds and good meals. The meat to be sure is generally cooked in a different way from what I have been accustomed to, and so disguised with various flavorings [and] seasonings that I can't . . . always tell whether it is beef, mutton, veal, pork, bear, rhinoceros or alligator. But it generally hits the palate in about the right place, and others eat it and don't die, and so I wade in." Now he was more dependent on Wilton than previously, commenting that his son's limited knowledge of German "is of immense advantage. I do not know what we could have done without it, in places in the interior of Germany, where there were none who spoke English." Uriah maintained his moralistic stance, noting that in contrast to Vienna's grandeurs, "the trail of the serpent of sin is still visible. Beggary in the streets, dens of temptation along the thoroughfares, and the marks of debauchery, depravity, disease, and imbecility upon the faces of many of the people." In a letter to Harriet Uriah wondered about the reaction to his *Review* reports. "Does anyone take an interest in them?" he asked. "And have you any means of knowing whether they in anywise meet the expectations that were raised in reference to them?"[35]

On September 10 father and son traveled to Budapest. About this time they seem to have come under the auspices of the Cook Company, for Wilton stated that they "stopped at the Grand Hotel Hungaria on Cook's coupons. It is quite a magnificent affair." They spent much of the next two days walking around the city, observing workers on the river and viewing the buildings. September 12 they visited Andrew Moody, pastor of the Scottish Presbyterian Church, who told them that the Hungarian desire for freedom had prevented the Roman Catholics from maintaining control of religion. Wilton found Moody a pleasant "gentleman, but somewhat pompous, and he kept continually saying, 'o, yes,' with his peculiar drawl. He knew considerable of SDAs and their work." That afternoon they left for Belgrade, arriving at 10:20 p.m., where the Grand Hotel made them comfortable but, according to Wilton, "far below the style of Budapest." The next afternoon, September 13, the two men walked around the park and visited a dilapidated fortress nearby before boarding their train for Turkey.[36]

TURKEY AND THE MIDDLE EAST

About 10:30 the next morning the train came to the Turkish frontier, where officials removed the passengers and put them in a small room to be fumigated. "It smelled principally of carbolic acid," Wilton wrote in his diary. "There were large cracks and holes in the floor, I suppose for the germs to fall through as they were killed and dropped off. Out by the track they had a cylinder of disinfectant that they sprayed all over the baggage, mail and all; one fellow pumped and another did the squirting." Properly disinfected, the passengers waited in a large room until assigned to quarters for the night. Placed in an unpainted barracks, Uriah and Wilton nonetheless had a decent room with "two iron bedsteads, with sheet and blankets and pillows. Two good chairs were in the room." Not long after moving in, "a fellow came and by motioning to his mouth wanted to know if we wanted to eat. We nodded our heads, and soon he came with two trays, containing soup, bread, roast beef and potatoes, a bottle of wine and grapes and pears. It went first rate." Uriah commented that "it was all excellent, [and] the roast beef the best I have struck in Europe." Later that evening Wilton again recorded in his diary, "the gentleman with a red cap, baggy seated pants and feet tied up in moccasins came again with dinner. This time he had noodle soup, bread, meat and potatoes, chicken and potato, wine, grapes and pears. We did full justice to this. After we got through, the waiter would eat what was left. Perhaps he was not in the habit of getting such a good feed." The next morning the officials sprayed their rooms and luggage with disinfectant before sending them on to customs. They then boarded the train and continued their journey to Salonika.[37]

Uriah and Wilton had now entered a new world. "Stepping upon the street, one will perhaps first see some animated haystacks coming toward him," Uriah wrote in the *Review*. "On closer inspection, he will discover a little donkey nose just protruding from the front, and four little donkey feet beneath, giving the mass its motion. Woodpiles move about in the same way. Great baskets and sacks which almost hide the animals from view, filled with fruits and vegetables, constitute traveling groceries. Two pieces of wide board, fitted together like the roof of a house, placed astride a donkey's back, and having rows of hooks on which are hung all varieties of meat, exposed to the not-overclean dust of the street and the blazing rays of the sun, and receiving the sedulous attention of the flies, furnish perambulating meat markets, and if the people were at all fastidious in their tastes and feelings, they would be circulating libraries in favor of vegetarianism. In the same way, milk cans, crockery, flowers, coal, and all movable merchandise are transported through the streets, seeking purchasers among the people."[38]

More graphically, he wrote to Harriet that "the Turks have their trousers cut so that the seat comes down to the knee. It makes them look as if they had had an attack of cholera morbus and met with a misfortune. Wilton thinks that style, [and] this city takes the cake."[39]

From Salonika they took a steamship to Piraeus, the seaport of Athens, arriving after midnight on September 18. The next afternoon a guide took them through the sites of classical Athens, and on September 21 they began a four-day tour of Greece, seeing, among other things, the Acropolis, the Parthenon, Prophlea, the Erechtheum, and Mycenae. "What these all reveal of the past skill and achievements of the Greeks, and the grandeur of their temples and palaces, is wonderful indeed," Uriah wrote in the *Review*.

"The imposing structures they reared, the stones of prodigious size and weight brought from distant quarries, and raised to great [heights] in their buildings, the skill and labor exhibited in carving them into elegant and graceful forms, the true proportions of symmetry and beauty into which they were shaped, the great number of statues erected to their gods, the vast treasures devoted to their gifts and offerings, excite the wonder of every beholder." He concluded, however, that "the bright sunshine, clear skies, and pleasant seasons of Greece are left; but the glory it once enjoyed is no more."[40]

On September 25 the Smiths boarded a Russian steamer at Piraeus, which arrived at Smyrna about 1:30 p.m. the next day. Wilton and Uriah hired a guide to show them around the city. After some walking, the guide obtained some donkeys and took Uriah and Wilton "up quite a high hill overlooking the city, sea, and surrounding country, on top of which are the remains of quite an extensive Roman fortification." Wilton said that he felt "somewhat awkward" riding the donkey but "tried to appear natural and easy and used to the business." After staying overnight on board their ship, they spent a couple more hours the following day exploring the city. Uriah found watching the process of fig-packing interesting but advised his *Review* readers to wash or steam the fruit before eating it. He also observed that while the French were good at developing harbors, roads, and railroads, he doubted that they could colonize, an ability that he believed belonged exclusively to the Anglo-Saxon race. About 4:00 p.m. the ship once more started on its way, passing during the next few days the islands of Rhodes and Cyprus, among others, before arriving at Beirut on October 1.[41]

A Cook agent met them on the boat and took them to the hotel, where they met their dragoman (who would serve as their interpreter and organize their tents and food on their journey through Palestine), a Mr. Abraham Lyons, who had been highly recommended by Elder Tenney. After obtaining extra Turkish police passports from the American consul, they took a ride around the city, viewing the American College and some ancient inscriptions on an old Roman road. The next day, October 2, after some discussion, they decided that Uriah should ride in a palanquin (a sedan chair usually carried on poles by two or more men but in this case apparently by mules) rather than on horseback, which would have been both fatiguing and dangerous. At 1:30 p.m. they began their 30-day tour, ascending about 3,000 to 4,000 feet up Mount Lebanon, stopping about 5:00, where, Wilton recorded in his diary, "our camp was already pitched for us and the American flag flying from our tent." The following night they camped at the Christian city of Zahleh. It had been a hot day, which Wilton recorded had given him a headache to accompany his "sore behind from so much riding." Soon after leaving Zahleh at 8:00 the next morning, they visited the alleged tomb of Noah and then made their way to Baalbeck, which Uriah described as the first objective of their journey. Along the way they viewed the remaining six columns of the Temple of Jupiter and an old stone sarcophagus. After camping the night in Baalbeck, the next morning they toured the temple ruins, following the instructions in their Baedeker guide. During the afternoon they visited a spring about a half-hour's ride from the city and a Presbyterian school, which had about 30 young boys.[42]

ILLNESS

The following morning, October 6, a Sabbath, both Wilton and his father woke up feeling ill. Wilton attributed his "bellyache" and "wind on my [stomach]" to something that he had eaten, and by the evening he "began to feel like myself again." Uriah, however, had a chill, fever, and sweats. Initially they attributed it to his sleeping in a draft. Unfortunately, they had arrived at Baalbeck in the midst of what Uriah later called "an epidemic of Syrian fever," namely malaria. The following day he thought that he was well enough to continue. They went down into the Plain of Bekaa and began climbing the Anti-Lebanon Mountains, but soon Uriah "vomited up his breakfast and felt completely exhausted." At lunchtime Wilton made a bed for his father to rest on, but by 1:30 p.m., the time the group was set to travel on "he was so weak he could hardly stand." After camping the night near the village of Sargiya, Uriah still was not feeling well on October 8, so they "got him dressed and into the palanquin, making it as comfortable for him as possible, with blankets and pillows." They passed through the Valley of Zebedane. When they stopped for lunch, Uriah still could not eat. That night they camped at El Hoosiniye, where Uriah went to bed almost immediately. With him so weak that they had to place him in the palanquin while it was on the ground and then lift it onto the mules, they left their baggage to follow for Damascus, arriving there about noon. Some men carried Uriah to their room, where they put him to bed, and Wilton summoned a physician. Dr. Mackinnon came about 4:00 in the afternoon, gave Uriah some medicine, and said that he would call again in the morning.[43]

Although Uriah had no fever the next morning and the doctor thought that with a careful diet and rest he would soon be able to get up, the fever returned again that afternoon, continuing throughout most of the night and causing Uriah to roll and toss "in sort of a [delirious] stupor and great misery." The next two days were difficult. "The deep red spots on each cheek glowed like balls of fire through the flushed, hot features," Wilton recorded in his diary. "His throat was parched and sore so that he could hardly swallow or speak and kept constantly calling for ice in a scarcely audible whisper." Starting October 11 Lyons stayed up with Uriah several nights, something that obviously was not part of his duties. The fever broke sometime on the night of October 12, but when the doctor came the next morning, Uriah's "temperature was way below normal and his pulse could hardly be felt at all. A cold clammy sweat gathered on his brow and hands, and he complained of numbness in his foot." Dr. Mackinnon was alarmed and, in addition to medicine, told Wilton to give him two ounces of milk with a teaspoon of brandy every half hour. He also arranged for a Christian nurse, Matilda T. Atthill, to stay in the room overnight. On October 14, a Sunday, Wilton recorded that Uriah "was so completely exhausted he thought he was going to die and wanted me to take his body home in a metallic casket. Passed a very restless day and night, cool and feverish by spells. Still continued the brandy and milk."[44]

The next day Uriah had slightly improved, but someone needed to watch him "almost every minute to fan him, give him ice or drink, or keep the clothes in place. There is not the least light or expression in his eye, and one or two attempts at a smile were ghastly and haunting." The situation was taking its toll on Wilton, who said that "along toward morning I felt so weary from lack of sleep that I frequently found myself nodding and dreaming as I stood by the bedside or sat on the foot of the bed." During the next few days Uriah's condition gradually improved. To give Wilton a break, Dr. Mackinnon invited him to his house for tea. By Friday Uriah had progressed enough that Wilton attempted to seat him in a rocking chair, "but his head dropped to one side and he soon complained of a terrible pain in his right side." The next day the doctor prescribed a "pick me up" tonic. "It was a bitter, greenish liquid, containing some nux vomica, which father abhors," Wilton wrote in his diary. "He calls it the 'green devil' and always kicks about taking it." On Sunday Uriah was able to eat a little toast soaked in chicken broth and sit up for a couple hours. By Wednesday he was sleeping well, eating more heartily, and even laughing, and the following Sunday was able to take a short carriage ride. Meanwhile, Wilton wrote to a Dr. Graham of the Beirut Hospital about bringing Uriah there for a few days. Tuesday the fever and vomiting returned, but Dr. Mackinnon recommended that they leave for Beirut the next day, despite the risk. Wilton and Lyons arranged his seating in a diligence, a two- or four-horse-drawn vehicle, which took them most of the way to Beirut, with a landau, another horse-drawn carriage but with a convertible top, meeting them about 45 minutes from the hospital. They obtained a "fine large room, commanding a magnificent view of the mountains and the sea" for Uriah while Wilton found a room at the hotel. On November 1 "Lyons took his leave, tears coming to his eyes as he said goodbye."[45]

The worst was past, but Uriah still had ups and downs during the next couple weeks, although the doctor said that he could sail for Jaffa in mid-November. While Wilton found a few diversions, his days were pretty routine: "Get up at any time it happened, from 7-9, eat my breakfast of bread and butter, and jam or honey, coffee and a couple of eggs, when they were not so rank I couldn't. Sit around a little and go up to the hos-

pital. Stay with father till noon, come back to lunch, sit around a little, go
to the hospital again, stay till six, return for dinner, sit around a little while
and go to bed. Ambition running at a very low ebb."[46]

At one point Dr. Bliss, president of the American College, paid them
a visit. "He is a fine old gentleman and entertaining talker," Wilton said.
On November 15 he took Uriah riding in the afternoon, which became a
somewhat regular activity. Uriah also was strong enough to begin dictating
his *Review* reports and letters and to walk in the garden next to the hospital. "I enjoy strolling about in it," he wrote Harriet, "and marking the great
variety of everything that meets the eye. You would be delighted. Lemons
on trees, orange trees, loaded with fruit, now just ripening, tea roses of the
loveliest, water lilies in the numerous tanks and fountains scattered over
the grounds, cacti of all kinds, from the great giant, to the small runners,
creeping plants such as I never saw before, the Egyptian lotus, a large bush
(almost a tree) covered with flowers, as large as a clematis, of the most
intense red, and making a wonderful show, and many other blossoming
plants, red, yellow, and blue, such as we do not have in America."[47]

By November 18 Uriah was eating so heartily that Wilton, concerned
about periodic vomiting spells, "kept admonishing him not to eat too
much until he thought I was a regular crank." Their journey through Palestine having been brought short by illness, they boarded a ship for Jaffa
on November 21, but both became seasick by the next morning.[48]

The seas were rough as they approached Jaffa on November 22, and for
a time it was doubtful whether they could land, but the weather calmed a
bit. Nonetheless, because Jaffa was what Wilton called the "worst port" in
the Mediterranean and a portion of the wharf had washed away, passengers had to board small boats that took them from the steamer to the land.
It made things difficult for Uriah, because of his artificial leg. Nonetheless,
he jumped from the steamer into the arms of two Arab boatmen. When
they reached the broken wharf, "a stout Arab took me up upon his back,
and carried me over the place to a safe landing, in which transaction I
must have made quite a spectacle," Uriah reported to Harriet. After staying
overnight, accompanied by Mr. Clark, the Cook agent for Palestine who
"made very good company," they left the next day by train for Jerusalem,
arriving that evening about sunset.[49]

After two days of rain, during which they stayed inside to write and read, they hired Abraham Lyon's father-in-law as their dragoman and an Indian chair with four carriers for Uriah and began their tour of Jerusalem. That day they visited the Armenian chapels on the site of Caiaphas' palace, the Wailing Wall, the Via Dolorosa, and the Garden of Gethsemane. Regarding the garden, Uriah wrote that "it is easy to believe that under one of these trees the Savior poured forth His soul in agony and bloody sweat under the weight of the sins of the world." At the Mount of Olives Uriah sought to climb a building with a high tower against Wilton's "express wishes, but only went up one flight but he got reeking with sweat and I was terribly afraid he would catch cold. He thought I was a regular crank I made such a fuss." The following day, November 27, they visited the Mosque of Omar and the Church of the Holy Sepulcher, followed on the twenty-eighth by trips to the Pools of Solomon and Bethlehem, where they saw the Church of the Nativity. On Thanksgiving Day, November 29, they visited the "tombs of the kings" and Golgotha. In his *Review* reports Uriah expressed skepticism about the "foolish" traditions attached to the various places, but he appears to have eventually come to terms with them. "Christians seem to have considered it a sin not to be able to identify every spot where any event mentioned in the Scriptures connected with the life of Christ has taken place. . . . But what matters it? The general localities are there beyond dispute, and to fix upon the exact spot where the events occurred gratifies the passion some men have for deciding such questions, and furnishes food for the credulity of those who wish to believe them." But Smith seems to have felt that his visit to Jerusalem was invaluable. "One can get no idea of the place [and] the scenery round about without a personal visit," he wrote Harriet.[50]

On November 30 Uriah and Wilton returned to Jaffa by train, Abraham Lyons accompanying them. They boarded a steamer for Port Said, arriving there the next morning and taking a train to Cairo. Using Cook Company coupons, they stayed in Cairo at Shepheard's Hotel. "It is filled up with English aristocracy who have come here to spend the winter," Uriah wrote to his wife. "Silks [and] satins, jewels, [and] dress coats—the toniest place I was ever in." On December 3 he and Wilton took a carriage to visit the tombs of the Mamelukes and the Mosque of the Citadel, but unfortunately Uriah experienced a relapse of his illness the next morning and, on a doctor's advice, stayed in his room the next two days. But then feeling well again, he and Wilton visited the pyramids on December 6. Wilton climbed one of the pyramids and went inside one of the chambers. Uriah, of course, did not attempt to get so close. "I might about as well try to go to the moon," he commented to Harriet, but viewed the structures from his carriage. "When on the top, Wilton did not look as large as Tom Thumb from where I sat," he wrote. Uriah was impressed with the degree to which Cairo had "taken on European manners and customs."

Again the following day he was feeling ill, and he mostly stayed in his room for the next three days, although on December 8 he enjoyed listening to a military band play on the hotel's lawn.[51] Always sympathetic to things English, he observed that "the influence of England has greatly helped the country. They have improved the laws, restored confidence, lowered the taxes, relieved the people of oppression, and made great improvements in both city and country." It contrasted with the areas ruled by Turkey, which he called the "Great Eastern Paralytic," a government that seemed to have as its purpose to "prevent improvements, arrest progress, keep the people in ignorance, and draw money into their own pockets."[52]

FROM ROME TO PARIS

On December 10 they took a train to Ismailia, where they boarded a steamer about an hour after midnight, arriving at Brindisi about 10:00 that morning. Initially planning to take a train straight to Paris, Uriah felt better after the sea voyage, and he and Wilton decided to go to Rome. Nonetheless, he was obviously thinking about his trip's end, describing to Harriet that their travels now were "the hop-skip-and-jump for home." He reported that "my health is improving right along, [and] my appetite is coming back like a tidal wave, but it is more for things such as I get at home, which I haven't seen a shadow of since we struck the continent of Europe." Combining both nostalgia and humor, he told his wife that "we find that pie is an American institution. We have seen nothing resembling it in Europe, Asia, or Africa. So I shall want some pie—custard pie, pumpkin pie, apple pie, [and] mince pie. We have seen nothing like our gravied toast, so I shall want some cream toast, and cracker toast. We have found nothing like dried beans or peas; so I shall want some baked beans with potato salad [and] some split peas. We have found nothing resembling pancakes, so I shall want some buckwheat pancakes, [and] fine flour pancakes, with the usual accompaniments. We find no American doughnuts, so I shall want some of them; and then I want some of those nice griddle cakes you make, a bowl of hasty pudding and milk, [and] perhaps finish up on a bowl of oysters. This will do for the first meal, and afterward we can plan for the second, if I survive this!"[53]

After spending the Sabbath, December 15, then writing and walking around Brindisi for a while, the next morning they boarded a train to Naples. It was a cold and hungry trip, for the only heat in their railroad coach was a can of hot water for their feet and their only food a loaf of bread. Arriving in the city at 5:30 p.m., they experienced a rough omnibus ride to their hotel, which, after the somewhat difficult day, was "a very quiet pleasant place." On Monday they took a carriage to Pompeii, where they acquired a sedan chair for Uriah and spent a couple hours touring the ruins. Uriah found Pompeii "wonderful to look upon" and, after describing the ruins in some detail, told his wife that "it is a rare object lesson on old Roman habits [and] customs." The following day they traveled to Vesuvius, which proved to be a little too exciting for Uriah. Describing the explosions that thrust steam and rocks up from the crater, he told Harriet that "I confess I did not care to have the volcano any more 'active,' while I was so near. . . . It was to me an awful place. I never felt much more skittish in my life, [and] was very thankful when we were safely down."[54]

After Uriah rested Thursday, December 20, he and Wilton caught a morning train to Rome, arriving about 1:30 p.m. The following day they acquired a guide and spent the next four days touring the city, seeing, among other things, St. Peter's Basilica and St. Paul's Cathedral, the Colosseum, the catacombs, the Appian Way, the Vatican, and several churches and museums. Interestingly, despite his usual impulse to criticize Catholicism, his visit to Rome prompted him only to observe to his wife that "Rome is largely a modern city, with fine streets [and] handsome business blocks, swept, clean, and greatly improved, since it went out of control of the popes, [and] came into the hands of the Italian government in 1870." His reports in the *Review*, where his anti-Catholic sentiments typically appeared, devoted themselves entirely to descriptions of the places he visited. Perhaps illness and weariness from his long travels weakened Uriah's natural proclivities.[55]

On Thursday, December 27, the two men left for Paris. Wilton com-

mented that "this was third day on the cars, and it was growing very mo-
notonous, especially as the cars were uncomfortably cold." Their hotel
room was apparently not much warmer, for Uriah told his wife that their
outside room had the "wind whistling in through the cracks in the doors
and windows, as while we are roasting one side the other is getting more
or less frostbitten." A move to the reading room to write a letter did not improve things much. "Though they have an imitation of a fire in the room,"
he observed to Harriet, "[and] call it a warm room, my fingers are so much
with cold that I can hardly write."[56]

Although they spent two days in Paris, neither Uriah nor Wilton said
much about what they saw there, except that Uriah did describe the city
as "the gayest and handsomest of the capitals of Europe. Its well-paved,
broad, and beautiful streets, and elegant business houses, make a constant
attraction to the visitor." He visited Notre Dame Cathedral and the Church
of the Madéleine, where, he observed, "it was amusing to see rich-robed
ladies, with their delicate gloves, come in and apparently dip their finger
into the font of holy water, which they were very careful not to touch, and
then make a sign of the cross on their foreheads! Perhaps they thought that
deceiving the people by going through the motions would satisfy the Lord
as well as [not] to spoil their dainty gloves."[57]

RETURN HOME

They left Paris for London on December 31. The trip across the English
Channel, fortunately, took only two hours, for as Uriah observed, "this
boat seemed to take special delight in assuming any and every position but
that of the horizontal." In London they again stayed with Uriah's son Leon
and his wife, Meda, who had acquired better quarters than the apartment
they had had upon his arrival in the city several months previously. Nonetheless, Uriah expressed concern that Leon had lost weight, which his
son attributed to an illness some two weeks previously. Uriah, however,
did not think that the English climate was good for him and hoped that
Leon would be able to return to the United States soon. Regarding his own
health, he told Harriet that it was "good again, [and] Wilton appears to be,
[and] says he is, in the best of health. He steps around as if he was walking
on springs, [and] propelled by electricity."[58]

After more than a week in London, Uriah and Wilton boarded the *August*

Victoria of the Hamburg line, which left port at 10:00 a.m. on January 9. A day and a half out they ran into a furious storm that lasted two days. "The wind blew with such violence that it swept the spray from the breaking caps of the lofty billows till it seemed that the whole heavens were filled with a driving snowstorm," Uriah reported. "The rear flagstaff of our boat was broken off, and a portion of the deck railing was carried away; while the motion of the ship was such that on one occasion at least we were sharply reminded, by being thrown down the stairway, that it was not altogether safe to try to pass from point to point." On January 18 they arrived in Jersey City, where T. A. Kilgore met them, and then they traveled on to Battle Creek the following day. The *Review* reported that "although travel worn and somewhat bruised, the result of being flung down the stairs headlong by a violent lurch of the ship during the storm of last week, Brother Smith is in good health and spirits, and says that he is ready for work."[59]

Despite the optimistic report about him returning to work, Smith "experienced a reaction of weakness and exhaustion to which he was hardly aware that his weary travels and uncertain fare following his severe illness in Syria had reduced him." Consequently, Uriah entered the sanitarium for three weeks of treatment to eliminate the "seeds of malaria." Editing the *Review* would have to wait a bit.[60]

[1] WS, diary, May 1, 1894-May 15, 1894; *RH,* May 22, 1894, p. 328.
[2] WS to AS, May 25, 1894; WS, diary, May 16, 1894; *RH,* June 12, 1894, p. 376.
[3] US to HS, May 22, 1894.
[4] WS to AS, May 25, 1894.
[5] WS, diary, May 23-25, 1894; WS to AS, May 25, 1894; US to HS, May 25, 1894; *RH,* June 12, p. 376; OAO to WCW, Mar. 17, 1893.
[6] WS, diary, May 25-May 31, 1894; US to HS, May 29, 1894; WS to HS, June 5, 1894.
[7] WS, diary, May 31-June 2, 1894; WS to HS, June 5, 1894.
[8] WS to HS, June 5, 1894; WS, diary, June 2-5, 1894; US to HS, June 18, 1874.
[9] *RH,* July 17, 1894, pp. 456, 457; WS, diary, June 7-11, 1894.
[10] WS, diary, June 12, 1894; US to HS, June 12, 1894; *RH,* July 24, 1894, p. 472.
[11] *RH,* July 31, 1894, p. 488.
[12] WS, diary, June 17, 18, 1894.
[13] US to HS, June 24, 1894; *RH,* July 31, 1894, p. 488.
[14] WS, diary, June 21, 1894; *RH,* July 31, 1894, p. 488.
[15] WS, diary, June 10, 1894; June 24, 1894 (the transcript has both Sunday and

Monday identified as June 24); *RH*, Aug. 7, 1894, p. 504; WS to AS, June 24, 1894.

[16] US to HS, July 4, 1894; WS, diary, June 25, 1894.

[17] *RH*, Aug. 14, 1894, p. 520.

[18] WS to AS, July 28, 1894.

[19] WS, diary, June 27, 28, 1894; WS to AS, July 28, 1894.

[20] US to HS, July 4, 1894.

[21] WS, diary, June 28-July 1, 1894; WS to AS, July 28, 1894; US to HS, July 4, 1894.

[22] WS, diary, July 3, 1894; WS to AS, July 28, 1894.

[23] WS, diary, July 4-11, 1894; WS to AS, July 28, 1894; *RH*, Aug. 21, 1894, p. 536.

[24] WS, diary, July 12-14, 1894; *RH*, Aug. 28, 1894, pp. 552, 553.

[25] WS to HS, Aug. 18, 1894; WS, diary, July 14-25, 1894; *RH*, Sept. 9, 1894, p. 568.

[26] WS, diary, July 26-30, 1894; WS to HS, Aug. 18, 1894. Wilton's diary indicates that they attended the beer garden concert on Sunday evening while his letter to his mother identifies it as Saturday evening.

[27] WS, diary, July 30-Aug. 16, 1894; US to HS, Aug. 5, 1894.

[28] WS, diary, Aug. 3, 1894.

[29] WS to Charles Smith, Aug. 18, 1894.

[30] WS, diary, Aug. 19-24, 1894; *RH*, Oct. 9, 1894, pp. 632, 633.

[31] WS, diary, Aug. 26, 27, 1894; *RH*, Oct. 9. 1894, pp. 632, 633; Nov. 6, 1894, p. 696.

[32] WS, diary, Aug. 28-30, 1894.

[33] *RH*, Oct. 30, 1894, pp. 680, 681.

[34] *Ibid*.

[35] WS, diary, Aug. 28-Sept. 9, 1894; US to HS, Aug. 30, 1894; US to HS, Sept. 2, 1894.

[36] WS, diary, Sept. 10-13, 1894; *RH*, Nov. 6, 1894, p. 696.

[37] WS, diary, Sept. 14, 15, 1894; US to HS, Sept. 16, 1894.

[38] *RH*, Nov. 13, 1894, p. 712.

[39] WS, diary, Sept. 15, 16, 1894; US to HS, September 1894; *RH*, Nov. 13, 1894, p. 712.

[40] WS, diary, Sept. 17-24, 1894; *RH*, Nov. 20, 1894, pp. 728, 729.

[41] WS, diary, Sept. 25-Oct. 1, 1894; *RH*, Dec. 18, 1894, p. 792.

[42] WS, diary, Oct. 2-5, 1894; *RH*, Dec. 25, 1894, p. 808.

[43] WS, diary, Oct. 6-9, 1894; *RH*, Dec. 25, 1894, p. 808.

[44] WS, diary, Oct.10-14, 1894.

[45] WS, diary, Oct. 15-31, 1894.

[46] WS, diary, Nov. 7, 1894.

[47] US to HS, Nov.18, 1894.

[48] WS, diary, Nov. 1-22, 1894; WS to HS, Nov. 7, 1894; WS to AS, Nov. 27, 1894.

[49] WS, diary, Nov. 22, 23, 1894; US to HS, Nov. 24, 1894; WS to AS, Nov. 27, 1894.

[50] WS, diary, Nov. 24-29, 1894. The diary entry for November 29 is mislabeled November 24. *RH*, Jan. 15, 1895, pp. 40, 41; Jan. 22, 1895, p. 56; Jan. 29, 1895, pp. 72, 73; Feb. 5, 1895, p. 88; Feb. 12, 1895, pp. 104, 105; Feb. 19, 1895, p. 120; US to HS, Nov. 29, 1894.

[51] WS, diary, Dec. 1-9, 1894; US to HS, Dec. 4, 1894; US to HS, Dec. 9, 1894.

[52] US to HS, Dec. 9, 1894; *RH*, Feb. 26, 1895, p. 136; Jan. 1, 1895, p. 8. In a short article H. W. Carter recounts a story from a "Sister Mackey" telling of Uriah Smith's visit

to India (see *RH,* Feb. 22, 1940, pp. 19, 20). Stella Parker Peterson also refers to the alleged India trip (*RH,* Dec. 28, 1944, p. 8; see also, EFD, *Yours,* p. 184). Given that we have a virtual day-by-day recounting of Smith's trip in Wilton's diary and other documents, that Smith was considerably weakened by his attack of malaria, and that neither Uriah nor Wilton make any mention of an India trip, it does not seem possible that the account is correct. Furthermore, it mentions that Smith's wife was traveling with him, which certainly did not take place. Perhaps after the passage of time, Sister Mackey confused Smith with someone else.

[53] WS, diary, Dec. 10-14, 1894; US to HS, Dec. 15, 1894.

[54] WS, diary, Dec. 17, 18; US to HS, Dec. 20, 1894; *RH,* Mar. 5, 1895, p. 152.

[55] WS, diary, Dec. 20-24; US to HS, Dec. 28, 1894; *RH,* Mar. 12, 1895, p. 168; Mar. 19, 1895, pp. 184, 185; Mar. 26, 1895, p. 200; Apr. 2, 1895, p. 216.

[56] WS, diary, Dec. 27, 1894 (Wilton Smith's diary has no further entries except for an expense account under the date of December 28); US to HS, Dec. 30, 1894.

[57] *RH,* Apr. 9, 1895, p. 232.

[58] US to HS, Jan. 3, 1895.

[59] *RH,* Apr. 9, 1895, p. 232; Jan. 22, 1895, p. 64. This *RH* report gives the dates of Smith's return to the United States and Battle Creek as January 17 and 18 while Uriah's has the dates as January 18 and 19.

[60] *RH,* Jan. 29, 1895, p. 80; Apr. 9, 1895, p. 232.

CHAPTER IX

"I STILL ADHERE TO THE OLD PATHS"
1895-1903

Despite his treatments at the sanitarium, Smith continued to feel the effects of his bout with malaria. He told W. C. White in June that he had been unable to attend any of the General Conference meetings and that he had been laid up for seven or eight days in late May but hoped to "have no more pull-backs of this kind." By the end of November he was well enough to attend meetings in Ann Arbor, where he spoke on a Sunday evening on the relationship of the Sabbath to the Second Coming.[1]

Meanwhile, the Review and Herald Publishing Association board,[2] apparently recognizing his weakened condition, voted that fall to release him from responsibilities for the journal for several months so that he would have time to revise *Daniel and the Revelation* and his book on the sanctuary. He completed his revision of *Daniel and the Revelation*, which he had worked on more than a year previously. George Amadon described it as "restating some points and carefully guarding others where there seemed to be some difference of views." Smith also wrote a pamphlet on spiritualism, a longstanding concern of his, before leaving for Florida on January 20, 1896. Uriah had wanted to go to a warmer climate for the cold months, saying that "I think the climate will be very beneficial to me. I like it much here so far, and find its quiet and retirement very favorable to my work." While in Florida he stayed at George I. Butler's house, although it is unclear whether he shared the home with his daughter, Annie, who had preceded him, and/or a "[Brother] and [Sister] Brunson." Smith said nothing about Harriet, but she presumably accompanied him. At the moment he did not know whether on his return to Battle Creek in May he would work again at the *Review* or continue writing books and pamphlets. "Nothing was said to that effect, at the board meeting referred to," he told W. C. White. "But it was intimated that there would be enough to keep my pen busy in the line of tracts, pamphlets and books. Well, if I can do acceptable work in that field, it will suit me just as well."[3]

While in Florida he received a letter from Stephen Haskell encouraging his effort to maintain traditional Adventist theology. "It is beginning to be found out," Haskell stated, "the old principles of the third angel's message are right and so there is quite a whirligig in that direction." He expressed his satisfaction that Smith was having the opportunity to revise some of his earlier books as well as write new ones and renewing contact with George Butler "and by so doing not commit [sacrilege]." Haskell advised Smith not to resign from the *Review* and observed that "it would not be any thing strange if you would be the editor in chief again."[4]

Although he had returned to the *Review*, Uriah sensed that the General Conference leaders were not entirely happy with his performance. He told W. C. White that his trip to Europe and the Middle East "was a wonderfully instructive one to me, and I appreciate the advantages I derived from it, as I can take in the situation so much better when I read or study about those parts. But the calculations of the brethren concerning it [the trip] did not materialize as they anticipated, or at least as they said they did, and if, in the providence of God, I am ever able to reimburse them for what they invested in it, I shall do so."[5]

But his feelings went much deeper than such comments indicate. Later that year Smith wrote a long letter to Haskell that suggested that he was experiencing what today we would call depression. Apologizing for not writing more often, he said that when he felt "particularly downhearted, and low spirited," he did not think that his letters could be of much edification. As he viewed world conditions and experienced the toll of passing time, he could not see much to be pleased about.

"Looking out upon the world there is so much of suffering and sorrow, so much poverty, distress, and crime, so much imposition upon the poor and weak and needy, [by] those who can take advantage of them, so much oppression upon the ignorant and helpless, by those who might help them, so many bright hopes suddenly dashed to atoms, so many who are the stay and staff of others, taken away by bereavement, so much love and confidence and hope betrayed, so much friendship estranged, so much light turning suddenly to darkness, so much disappointment and failure and despair, that nothing seems of much worth in this life."

Writing more personally, he stated that "at my age there is more behind than there is before, and everything that comes within the field of memory is tinged with regret rather than gladness. I know the apostle speaks of forgetting those things which are behind, and reaching forth to those things which are before; but it does not seem to me that there is much for me to reach forth to; and as I look over the past there are many things that I cannot help wishing had been different."

Like many people looking back over their lives, he saw opportunities missed. "Away back when I was going to school, if I could only have had a sense of the possibilities of life, and what I might and should have made of myself, I see how I could have put in my time to better advantage, and improve opportunities and privileges as I did not do, and which has caused me to labor under disadvantages and inefficiency [ever] since."

Reflecting on his experience with Seventh-day Adventism, he revealed the emotional cost of the many conflicts that had occurred through the years and his increasing sense of isolation from a new generation of denominational leaders who had not been present during the pioneer days.

"And since I have been associated with this work, it has not been much better. So my whole life, compared with what it might have been, seems like a poor failure. I have, to be sure, written some books; but that is perhaps more owing to my having had friends back there than anything else. I am sure that if I had had no more friends then than I have now, I should never have been encouraged to write them. But Brother White I think was my friend. At least he took a great interest in some of the books that I got out. You have spoken of the good you thought the book on Daniel and Revelation was doing; and I hope it has done some good, and will do more; but whatever it has done or may do will stand largely to the credit of Brother White, as I am willing it should."

Referring to his tensions with James White, he said that "of course circumstance sometimes occurred to bring us into severe trial, as you know; but in general, I consider [Brother] White to have been a largehearted man. But the past cannot be recalled. All we can do is to make the most of what is left." Expressing irony regarding his present relationship with denominational leaders, he said that he often wondered "why circumstances should so have come around as to bring me into association with this work, unless it was that I might be a trial to my brethren; in which case, if that was the design, I may have made something of a success." Nonetheless, he sought to end on a hopeful note: "But I am thankful for the statement of the Scriptures, that the Lord is pleased with those that 'hope in His mercy.' I certainly have need enough of it, and shall try to serve Him in that way."[6] It was an extraordinarily revealing letter for an editor who week by week had to present a public image of self-confidence in his paper.

Smith's short book on spiritualism appeared in 1896. Repeating many of his themes of previous years, he recognized that fraud had existed in the movement, but that also "there have been manifestations of more than human power, the evidence for which has never been impeached." Because, according to Smith and Adventist belief, the Bible teaches that the soul is not immortal, spiritualism must be wrong. "If the Bible is true, the whole system rests upon deception and falsehood. No one who believes this will tamper with Spiritualism. One cannot have Spiritualism and the Bible, too."

Quoting extensively from spiritualist literature, particularly its journal *Banner of Light*, Smith noted erroneous doctrines taught by the spirits, such as their denial of the distinction between right and wrong, and then placed the movement in an apocalyptic context. Spiritualism was invading the popular churches and, in view of Revelation 16:14, was going "to the kings of the earth to gather them to the battle of the great day of God Almighty."[7]

A. T. JONES

Smith's uncertainty about his position at the *Review* would soon be confirmed. After he returned from Europe, administration appointed him and George C. Tenney joint editors of the journal, although in both 1896 and 1897 Smith also was elected a member of the publishing board. In October, however, the *Review* published an "Important Announcement." The board had added Smith's longtime theological nemesis, the flamboyant A. T. Jones, to the editorial staff and made Smith an associate editor. "Elder Smith will continue as associate editor; and as he has recovered from the serious illness which was incurred in Syria, and which has troubled him more or less since his return, in 1895, we hope to have much more from his pen filled with the old-time fire of the message," the board's announcement read. "Elder Smith's long experience in the cause enables him to write as but few can. He is one of the only two or three of the old pioneers of forty years' labor in this work who are left to us."[8]

Jones, along with A. F. Ballenger, who traveled around the United States as a General Conference evangelist, was leading a Holiness revival within Adventism that had begun about 1894. Under the phrase "Receive Ye the Holy Ghost," the movement emphasized the need for Adventists to ask for the "latter rain" of the Holy Spirit and within a short time was also directing attention to physical healing. As editor of the *Review*, Jones closed nearly every editorial with a call to "receive ye the Holy Ghost." The movement continued until about 1900, when the emergence of the "holy flesh" theology in Indiana brought it into disrepute.[9]

Although it is unlikely that the rationalistic Smith had much enthusiasm for the Adventist version of Holiness, he did write a favorable notice of Ballenger's and Jones's Battle Creek meetings in the fall of 1897. More significantly, Holiness themes appeared from time to time in his editorials. Adopting another phrase popular in the movement, "the shout of victory," Uriah in November 1897 placed the concept within a Second Coming framework. "The shout of victory, *then*," he wrote, "depends upon the shout of victory *now*. Meet every assault of the enemy with courage, and go into every conflict with the shout of victory on your lips." A couple months later he wrote about the need for internal spiritual experience, emphasizing "Christ *dwelling* in the heart" and the necessity to be "filled with the *fullness* of God." In August of 1899 Smith argued that "preparation for the great day of the Lord lies not in a mere knowledge of the doctrine that that day is at hand, and an assent to the evidences that support that view, but it lies in having a vital connection, and union, with Him who then comes without sin unto salvation for those who are truly looking for him."[10]

Uriah also related the new emphasis on the Holy Spirit and spiritual experience to salvation. Early in 1898 he said that Jesus is praying while the Holy Spirit is making intercession for us. Then about a year later, in contrast to his usual emphasis on the law in the relationship between God and the individual person, he spoke of God's love as the ultimate force. "Love is the attractive power between God and the sinner," he wrote, "moving God toward the sinner, in his lost and hapless state, and the sinner toward God, in gratitude for His loving-kindness and great condescension in delivering him from his sin and its consequences."[11]

If asked, Smith probably would have said that he had believed in the need for the Holy Spirit and the power of God's love for decades, but such themes had never previously made a significant appearance in his writings and most likely did so now because of the "Receive Ye the Holy Ghost" movement and the editorial influence of Jones. We should note, however, that we have no record of Uriah accepting or supporting the healing emphasis of this movement when it appeared. Furthermore, he did not shrink from asserting the necessity of human effort in the quest for salvation. He argued that "Christ came in the likeness of sinful flesh, to demonstrate before all parties in the controversy that it was possible for men in the flesh to keep the law. He demonstrated this by keeping it Himself." In his mind such a position did not conflict with belief in righteousness by faith, for human beings "by the freely offered help of Christ in [their] fallen condition can do so still." Consequently, "life is a warfare," he wrote in May 1899. "We are not to shrink from its conflicts. Like faithful soldiers, we should discipline and exercise ourselves for victory."[12]

Attention to Holiness themes did not detract from Smith's concern with last-day events. World conditions pointed to worsening instability. Expressing skepticism regarding a possible alliance of Japan, Great Britain, and the United States, he observed that "in the age of the world that we have reached, there can be no permanent cohesion between peoples and nations." The Dreyfus case, in which a Jewish army captain was unjustly convicted in 1894 of betraying military secrets, drew Uriah's observation "that the stability of governments rests upon fraud and lying, which God hates . . . —has not the time come for the King of kings to don the garments of vengeance, and dash such nations in pieces like a potter's vessel?" Even the economic effects of European beet sugar on the West Indies sugarcane industry caught his notice: "So it seems that there are other sources of trouble and distress for this old world besides wars, pestilences, famines, and tornadoes."[13]

Referring specifically to the United States, Smith noted the fiftieth anniversary of Spiritualism, and asked what good it had done humanity. He also called Christian Science a fraud and "a modified form of Spiritualism." Turning from religion to society, he expressed his bias in favor of Northern Europeans as he commented on the immigrants, particularly from Eastern and Southern Europe, that had begun pouring into the country in the 1880s. "While some [immigrants] are very desirable, giving promise of making citizens of industrial, mental, and moral worth," he wrote, "others are of far less worth in these respects." Consequently he endorsed laws restricting immigration and, like other supporters of such legislation, cited crime statistics for various groups. "There is no better class of immigrants coming to this country than the Swedes and Norwegians," he concluded.[14]

Smith expanded on such editorial thoughts in a pamphlet, "America's Crisis," published in 1898. The first several pages covered Bible prophecy, concluding with the interpretation that the United States was the two-horned beast of Revelation. He saw the prophecy being fulfilled before his eyes as religious groups sought, through the ballot box and threatened boycotts, to establish in law the concept that America was a Christian nation. Sunday laws were the crucial element in such an effort, but they were, in his view, "contrary to the Constitution of the United States, and the constitutions, or bills of right, of the different states of which the nation is composed." Referring to the arrest of Adventists for breaking these laws, he asserted that "the great crisis of human history is upon us, and the decisions of eternity are hanging in the balance. Here and now, in the movements with which it is the lot of the men of this generation to be connected, is to be decided the great controversy which commenced with the defection of the archrebel before time began."[15]

Through his *Review* editorials Smith emphasized the apocalyptic interpretation that he had held since the early 1850s and was as convinced as ever that he was living in the "last days." In 1899 he announced that the final generation had commenced. The following year he responded to the idea that 50 years was too long a period for the investigative judgment, which Adventists believed had begun in October 1844. "Beware! Remember that the work covers the entire human family; and the decisions are for eternity," he warned those inclined to skepticism. "But we know that it [the end] is stealing swiftly and silently upon a world intoxicated with pleasure, and dreaming of peace and safety. And what is our attitude? Are we watching and preparing?" As the twentieth century dawned, he pre-

dicted that it would be characterized by the oppression of the church by
Catholicism, and stated confidently that "we shall not have entered far into
the century before all these things will be accomplished."[16]

The year 1898 also saw the publication of *Looking Unto Jesus*, which Smith
had worked on in Florida. A revision of his earlier book on the sanctuary,
Uriah opened the book with an explanation of his Arian understanding
of Jesus, a view that had not changed much over the years. Only God, in
his thinking, had no beginning. Through "some divine impulse or process
. . . the Son of God appeared. And then the Holy Spirit," which he described as "the divine afflatus and medium of their power representative
of them both." Although the Father and Son were equal beings, the Holy
Spirit was not part of the deity, for "with the Son, the evolution of deity,
as deity, ceased." All the remainder of creation, animate and inanimate,
came through the Father as the antecedent cause and the Son as the "acting agent."[17]

Having established the nature and status of Jesus, Smith turned to the
problem of sin. Because the law demanded perfect obedience, and humanity had transgressed the law, Jesus as the creator of that law could meet its
demand on behalf of His creatures. Prompted by infinite love, rather than
by blind vengeance, Jesus "condemned sin in the flesh, by living Himself
in the flesh and doing no sin, showing that it was possible for man thus to
live." God, therefore, had made no unjust demands.[18]

Then came the heart of the book, the discussion of the heavenly sanctuary. On the cross, Jesus was "acting in the capacity of a sacrifice." Although
His sacrifice was and is available to everyone, it "does not save all indis-
criminately, and make the doctrine of universal salvation true; for man is a
free moral agent, and his acceptance of the gift of God must be voluntary,
not forced." It is at this point in the plan of salvation, according to Smith,
that the sanctuary as a type in the Old Testament and an antitype in the
New helps us understand the atonement.[19]

Just as the priest ministered in the Old Testament sanctuary, so Jesus
ministers in the heavenly sanctuary depicted in the book of Hebrews.
"Where is now our Priest? In heaven. Where is now our sanctuary? In
heaven. Is the sanctuary in heaven a literal sanctuary? Just as literal as the
Priest, our Lord Jesus Christ, who ministers therein." At some point in His
ministry, Jesus, as with the Old Testament priests, must move from the

holy to the Most Holy Place of the sanctuary, "to perform a special ministry there . . . on the day of atonement." Just as the sins of the people were taken into the Old Testament sanctuary through the blood of animals, so now they are borne into the heavenly sanctuary through the blood of Christ.[20]

Jesus' transfer to the Second Apartment, or Most Holy Place, of course, took place on October 22, 1844, according to Adventist understanding. From that point of time He has been engaged in cleansing the sanctuary, or blotting out sins, which "involves the examination of all the deeds of our lives. It is an 'investigative judgment.'" Christ is determining whether we have repented of our sins, of which a faithful record has been recorded, and subsequently lived a life of obedience and faith.

"If we secure the pardon of our sins, the time comes, just before the end, when these sins are blotted out of the books, and our names are retained in the Lamb's book of life, and the Savior confesses our names to the Father as those who have accepted of salvation through Him. Our cases are then decided, and we are sealed for everlasting life. If, on the other hand, we do not repent, our sins are not blotted out of the record where they stand, but our names are blotted out of the book of life, and Christ denies our names before His Father, as those who have slighted His mercy, and are not entitled to everlasting life through Him."[21]

Battling the doctrine of universalism, the teaching that everyone will ultimately be saved, which he saw as inherent in the idea that Christ's death brought atonement on the cross, Smith stated clearly that "the death of Christ and the atonement are *not the same thing*. . . . Christ did not make the atonement when He shed His blood upon the cross." Atonement is Christ's last act as our high priest. "'Forgiving sin' and 'blotting out sin' are not the same. Forgiveness is conditional; the condition being that we comply with certain requirements upon which it is suspended, till the end of our probation. If we fail, we stand at the last unforgiven, and no atonement can be made for us." In short, the cross offers us forgiveness, but that forgiveness does not remove our sins from the heavenly record books until Christ has judged our faithfulness favorably and blots them out.[22]

Once Christ has completed His work of judgment, the seven last plagues will strike the earth, after which Jesus returns to receive His saints. Satan gets cast into the bottomless pit for 1,000 years. Responding to criticisms that Adventists with their understanding of the scapegoat made Satan a participant in the atonement, Smith asserted that he had "no share in the work; but our High Priest has something to do *with* him in carrying out the result of his work, by making him bear away the sins which have been taken from the sanctuary, that he may perish with them, and thus a final disposition be made of both them and him. It will be seen that the atonement is all made, and every case decided before Satan comes into the program."

After Satan, sinners, and their sins have been destroyed, the great controversy will end. Thus closed Smith's last major contribution to Adventist theology.[23]

FAMILY LIFE

Although not much information is available regarding Smith's home life during this time, he did conduct the wedding of his daughter, Annie, to George Walker Bovee at the Smith residence on October 26, 1898. The following year the newlyweds joined the Smith family for Thanksgiving. "George has promised to bring a duck to grace the occasion," Uriah wrote to Wilton, inviting him to join the dinner. For some reason Wilton was unable to attend and Harriet was feeling poorly, so they sent the ducks back, expecting to have them for Christmas instead. In 1900 Harriet reported to her daughter that she had been relieved from making midday meals for Uriah and Wilton, who were taking their dinner at the "Hygienic," perhaps the dining room at the sanitarium, "but they do not enjoy it very well." The following year Parker left on February 7 for a teaching position at an Adventist school on St. Andrews Island, Colombia.[24]

Also, sometime in the late 1890s Smith, ever the tinkerer, developed his strangest invention, though whether he took it seriously or simply saw it as a bit of whimsy is not clear. According to Mary Landon, who had been a stenographer at the Haynes-Apperson automobile company in Kokomo, Indiana, Uriah arrived at the factory one day and convinced Mr. Apperson that placing a horse's head at the front of his automobiles would prevent the horseless "carriages" from frightening real horses. Asked by Apperson to take the head for a trial run, Mrs. Landon's husband, John, drove around Kokomo. "Presently he met a horse, which took one look at the odd apparition confronting him, moaned piteously, backed away, then shrieked and took off southeast toward Pumpkinville Pike, as fast as legs would carry." After other horses responded similarly, Apperson shipped the horse's head back to Smith. A picture of the horse's head appeared in the magazine *Motor Age* in 1899. Smith's grandson later stated that "while that patent was the least useful of the more than seven patents issued to him during his inventive years, Uriah Smith's fame is greater for his whimsical horse's head than for most anything else."[25]

EDITOR AGAIN

Although Jones's editorship of the *Review* enlivened the journal and by early 1898 had increased subscriptions by 20 percent, he soon wore out his welcome. He sought to reform the Review and Herald Publishing Association, particularly regarding the issue of royalties, and played an important role in bringing E. A. Sutherland to the presidency of Battle Creek College, which led ultimately to the school's move to Berrien Springs, Michigan, and a radical change in its curriculum and overall operation. Although General Conference leaders and Ellen White generally supported Jones's reform efforts, they faulted him for his frequently sharp language and high-handed methods. In 1901 the Publishing Committee removed him as editor, replacing him with Uriah Smith.[26]

Smith continued with the apocalyptic themes he had been sounding throughout his adult life. Addressing Roman Catholicism, he declared the church as un-Christian, for it took the place of God on earth. Seeking to distinguish between institutional Catholicism and its adherents, he urged "uncompromising opposition to the errors, the workings, and the tendency of that system of religion, but a recognition of every good quality in individual members, and a desire to do them good, and to persuade them to better things." But he was also concerned with the direction of the American federal government. Strongly opposed to imperialism, he criticized the Cuban policy of the United States following the Spanish-American War of 1898, saying that the stain on the honor of the United States could only be erased by repealing the Platt Amendment and allowing Cuba self-determination. In even stronger language, he condemned the American policy toward both Cuba and the Philippines, arguing that the United States had repudiated its own constitution. "The United States has shown itself willing to extend its jurisdiction over subject peoples," he wrote in January 1902, "while at the same time it denies to them the civil and religious rights which the Constitution guarantees to all people. This is national apostasy."

Applying his principles more closely to home, he noted the violence against and disenfranchisement of African Americans, a process that had gained momentum in the 1890s. "The principle of government by consent of the governed has been as fully repudiated in one section [the North] as in the other [the South]." At the time of the Civil War he had predicted that slavery would continue to the end of time. Apparently interpreting the contemporary oppression of African Americans as a form of slavery, he again foretold that "there will be negro slaves when probation ends, and some of them will be numbered with those whom God accepts." Despite Smith's radical views of both imperialism and race relations, however, we find no indication that he ever rethought his opposition to Adventist political involvement. Rather, such issues were signs of the coming apocalypse, which should stimulate Adventists to press their warning message even harder. In October 1901 he commented on the fifty-seventh anniversary of the Great Disappointment and asked how much longer time could last. "Get ready for the culmination of the work," he stated. "Make more of this anniversary."[27]

Uriah also maintained his concern with proper belief and obedience to the law. In April 1901 he urged his readers to compare their moral habits "one by one" with God's commandments, and test honestly whether they conformed with "the spirit and genius of the gospel." "And there must be *self-discipline*, as well as self-examination." Christians must combine such examination with proper belief. "Without doctrine or dogma, setting forth Christ's existence, His nature, and His attitude of love and mercy toward mankind," Smith observed, "He could not be recognized and loved as He has revealed Himself, and as He is. Dogma or doctrine lies at the foundation of the truth as it is in Jesus."[28]

Meanwhile, in addition to his editorial duties, Smith was assisting Stephen N. Haskell with his book *The Story of the Prophet Daniel*. Wanting to write on the biblical books of Daniel and Revelation, Haskell had talked with Smith in 1899 about the project. Agreeing to help in any way he could, during the next year or so Uriah reviewed Haskell's manuscript to determine the accuracy of its dates and other historical references. Stephen told Ellen White that Uriah did not want to write anything himself nor enter into the interpretive questions, but rather corrected errors and made editorial suggestions. Apparently Smith retracted his refusal to write, for he contributed an introduction to the book, which was published in 1901. "He has taken an interest in it [the book] from the beginning," Haskell reported to Ellen White. "He also has given me the best notice of it of anyone."[29]

At about the same time, Uriah was also thinking about retirement. Correspondence with a W. H. Hall convinced him "that Florida offers the best show for me, when I lay off the harness, and go out to grass, as I shall soon have to do. The winter here has not been very cold, since you left, but it is just as disagreeable as ever, with its dull cloudy days." A month later he again told Hall that he was "more and more inclined to think that I will make Florida my last stopping place before leaving this world. But the way does not seem to be opening up for me to leave here yet."[30]

Although he did not explain the obstacles, finances probably played a crucial role. The denomination had no retirement plan at the time, and royalties on his books had declined to almost nothing. In 1894, while traveling in Europe, he had written Ellen White that his entire royalties for the past year had been $56. Furthermore, by 1897 the Review and Herald management had reduced the royalty percentage that they paid authors. Smith told W. C. White that James White had divided evenly the income from books between the publisher and the author. At some point the publishing house reduced it to 10 percent. By the time *Daniel and the Revelation* was published, Uriah was receiving 10 cents a book. Moreover, in 1897 the Review management began pushing the idea that authors employed by the publishing house should receive no royalties at all, for all of their writing was its property. "It is my opinion that much profitable work has been driven away from the office which would have been of financial benefit to the institution," Uriah wrote to W. C. White, and of advantage "to the cause, from this hostility to the idea that an author should reap a proportional benefit from his labors." Two years later the situation had not improved. Smith wrote to his son Wilton stating that salaries had been cut, and went on to observe that "there has been such a turn in the book business that I look upon the further circulation of my books, [*Daniel and the Revelation*] and others, as practically nil; and it looks to me that my best course is now to get what I have in a shape that it will bring me in a little, instead of being a constant expense, and then go to some locality where the climate is mild, and living easy, and then not depend on constant labor for a living."[31]

In 1900, with a new management in place, Haskell attempted to help Smith collect royalties due him. Stephen reported that Uriah had pledged to give $1,000 to the church in Australia from his income on *The Marvel of Nations*, but that the publishing house had "jewed him down to $1000, saying that *The Marvel of Nations* had had its day and that not many more of them would be sold." However, the book had sold an additional 100,000 copies, on which Smith proposed to take a royalty of 2.5 cents, half of his previous five cents. In addition to the pledge to Australia, Smith also planned to pay for his trip to Palestine and some excess wages he had received.[32]

What became of his plans is not known, but it is apparent that the Review and Herald Publishing Association, in addition to being affected by the economic depression that had hit the country in 1893, had become a dysfunctional institution in the 1890s. G. W. Amadon reported to Ellen White that the foremen and leaders of the publishing house held many meetings in addition to the entire staff attending Sunday morning meetings and departmental sessions scheduled on Thursday mornings. He said that Smith rarely attended them, spending part of each day at the office but doing most of his work at home. Furthermore, A. R. Henry, a financial officer, though retaining an office at the publishing house, had little to do with its operations and "always looks thoughtful and sad." What treasurer Harmon Lindsay did, he did not know. Beyond those signs of personal disaffection, friction continued over both royalties and wages, a lawsuit over alleged libel by A. R. Henry, resignation of employees that led to the hiring of "tramp printers," some of whom had been in jail for drunkenness, and a severe decline in the subscription book business. In 1901 A. G. Daniells wrote that "it makes my heart sick when I see the great stacks of books piled up in the Review and Herald office. They have $70,000 worth of our publications stacked up on their shelves. Of course the books are doing nobody in the world any good lying there, and they represent an enormous amount of money." Among the volumes were Smith's *Daniel and the Revelation* and Ellen White's *The Great Controversy*.[33]

Not surprisingly, Smith was still concerned with maintaining traditional Adventist theology. Writing to W. H. Littlejohn, pastor of the Battle Creek

church, with regard to his interpretation of 666, which some were criticizing, he stated that "modern cranky notions have unsettled almost ev-
erybody. But I still adhere to the old paths."[34] Uriah's traditionalism was
nowhere more true than with the issue of the law in Galatians. Even while
working under Jones in 1900 he had written a lengthy explanation of his
position to a correspondent:

"I have never seen occasion to change my position since 1856. [Brother]
J. H. Waggoner in . . . *The Law of God,* published in Rochester, N.Y.,
took the position that the law in Gal. 3:10 referred to the moral law. The
[brethren] in Vermont felt so deeply over it, that Elder Stephen Pierce
came on to Battle Creek, to have an investigation of the question. Meetings were held some three days studying the subject, in which we all
became satisfied that the position of [Elder] Pierce was correct. [Brother]
and [Sister] White both [agreed?] to it. [Brother] Pierce's position was
that the law in [Galatians] referred to the whole law system; and the law
system was the moral law as a rule of life, and the ceremonial law as a
means of recovery from sin, or justification from sin, or the transgressions
of that moral law. According to this, the law that was 'added,' and that
was 'our schoolmaster,' was the ceremonial, or 'remedial law.' [Brother]
Waggoner would not attend the discussion and would not yield a parti-
cle. A few days afterward, [Sister] White had a vision, in which she saw
in regard to this investigation, and wrote to [Brother] Waggoner, 'I see
that your position was wrong.' When [Brother] Waggoner requested its
republication, [Brother] White said, No! until you will change position
on the law in Galatians. But this [Brother] Waggoner would never do;
and so the book was not republished. But now a great many do know,
not that Dr. W. has ever seen anything on this question. This is why I
understand [the brethren] now are advocating the views they are. At the
conference in 1888, I attempted to explain these things, and was at once
charged with denying justification though Christ, as false a view and as
unjust a charge as could possibly be made. I then gave up this question
in discouragement, and do not intend to say anything more on the subject."[35]

About a year later Smith recounted the story similarly to another correspondent, adding that "I was then quite young in the truth, and as these
meetings were new to me, I, including both [Brother] and [Sister] White,

became convinced that [Brother] Pierce had the right view, and J. H. [Waggoner] was wrong." Noting that Waggoner's book was never republished, he went on to say:

"The next we heard of it was when E. J. [Waggoner] came out in the *Signs* and *Instuctor* and taught in Healdsburg College taking the old position of his father, which [Sister White] had pronounced wrong. This stirred up [Brother] Butler to correspond with [Sister White] who was then in Switzerland, and called forth the letter from her to [Brother] Butler, a copy of which you enclosed. This course of E. J. [Waggoner] opened up the whole question again, and the determined men on that side of the question have carried quite an influence and those who have had charge of our publications have given them the field, but those who know the history that I have related cannot change on that account. When men, to save their position, have to take the position as E. J. [Waggoner] and others do, that the SEED [Jesus] HAS NOT YET COME, they are in a pretty tight place in my opinion. Some try to make it appear that when [Sister White] said to J. H. [Waggoner] that his position was wrong, she did not mean his position on the law in Galations; but I was there when the investigation took place and know that the only issue involved was whether the law Paul speaks of as 'added' was the moral law or not. Waggoner said it was the moral law. Pierce said, No, but that it included more. The Jews had come to believe that they could be justified from everything wrong by the law of Moses. Acts 13:39. So, when Paul preached Christ as the sole means of justification, the Jews said, No, we can be justified by circumcision, offerings, our priestly atonement, and other services. So to make way for Christ, Paul had to take these all out of the way, saying they were only designed to continue till the SEED should come, and they were an object lesson leading and pointing the way to Christ. I could say more; but this will probably be sufficient. I hope the truth will prevail."[36]

Such private letters clearly reveal that Smith had not reconciled himself to the 1888 teaching of Waggoner and Jones. Nonetheless, with one exception he did not push such ideas on *Review* readers. That instance occurred in the winter of 1902, when the *Review* ran a series of articles on Galatians by William M. Brickey,[37] which Daniells described as "openly and squarely against the message that came to this people of Minneapolis, that has been embraced by thousands of our people and openly and repeatedly endorsed by the Spirit of Prophecy."

Although he had not been involved in the 1888 controversy, Daniells was a strong administrator who sought to establish unity throughout the denomination. He was concerned that opposition to the 1888 message had continued in several Western and Central states, and he did not find the articles helpful.

"Many of our ministers were perfectly astonished that the *Review* would publish them. They could not believe that they had been read by the editor, and so wrote him. Some of them gave warning that if the *Review* continued to publish such theology, it would be necessary for the state conference committees to take their stand against the *Review* and use their state papers and other local facilities to place the situation truly and fairly before their brethren. I stand in a position to know that serious injury has been wrought by these articles. And I know that the *Review* could not stand with our brethren if it continued that course."[38]

At some point, Daniells spoke to Smith regarding the Brickey articles, suggesting that one of his subordinates had inserted them. But an unrepentant Uriah responded that such was not the case, that in fact he had "read them himself, and published them because he believed they set forth the truth." Responding to a correspondent who had written criticizing the articles, Smith stated that it appeared to him "that if any *dissatisfaction* was aroused, or any *injury* done, it should have been when this view was ruthlessly broken into by the articles in the *Signs of the Times*, and the lectures in Healdsburg College, and subsequent articles in the *Youth's Instructor* and *Review*." Daniells said that he wanted no controversy with Smith but that he could not "endorse this recent development. It is not right. God has put His seal of approval upon the message that came at Minneapolis, and I cannot understand how a man can proclaim his unbounded confidence in the Spirit of Prophecy, and reject the Minneapolis message."[39]

The GC president was also upset with Uriah about articles that had appeared in the *Review* addressing the "color question." Adventists had begun significant work among Blacks in the South in the 1890s with Edson White's *Morning Star* boat mission on the Mississippi and Yazoo rivers. Because of threats of violence the Adventist preachers had adopted what they thought would be a temporary practice of segregation in their meetings, but as White Southerners also joined the church, the pragmatic approach became standard policy. Daniells, primarily concerned with the smooth working of denominational efforts, opposed any effort to change Southern racial practices. Thus, when during the Fall Council of 1901 the *Review* appeared with an editorial apparently opposed to segregation, Southern delegates were "offended." As a result, Daniells called the managers and editors of the *Review* to a meeting in which the "Southern delegation made it very plain to the editors that these articles had done our people much harm in the South, and that if they continued, the *Review* would be cut off from that part of the field." The shipment of the journal was still in mailbags at the railroad station, which enabled the *Review* management to phone the station and have the bags returned to the publishing house. The editors removed the offensive article and replaced it, all of which cost the publishing house quite a bit of money. Nonetheless, about two months later another article appeared "in which offensive statements were made regarding any recognition whatever of the color line."[40] That time Daniells reported that Smith had not seen the article and neither of his associates admitted knowing about it either.[41]

In another incident, an article appeared severely criticizing the Battle Creek church choir, which responded by demanding a retraction, otherwise the entire group would resign. Although Daniells had told the choir not to pursue the matter, it did not accept his advice. Smith wrote an article defending the group and published a rebuke of the author of the original article.[42] The various incidents convinced Daniells that Uriah was not managing the journal appropriately. He described Smith as never being "well and strong since his return from Europe. During the last year he has failed a great deal" and therefore had turned over much of his responsibility to his subordinates. "Although Brother Smith was nominally at the head of the paper," the General Conference president stated, "he did not really manage it, at least this is the view taken by those who were in a position to make the closest observations. He wrote his editorials, and examined some of the articles that went into the paper; but many of the articles, including editorials, were not read by him either before or after their publication. The young men put in what they chose. Some of the articles they published were not helpful to the people, and some were positively offensive."[43]

DEMOTION

Not surprisingly, such dissatisfaction led Daniells to push for Smith's removal as principal editor. On February 15, 1902, a "Minority Meeting" of the General Conference Committee convened at 7:00 p.m. in Daniells' office in the General Conference building. The first item of business was the editorship of the *Review*. I. H. Evans, president and manager of the Review and Herald, moved that W. W. Prescott, chair of the Review and Herald Publishing board, be made editor in chief of the *Review*, a motion seconded by W. A. Spicer, secretary of the Mission Board. The minutes recorded that "this important question was discussed freely by the brethren present, and there was a remarkable unanimity of opinion as to the propriety of this action." Although the committee made its decision in mid-February, George Butler, apparently receiving information from someone in Battle Creek, claimed that Smith was not told until nearly a week later. In the February 25 issue Evans announced the decision to add Prescott to the editorial staff. The masthead now listed Smith, W. W. Prescott, and L. A. Smith as editors, but did not indicate that Prescott, who had long been critical of the editing of the *Review*, was the lead editor.[44]

George Butler and others severely criticized the General Conference Committee for what they perceived as its ill treatment of Smith. Butler's letter to Ellen White focused on the "falsified" picture presented in the *Review*, which continued to list Smith as first among the editors while the General Conference Committee minutes clearly showed that it had voted Prescott as editor in chief. W. B. Woodruff, a dentist in Denver, Colorado, who had worked at one point with Smith, wrote saying that he "would like to see the name of Uriah Smith as the *nominal* editor in chief of the *Review* so long as he lives. It grieves me every week when the Review arrives to see the evident effort to shelve him."[45]

Daniells wrote to Butler strongly defending his actions. "I cannot see how our action was unkind toward Brother Smith. We did not attempt to cut him off from the *Review*, we did not reduce his pay, nor limit his field of usefulness. We did not even desire to place his name second in the list of editors." He claimed that Evans and other members of the publishing board had talked with Smith and that everyone was pleasant at the meeting. "I did not know from his appearance, nor from anything he said, that Brother Smith's feelings were hurt because of our recommendation." Prescott, who expressed surprise at being appointed to the editorial staff, although he was part of the committee that took the action, similarly wrote to Ellen White that "we did all that we possibly could to make the change without hurting [Brother] Smith's feelings. I had a good personal talk with him about it and explained my plans and ideas to him, and it was at my own personal request that his name was placed at the head of the list of editors. So far as I know there has been no personal friction in any way since I went into the office, and I do not intend that there shall be." Both Daniells and Prescott wrote their letters in April, some two months after making the changes in the editorial staff. Although by now Daniells admitted hearing from others that the action had offended Smith, neither he nor Prescott mentioned that the night after learning of his demotion Uriah had suffered a stroke, something that both of them must have been aware of and which Ellen White knew from Butler's letter and perhaps from others.[46]

Writing to her sister a year after the events, Harriet Smith offered a picture that differed considerably from that given by the church administrators. Obviously biased in favor of her husband, she said that the demotion "did seem a cruel thing that his brethren did, and so uncalled for," then went on to describe the events of the evening after he had learned of the General Conference Committee's decision. "He fairly staggered home that night, as was noticed by some who saw him pass," she wrote. "He said nothing to us about it, but when later in the evening it leaked out, we tried to make the best of it as he would be released from such responsibility, and he made no complaint whatever, though he said afterward he felt as though a blow had struck him on the head."

His statement was truer than he realized, for when he awoke the next morning, he could neither swallow nor speak distinctly, but within a few days the greatest danger had passed. "The fingers of his right hand have never felt natural since," Harriet wrote. "But his general health seems good, and he is very comfortable in most respects, though his lameness, which he used to mind so little, now greatly disables him." In short, she concluded, "he has become old before his time, but I am thankful he still lives, and still has some friends who hold him in loving remembrance."[47]

Daniells reported that the European leaders were pleased with changes that Prescott had initiated in the *Review*, particularly its increased attention to missionary activities, and claimed that "relations between Brother Smith, Brother Prescott, and Leon and myself have been of the most pleasant kind possible." Whatever offense Smith may have felt in February did not appear a few months later in an editorial that he wrote concerning his seventieth birthday and his 50 years with the *Review*. "But next to life itself, we prize the privilege of being called to a knowledge of the truth which God is sending forth to the world in these last days, and having the opportunity of acting some humble part therein," he said. "Over fifty years have been spent in this relation; but, alas! how far short of the standard have they been! May 1, 1902, completes fifty years of connection with the *Review* office."[48]

In his other editorials Uriah perhaps placed more emphasis on Jesus and the assurance of salvation than he had previously. During June he wrote that "Christ does not stop with any halfway work. When He forgives sin, He forgives it *all*." The following month he stated that because Jesus was in heaven as their high priest, "the saints may consider themselves as possessed of their rights." Jesus "has a gracious sense of all our frailties, griefs, trials, temptations, and fears. He presents our cases continually to His Father. If we cleave unto Him, His resurrection power and glory are secured unto us." Then in October he described Jesus as "the [clue] of the universe, its center and explanation. All things are to be seen in the light of the cross. And all things reflect light on the cross." We need to understand all of his statements within the context of the Adventist sanctuary teaching that he had done so much to explain through the years. Pointing out an "Important Anniversary," Smith reminded his readers that for Seventh-day Adventists, October 22, 1844, "was the most important day in the world's history since the resurrection of Christ." Perhaps his reference to the Resurrection as well as Christ's entrance into the Most Holy Place of the heavenly sanctuary was significant. Smith had always protested that he believed in salvation by faith, but in 1902 he appears to have shifted somewhat from emphasizing the law to emphasizing grace.[49]

ILL HEALTH AND DEATH

On December 30, 1902, a fire destroyed the Review and Herald Publishing Association building. Smith had the unhappy duty of telling the church at large about the catastrophe. "Fire has wiped from the face of the earth the visible symbol of what has long been regarded as an object of love and veneration. But God lives, and His truth endures."[50] The longtime editor did not record his personal thoughts regarding the disaster, but one can imagine that the loss of the building in which he had spent so much of his life had a strong emotional impact.

Although he continued to write his editorials, Uriah was not well. In 1899, about two years before his stroke, Dr. John Harvey Kellogg had written to him saying that he was looking "much worn and thin" and recommended that he come to the sanitarium every day for a "good tonic bath [and] a massage." Nonetheless, he also observed that "you have naturally such a great fund of vitality you ought to be good for 20 years work yet." After Smith's death in 1903, Daniells reported that the editor had been failing for the past year and that the winter weather had been hard on him. Although Uriah seems to have worked at home much of the time, he made a daily walk to the office. "Often when he has come down to the office his face has been as red as a beet," the GC president stated, "and the perspiration has rolled from his head. . . . Some of us have advised him not to venture out, but he has wanted to take his accustomed walk down each day, and see how things were moving and then walk back again to his house." Although Uriah was issued credentials to be a delegate at the 1903 General Conference session in Oakland, California, he determined that he could not attend. "He is too helpless to travel," Harriet told Ellen White, "and in some respects has not recovered from the shock of a year ago. Tchis [sic] affected his mind to the extent of unfitting him for any public service, on account of his thoughts becoming confused so that he cannot express them as formerly. When he writes it is not so, and now it seems that all the service which he can render to the cause he has loved so well is by his pen."[51]

Not being able to attend the session, Smith asked the denominational leaders if they would read to the delegates an appeal "to stand by the pillars of our faith, and to revive the Advent message and work among the people." Encouraged to write the appeal, on the morning of Friday, March 6, Smith began his daily walk to the *Review* office for the purpose of showing what he had prepared to his associates. On the way he stopped by the home of H. W. Kellogg and talked with the family about what he had composed. He also commented on his own health, stating that he felt like a young man. Continuing his walk to the office, however, when directly in front of the Battle Creek Tabernacle about 10:00 a.m., he fell to the ground, struck down by a stroke. Some of the publishing house workers rushed to his aid and, though he was conscious for a time, he could not speak and soon drifted into a coma. After he was taken to the *Review* office, a patrol wagon soon arrived and carried him to his home, where he died about 2:00 p.m.[52]

At the Battle Creek Tabernacle "appropriate reference was made to the sad stroke" at the next day's Sabbath services, and "the mourning emblems around the pulpit, and at the entrance to the office, spoke in eloquent silence of the sorrow which filled many hearts." On Sunday, March 8, viewing of the remains took place at the Tabernacle from 11:00 a.m. to 2:00 p.m. The local newspaper reported that "during the entire time the remains lay in state before the heavily draped rostrum, a constant stream of people passed in review before the casket, taking their last look at the kindly peaceful face of the man whose heart it could be well said bore malice toward none, but broad and unselfish charity toward all."[53]

Daniells and Prescott led the funeral service. After a quartet sang a hymn written for the occasion by F. E. Belden, an Adventist hymn writer, the GC president gave a life sketch and evaluated Smith's contribution to the cause. He observed that Uriah "reasoned calmly and logically, and always took his stand courageously in harmony with sincere and well-matured convictions. All his utterances, both by voice and pen, were clear, forceful, and pleasing; but the most beautiful and most prominent feature of his life was that tenderness, that gentleness, which was ever intermingled with his work." The quartet sang another hymn, followed by Prescott's funeral sermon, which emphasized the Advent hope: "I see no painful messages passing over that land, telling that a friend, a brother, a fellow laborer, has fallen beneath the cruel stroke of a relentless foe. I see no darkened room where the tide of a precious life is ebbing slowly away. I see no bosoms heaving with anguish, no badges of mourning, no funeral trains, no yawning, insatiate grave. But on the other hand, I see a glorious company who bear bright palms of victory over death and the grave."[54]

The following day Daniells wrote to Ellen White, stating that he had visited Harriet several times during the past two days. "You know something of his dignity, his gentleness, and of the high esteem in which he was held," he said, "and it seems to her that a part of the world has been removed." Making no reference to the tensions of the past two years, the GC president reported that "there is universal gladness to know that nothing has occurred in Brother Smith's life to dim the glory of the grace that has been given to him. He has grown old gracefully, or rather full of grace. He was ready to depart. He rests, but his manifold works will follow him. The seed that he sowed will still spring up and bear fruit. These considerations cheer his family, his closest associates, and the members of the church."[55]

Prescott also wrote a tribute to Smith published in the same issue reporting his death and funeral. The *Review* editor recounted that in 1884 at the Vermont camp meeting he had told Uriah that he wanted to play an active role in the church's work and that the older man's interest and sympathy helped produce a turning point in his life. Regarding his association with Smith on the *Review* editorial staff during the past year, Prescott commented: "Brother Smith had positive convictions of truth and duty, which gave a strong individuality to his work, but he uniformly exercised the utmost Christian courtesy toward his associates, which won for him the tender regard of his fellow laborers." In behalf of the General Conference Committee, A. G. Daniells stated that during the past two years it had "enjoyed very pleasant associations with this esteemed servant of God. It has been a personal blessing to me to be connected with him in the work during this time."[56]

Subsequent issues of the *Review* carried further tributes to Smith from longtime colleagues. G. W. Amadon described him as having a "genial social nature which so especially endeared him to those with whom he came in contact. . . . Being naturally of a buoyant and social turn, he made friends everywhere, whether at home, in the church, or abroad in the field." S. N. Haskell, fellow warrior in defending the Advent faith, stated that "his principal method of teaching was to go over the principles underlying present truth, and bring out those truths that would direct the mind to the times in which we live. In times of controversy upon points of present truth, Elder Smith's pen always stood in defense of the truth." Finally, John N. Loughborough observed that "it is safe to say that hundreds who are rejoicing in the light of 'present truth' first saw it while perusing *Thoughts on Daniel and the Revelation*, or some of his other books. Though he rests from his labors, these books, as they are circulated in the future, will multiply the fruits of his labors, and add stars to his crown of rejoicing in the great day when the final reward is given to the faithful."[57]

Meanwhile, more privately, Harriet told her daughter: "O if I had only known I was to have him so little time I could have done more for him and showed him more loving attention. But I know he would not have me mourn over my fortunes in this respect.

"My heart breaks over our [irreparable] loss. But it is his blessed gain. No more care or toil for him. No more weary faltering steps, wounded feelings or disappointed hopes. Sweet rest, sweet rest. Would I too could rest as sweetly by his side. But I will try to be brave and trust that God will care for me and bring us together again after a while."[58]

Smith, though, was not yet finished with his work. The appeal that he had been working on at the time of his death remained to be read at the General Conference session. In many respects it was a summary of the battles he had been fighting for the past 20 years that had brought him into tension with denominational leaders. He strongly aligned himself with the doctrines hammered out by the founders of the denomination, saying that "the main pillars of our faith, I adhere today as firmly as I ever did." He was disturbed, however, that recently the church "seemed to be giving way to a spirit of innovation and novelty, and turning away from the old and well-established views, speaking of them as 'back-numbers,' 'behind the times,' etc., with the result that no one now knows what Seventh-day Adventists believe." Mentioning such issues as the personality of God, the work of the Holy Spirit, the "daily," and the cleansing of the sanctuary, he observed, "What sentiments a Seventh-day Adventist may express now when questioned in regard to his faith is a matter of much uncertainty. These things ought not so to be."[59]

Unfortunately, we have no record that anyone actually read Smith's final appeal to the General Conference session held in Oakland in April. On Sabbath, April 11, it held a memorial service for Smith at 3:00 in the afternoon, which included comments by Daniells, Butler, Loughborough, S. H. Lane, and G. A. Irwin. It is possible that someone did present Uriah's address at the service, but the *General Conference Bulletin* report of the meeting does not mention it.[60] Honored though he might be, Smith's theological convictions may have reopened controversies about which the church administrators preferred to remain silent.

---

[1] US to WCW, June 7, 1895.

[2] Smith was elected a member of the publishing association board every year between 1896 and 1899. *RH*, Mar. 3, 1896, pp. 140, 141; Mar. 16, 1897, pp. 172, 173; Apr. 5, 1898, pp. 222, 223; Mar. 21, 1899, pp. 187, 188.

[3] *RH*, Mar. 21, 1899, pp. 187, 188; US to WCW, Feb. 10, 1896; GWA to EGW, Jan. 9, 1897.

[4] SNH to US, Mar. 20, 1896.

[5] US to WCW, Nov. 6, 1896.

[6] US to SNH, Nov. 10[?], 1896.

[7] US, *Modern Spiritualism: A Subject of Prophecy and a Sign of the Times* (Battle Creek, Mich.: Review and Herald Pub. Co., 1896), pp. 10, 64, 95, 145.

[8] *RH*, Apr. 2, 1895, p. 218; Mar. 3, 1896, pp. 140, 141; Mar. 16, 1897, pp. 172, 173.

[9] For discussion of the Adventist Holiness movement, see GRK, *From 1888 to Apostasy: The Case of A. T. Jones* (Hagerstown, Md.: Review and Herald Pub. Assn., 1987), pp. 167-171; Calvin W. Edwards and Gary Land, *Seeker After Light: A. F. Ballenger, Adventism, and American Christianity* (Berrien Springs, Mich.: Andrews University Press, 2000), pp. 32-64; and Gary Land, "At the Edges of Holiness: Seventh-day Adventism Receives the Holy Ghost, 1892-1900," *Fides et Historia: Journal of the Conference on Faith and History* 33 (Summer/Fall 2001): 13-30.

[10] *RH*, Oct. 5, 1897, p. 640; Nov. 2, 1897, p. 697; Jan. 18, 1898, pp. 45, 46; Aug. 15, 1899, p. 525.

[11] *RH*, Jan. 25, 1898, p. 63; Feb. 21, 1899, p. 121.

[12] *RH*, Mar. 16, 1897, p. 169; May 23, 1899, pp. 329, 330.

[13] *RH*, Sept. 13, 1898, pp. 586, 587; Oct. 4, 1898, p. 636; Nov. 8, 1898, pp. 715, 716.

[14] *RH*, July 26, 1898, p. 475; Dec. 27, 1898, pp. 833, 834; Apr. 18, 1899, p. 249; Jan. 25, 1898, p. 68.

[15] US, "America's Crisis," *Bible Students' Library* (Oakland, Calif.: International Tract Society, October 1898), pp. 23, 28.

[16] *RH*, May 30, 1899, pp. 345, 346; Aug. 7, 1900, pp. 506, 507; Jan. 8, 1901, p. 26.

[17] US, *Looking Unto Jesus, or Christ in Type and Antitype* (Battle Creek, Mich.: Review and Herald Pub. Co., 1898), pp. 10-17. On Smith's Arianism, which also appeared in *Daniel and the Revelation* and elsewhere, see Alexander Joseph Greig, "An Investigation of the Christology of Uriah Smith" (research project, Seventh-day Adventist Theological Seminary, Andrews University, 1961); Erwin Roy Gane, "The Arian or Anti-Trinitarianism Views Presented in Seventh-day Adventist Literature and the Ellen G. White Answer" (MA thesis, Seventh-day Adventist Theological Seminary, Andrews University, 1963), pp. 20-29.

[18] US, *Looking Unto Jesus*, pp. 19-30.

[19] *Ibid.*, pp. 38, 57, 111.

[20] *Ibid.*, pp. 115, 124, 140.

[21] *Ibid.*, pp. 222-224, 242, 243.

[22] *Ibid.*, pp. 237-243.

23 *Ibid.*, pp. 251-266.

24 Wedding invitation for Annie Arabelle Smith and George Walker Bovee, Oct. 26, 1898; US to W. H. Edward, Feb. 17, 1901; US to WS, Nov. 23, 1899; HS to ASB[?], 1900; US to WS, Nov. 30, 1899.

25 Thomas Morrow, "By the Way: Is She to Blame for It All?" Chicago *Daily Tribune*, July 24, 1957; Mark Bovee to Editor, Battle Creek *Enquirer and News* clipping—no date; "Grandpa Uriah Had Other Ideas," Battle Creek *Enquirer and News*, Aug. 5, 1963. This article lists other places, including Ripley's "Believe It or Not," that mentions Smith's horse's head. See also Amy South, "Looking Back: Uriah's Marvelous 'Horse Car,'" Battle Creek *Enquirer and News*, Nov. 14, 1971. South also states that Smith was one of the first residents of Battle Creek to purchase an automobile, but I have seen no other reference to it. Hoare also mentions the horse's head in her "Notes."

26 GRK, *1888 to Apostasy*, pp. 171-177.

27 *RH*, June 11, 1901, pp. 378, 379; June 18, 1901, pp. 395, 396; Jan. 28, 1902, p. 56; July 16, 1901, p. 458; Oct. 29, 1901, p. 704.

28 *RH*, Apr. 2, 1901, p. 217.

29 SNH to EGW, Oct. 3, 1899; SNH to EGW, May 18, 1900; SNH to EGW, Jan. 13, 1901; SNH to EGW, July 18, 1901.

30 US to W. H. Hall, Jan. 15, 1901; US to W. H. Hall, Feb. 17, 1901.

31 US to EGW, Aug. 16[?], 1894; US to WCW, June 18, 1897; US to WS, Nov. 1, 1899.

32 SNH to EGW, May 28, 1900.

33 GWA to EGW, Jan. 9, 1897; AGD to EGW, Sept. 2, 1901; AGD to EGW, Oct. 16, 1901.

34 US to W. H. Littlejohn, Sept. 12[?], 1902.

35 US to H. J. Adams, Oct. 30, 1900.

36 US to W. A. McCutchen, Aug. 8, 1901.

37 *RH*, Jan. 21, 1902, p. 36; Jan. 28, 1902, p. 52; Feb. 4, 1902, pp. 67, 68.

38 AGD to GIB, Apr. 11, 1902.

39 AGD to WCW, May 12, 1902.

40 AGD to GIB, Apr. 11, 1902. Daniells may have been referring to "Seeking Help From the Wrong Source," *RH*, Oct. 8, 1901, p. 656, which reported that Black Baptists in the South were thinking about turning to the Roman Catholics because of their social, political, and economic oppression by White Protestants.

41 Gilbert Valentine interprets this incident as offensive to Black delegates to the 1901 General Conference session. It is highly unlikely, however, that Black delegates attended. Rather, the articles in question are much more likely to have challenged church leaders' accommodation to segregation. See GMV, *The Shaping of Adventism: The Case of W. W. Prescott* (Berrien Springs, Mich.: Andrews University Press, 1992), p. 170.

42 *RH*, Dec. 17, 1901, p. 815; Dec. 31, 1901, pp. 850, 851.

43 US to L. F. Trubey, Feb. 11, 1902; AGD to GIB, Apr. 11, 1902.

44 Minutes, Minority Meeting of General Conference Committee, Feb. 15, [1902], 7:00 p.m.; *RH*, Feb. 25, 1902, pp. 120, 128; GIB to EGW, Mar. 24, 1902; OAO to EGW, Mar. 9, 1894.

45 GIB to EGW, Mar. 24, 1902; W. B. Woodruff to AGD, Aug. 24, 1902.

46 AGD to GIB, Apr. 11, 1902; W. W. Prescott to EGW, Apr. 23, 1902; GIB to EGW, Mar. 24, 1902. See also AGD to WCW, Apr. 14, 1902. In 1903 Daniells did acknowledge Smith's "shock." See AGD to ?, Feb 28, 1903.

47 HS to "My Dear Sister," Feb. 28, 1903.

48 *RH*, Apr. 29, 1902, pp. 3, 4.

[49] *RH*, June 17, 1902, pp. 3, 4; July 8, 1902, pp. 4, 5; Oct. 28, 1902, p. 4; Oct. 21, 1902, p. 7.

[50] *RH*, Jan. 6, 1903, p. 4; AGD to WCW, Mar. 6, 1903.

[51] J. H. Kellogg to US, Apr. 25, 1899; AGD to SNH, Feb. 12, 1903; AGD to WCW, Mar. 6, 1903; HS to EGW, Feb. 28, 1903.

[52] AGD to WCW, Mar. 6, 1903; *RH*, Mar. 10, 1903, p. 3.

[53] *RH*, Mar. 10, 1903, p. 3; "The Sable Plume," Battle Creek *Morning Enquirer*, Mar. 9, 1903.

[54] *RH*, Mar. 10, 1903, pp. 3-6.

[55] AGD to EGW, Mar. 9, 1903.

[56] *RH*, Mar. 10, 1903, p. 7.

[57] *RH*, Mar. 17, 1903, pp. 6, 7; Apr. 7, 1903, pp. 7, 8.

[58] HS to AS, n.d.

[59] US to General Conference of Seventh-day Adventists [1903].

[60] *General Conference Bulletin*, Apr. 13, 1903, p. 192.

AFTERWORD

After several months of illness Harriet Smith, stricken by cancer, followed her husband in death in 1911. Her obituary, written by son Leon, stated that she was known for her charitable work in Battle Creek. The Smiths' oldest son, Wilton, completed the dental program at the University of Michigan in 1900 and worked at the Battle Creek Sanitarium until its destruction by fire in 1902, after which he entered private practice. Long having had a problematic relationship with the Seventh-day Adventist Church, he left the denomination at some point after his father's death. He died in 1936 in Battle Creek at the age of 75. Annie worked as a proofreader at the Review and Herald Publishing Association until it moved to Washington, D.C., in 1903. She had married George W. Bovee, a farmer, in 1898 and lived in Battle Creek until her death in 1952. Charles S. Smith graduated from the University of Michigan and the College of Osteopathy in Kirksville, Missouri. Practicing medicine in Battle Creek, he became known for his success in treating influenza patients during the epidemic following World War I. He died in 1954. Leon Smith served the denomination in a number of editorial capacities, including many years at the Southern Publishing Association, where he edited its evangelistic magazine, *The Watchman*. After a long retirement, part of which he spent in California, he died in Nashville, Tennessee, in 1958. S. Parker Smith graduated from Battle Creek College in 1895 and with his wife, Bessie, began Adventist efforts in the Caribbean, where he served as a mission school director on St. Andrews Island from 1901 to 1903. The family then moved to San Fernando Valley Academy in California, where Parker taught from 1903 to 1918. Remaining in San Fernando, he then became a rancher/farmer until his death in his 90s in 1962.[1]

Uriah Smith left a mixed legacy to the church. His major contribution was through his editorship of the *Review and Herald*, which provided a unifying force to the denomination during its formative years. His writings also ensured that the church focused on prophecy and the second coming of Jesus. Shortly before his death he said that he had never had a misgiving about the doctrine of the Second Coming since accepting it in 1844. In his numerous writings on prophecy he had repeatedly stated his expectations regarding the future. But they failed to occur. The United States never passed a national Sunday law, and the National Reform Association faded away. Spiritualism, although continuing in existence in various forms, did not become the religious force he expected. Despite tensions, Catholicism gradually accommodated itself to American values of separation of church and state. Turkey, which he believed would soon disappear, still exists as a national state, despite the predictions of Adventist preachers who, following Smith, expected its demise during World War I.[2] And, most important of all, Jesus has not yet returned. We have no record of Smith addressing the failure of such predictions. Instead, he died expecting that the end would come soon. "And now the question arises how long a generation can continue, the youngest members of which are upward of seventy years of age," he wrote in 1903. "We have not to wait for a new generation to arise, pass its period of infancy, youth, and middle life, before we reach the end, but only for a section of the human family to retire its old men, already fast disappearing before all these things are closed up and finished. Happy they who have a part in this work now!" Of course, several generations have come and gone since he wrote those words.[3]

As an author he achieved a wide readership. Uriah's *Daniel and the Revelation* sold 180,000 copies by 1899, mostly through door-to-door salesmen, known as colporteurs. *Marvel of Nations*, also sold by colporteurs as well as used as a premium by *The Sentinel*, the Adventist religious liberty magazine, realized a distribution of 235,000 by the same year. Clearly those books reached far beyond the small Adventist market, although it is impossible to know what impact they had on their readers' beliefs.[4]

Smith also had a personal impact on the lives of several Adventist couples, performing a total of 129 marriages, including both his daughter Annie A. Smith to George W. Bovee and his son Samuel Parker Smith to Bessie Stowell. He conducted his last wedding in 1902 with the marriage of Arthur Wellesley Russell and Winnona Elizabeth Marvin.[5]

Doctrinally, the denomination shifted from some of Smith's interpretations. The church gradually abandoned his interpretation of "the daily,"

referred to in Daniel 11 and 12 and understood by early Adventist expositors as meaning Roman paganism, a view reinforced by Smith's commentary *Daniel and the Revelation*. When W. W. Prescott and others began in the
early twentieth century suggesting that "the daily" referred to Christ's ministry, they stirred up a controversy, largely because it involved the authority
of Ellen White's writings. But the new view eventually won out as members
of the old guard who defended the traditional interpretation passed away.[6]
With the emphasis on righteousness by faith that began in the 1880s, the
legalism that characterized early Adventism and, despite his denials, Uriah
promoted, softened considerably. Also, after 1888 the church moved fairly
rapidly from Arianism to Trinitarianism. W. W. Prescott brought the issue
into the open at the 1919 Bible Conference held in Washington, D. C.,
questioning how the church could continue to distribute Smith's *Daniel
and the Revelation* with its clear Arian position. In 1930 Alonzo Baker, an
editor at the *Signs of the Times*, wrote some interesting comments to an
inquirer. He noted several differences between W. W. Prescott and Smith,
including their views of the restoration of temporal power to the pope
and the Alemanni replacing the Huns as part of the 10 kingdoms. "Leon
Smith," he commented, "came to see that his father was altogether wrong
and hence made the needed correction." Prescott then assessed Uriah's
legacy: "Elder Smith was not infallible, and we must be careful not to
attribute infallibility to what he wrote. An angel indeed stood by his side
and helped him mightily, but this was no guarantee against a mistake here
and there."[7]

Smith's limited, even critical, view of Ellen White's inspiration and authority, particularly his insistence that her writings were subordinate to
the Bible and his distinction between her writings based upon visions and
those that were not, the latter of which he did not regard as inspired,
might have helped the church. Denominational leaders largely ignored his
cautions, however, and the church subsequently endured controversies
over Ellen White at the 1919 Bible Conference and later in the 1970s.

In retrospect, it seems that the denomination did Smith a disservice
when it placed him in executive positions, such as on the boards of the
Health Reform Institute and Battle Creek College. Both positions led him
into controversies he did not want or need, for he simply did not seem
to have been cut out for executive leadership. He appears to have been

a man who wanted peace, patience, and compromise in such situations, a perspective that conflicted with those such as James White and George I. Butler, who sought strong, definitive decisions. Uriah, however, was a man of thought and functioned primarily as a writer and editor. Addressing institutional conflicts decisively did not fit his nature, but as a loyal churchman he accepted executive positions when asked, even though they seem to have inevitably led to problems.

One curious thing about Smith is that the strong language he used regarding Roman Catholics, other Protestants, and social developments such as immigration and the conflict between capital and labor do not show up in his personal papers. Although he did not leave behind extensive copies of his correspondence, which would give us a more complete view, his letters to his wife and parallel reports in the *Review* during his visit to Europe reveal this discrepancy. The *Review* reports often strongly condemned Catholicism as he observed its historic cathedrals and shrines, but even when describing the same sites to Harriet, such critical language never shows up in his letters. Although undoubtedly Smith disliked Catholicism, one wonders to what extent his language on this and other issues in the *Review* was tailored to his audience's expectations. His surviving correspondence suggests that he was a much gentler man than his editorials, articles, and books might indicate.

Uriah Smith was a complex individual, strongly conservative in his views of theology and society but at the same time widely respected as a kindly person. His theology was apocalyptic and legalistic, yet he does not seem to have dealt with individuals with the heavy hand his outlook implied. He had both an artistic bent, as shown in his early artworks and occasional poetry, and a mechanical orientation that revealed itself through his several inventions. Although he worked long hours and traveled frequently, he was still a family man who seems to have regretted his time away from home. In the end, he helped mold nineteenth-century Adventism, and disturbingly to him, lived to see the first elements of that mold break apart in the 1888 controversy over righteousness by faith and its aftermath. But not everything changed, especially his historicist interpretation of biblical prophecy and rational approach to theological matters, which continue to influence the church. Smith's most important work, *Daniel and the Revelation*, was extensively revised in the mid-twentieth century by a committee, appointed by the General Conference, that sought to popularize its style, improve its historical accuracy, and soften its invective. But the committee did not change his views on such issues as the "daily" and Turkey as expressed in the volume, even though the church had long left them behind. The revised book was first published in 1944 and reprinted in paperback in 1972 and 1977, thus continuing its influence over Adventist thinking for more than a century after its original appearance. Today other commentaries have largely replaced Smith's work, but they reveal his influence through their continued commitment to his historicist approach. Most significantly, they have not gained the large readership that Smith enjoyed. In the end, Uriah's views on the Sabbath, the state of the dead, prophecy, and Christ's soon return still constitute the fundamentals of Adventism. Though much has changed, he would still recognize the twenty-first-century church as the one he helped shape.[8]

---

[1] *RH*, Mar. 30, 1911, p. 23; "Death Claims Dr. U. W. Smith at Age of 75," clipping from unnamed newspaper; "Life Sketch of Annie Smith," *RH*, Oct. 30, 1952, p. 22; *Lake Union Herald*, Sept. 23, 1952, p. 7; *RH*, Mar. 18, 1954, p. 28; *Lake Union Herald*, Mar. 23, 1954, p. 15; *RH*, June 19, 1958, p. 13; *Southern Tidings*, July 9, 1958, p. 7; "Uriah Smith's Son Dies at 94," clipping from unnamed Battle Creek newspaper; *RH*, Oct. 4, 1962, p. 25; *Pacific Union Recorder*, Aug. 20, 1962, p. 6; EFD, *Yours*, p. 34. The newspaper clippings and life sketch mentioned above are located in the Smith/Bovee collection.

[2] See Gary Land, "The Perils of Prophesying: Seventh-day Adventists Interpret World War I," *AH*, January 1974, pp. 28-33, 55, 56.

[3] US, "Former Things," *RH*, Jan. 6, 1903, pp. 4, 5.

[4] US to Arthur H. Chase, Dec. 11, 1899.

[5] "Copy of Marriages Performed by Uriah Smith." This document does not list the first 66 marriages performed by Smith.

[6] GWV, *W. W. Prescott: Forgotten Giant of Adventism's Second Generation* (Hagerstown, Md.: Review and Herald Pub. Assn., 2005), pp. 214-226, 232-235, 276-281.

[7] *Ibid.*; Alonzo L. Baker to W. M. Robbins, Feb. 13, 1930; WWW, Jerry Moon, and John W. Reeve, *The Trinity: Understanding God's Love, His Plan of Salvation, and Christian Relationships* (Hagerstown, Md.: Review and Herald Pub. Assn., 2002), pp. 190-203.

[8] EFD, *Yours*, pp. 223-234; Merwin R. Thurber describes the revision process in "New Edition of 'Daniel and the Revelation,'" *Ministry*, April 1945, pp. 13-15, and in "Uriah Smith and the Charge of Plagiarism," *Ministry*, June 1945, pp. 15, 16. In another article in the May 1945 issue of *Ministry*, "Revised *D & R* in Relation to Denominational Doctrine," he deals with theological issues in Smith's book (pp. 3, 4, 30).

APPENDIX

PUBLICATIONS OF URIAH SMITH

The following publications are listed in chronological order. Where the publication date is uncertain but can be estimated, dates appear in brackets. Items with no publication information appear at the end of bibliography.

The Warning Voice of Time and Prophecy (Rochester, N.Y.: James White, 1853)

The 2300 Days and the Sanctuary (Rochester, N.Y.: *Advent Review* Office, [1854])

The Four Universal Monarchies of the Prophecy of Daniel, and God's Everlasting Kingdom (Rochester, N.Y.: *Advent Review* Office, 1855)

A Word for the Sabbath: or, False Theories Exposed (Rochester, N.Y.: *Advent Review* Office, 1855)

The Bible Student's Assistant, or, A Compend of Scripture References (Battle Creek, Mich.: Steam Press of the *Review and Herald* Office, 1858)

Which, Mortal or Immortal? or, An Inquiry Into the Present Constitution and Future Condition of Man (Battle Creek, Mich.: Steam Press of the *Review and Herald* Office, 1860)

The Prophecy of Daniel: The Four Kingdoms, the Sanctuary, and the Twenty-three Hundred Days (Battle Creek, Mich.: Steam Press of the Seventh-day Adventist Publishing Association, 1863)

The Sanctuary and the Twenty-three Hundred Days of Daniel 8:14 (Battle Creek, Mich.: Steam Press of the Seventh-day Adventist Publishing Association, 1863)

Vindication of the Business Career of Elder James White, with G. W. Amadon and E. S. Walker (Battle Creek, Mich.: Steam Press of the Seventh-day Adventist Publishing Association, 1863).

Thoughts, Critical and Practical, on the Book of Revelation (Battle Creek, Mich.: Steam Press of the Seventh-day Adventist Publishing Association, 1867)

The Two Covenants (Battle Creek, Mich.: Review and Herald, [186-?])

An Appeal to the Youth: Funeral Address of Henry N. White (Battle Creek, Mich.: Steam Press of the Seventh-day Adventist Publishing Association, 1868)

The Visions of Mrs. E. G. White: A Manifestation of Spiritual Gifts According to the Scriptures (Battle Creek, Mich.: Steam Press of the Seventh-day Adventist Publishing Association, 1868)

Both Sides on the Sabbath and the Law: Review of T. M. Preble (Battle Creek, Mich.: Seventh-day Adventist Publishing Association, 1869)

To Whom It May Concern, with J. N. Andrews and E. S. Walker (Battle Creek, Mich.: n.p., [1869])

A Declaration of the Fundamental Principles of the Seventh-day Adventists (Battle Creek, Mich.: Review and Herald, [186-?])

Defense of Eld. James White and Wife: Vindication of Their Moral and Christian Character, with J. N. Andrews and G. H. Bell (Battle Creek, Mich.: Seventh-day Adventist Publishing Association, 1870)

Poems, with Rebekah Smith and Annie R. Smith (Manchester, N.Y.: John B. Clarke, printer, 1871)

A Declaration of the Fundamental Principles Taught and Practiced by Seventh-day Adventists (Battle Creek, Mich.: Steam Press of the Seventh-day Adventist Publishing Association, 1872)

The State of the Dead and the Destiny of the Wicked (Battle Creek, Mich.: Steam Press of the Seventh-day Adventist Publishing Association, 1873)

The Testimony of the Bible on the State of the Dead (Battle Creek, Mich.: Steam Press of the Seventh-day Adventist Publishing Association, 1873)

Thoughts, Critical and Practical, on the Book of Daniel (Battle Creek, Mich.: Steam Press of the Seventh-day Adventist Publishing Association, 1873)

Injustice of Eld. Miles Grant, Editor of the "World's Crisis," Toward Seventh-day Adventists, with J. N. Andrews and J. H. Waggoner (Battle Creek, Mich.: n.p., 1874)

The United States in the Light of Prophecy, or An Exposition of Rev. 13:11-17 (Battle Creek, Mich.: Steam Press of the Seventh-day Adventist Publishing Association, 1874)

The Biblical Institute: A Synopsis of Lectures on the Principal Doctrines of Seventh-day Adventists, with James White (Oakland, Calif.: Steam Press of the Pacific S.D.A. Publishing House, 1878)

The Great Commandment (Battle Creek, Mich.: Review and Herald, [187-?])

Day of the Crucifixion and Resurrection of Christ: How Long Did Christ Lie in the Grave? (Battle Creek, Mich.: Review and Herald, [187-?])

The Seven Heads of Revelation 12, 13, and 17 (The Author, [187-?])

A Greek Falsehood: Ignorance or Dishonesty? Which? (Battle Creek, Mich.: Review and Herald, [187-?])

Parable of the Ten Virgins (Battle Creek, Mich.: Review and Herald, [187-?])

In Memoriam: A Sketch of the Last Sickness and Death of Elder James White, Who Died at Battle Creek, Michigan, August 6, 1881, Together With the Discourse Preached at His Funeral, with W. C. Gage and John Harvey Kellogg (Battle Creek, Mich.: Review and Herald, 1881)

Key to Smith's Diagram and Parliamentary Rules: Together With Concise Hints and Directions for Conducting the Business of Deliberative Assemblies (Battle Creek, Mich.: Review and Herald, 1881)

Thoughts, Critical and Practical, on the Books of Daniel and the Revelation: Being an Exposition, Text by Text, of These Important Portions of the Holy Scriptures (Battle Creek, Mich.: Review and Herald, 1881).

Man's Nature and Destiny, or, The State of the Dead, the Reward of the Righteous, and the End of the Wicked (Battle Creek, Mich.: Review and Herald, 1884)

Our Country's Future: The United States in the Light of Prophecy, or, an Exposition of Rev. 13:11-17 (1884)

Synopsis of the Present Truth: A Brief Exposition of the Views of S. D. Adventists (Battle Creek, Mich.: Seventh-day Adventist Publishing Association, 1884)

The Marvel of Nations: Our Country: Its Past, Present, and Future, and What the Scriptures Say of It (Battle Creek, Mich.: Review and Herald, 1885)

Tabernacle Lecture Course: Comprising a Series of Discourses Setting Forth the Doctrines of Seventh-day Adventists, Delivered at the SDA Tabernacle, Battle Creek, Mich., and Reported for the Battle Creek Daily Journal (Battle Creek, Mich.: Review and Herald, 1885)

An Exposure of Fanaticism and Wickedness, with Geo. I. Butler (n.p., [1885])

Without Excuse (Oakland, Calif.: Pacific Press, 1889)

America's Crisis (Oakland, Calif.: Pacific Press, 1895)

Modern Spiritualism: A Subject of Prophecy and a Sign of the Times (Battle Creek, Mich.: Review and Herald, 1896)

Is Sunday Called the Sabbath in the New Testament? An Examination of the Greek of Matt. 28:1 and Parallel Passages (Oakland, Calif.: Pacific Press, 1896)

Seventh-day Adventists and Their Work (Oakland, Calif.: International Tract Society, 1896)

Trine Immersion (Oakland, Calif.: International Tract Society, 1896)

Here and Hereafter; or, Man in Life and Death (Battle Creek, Mich.: Review and Herald, 1897)

Brief Review of S. W. Gamble on the Sabbath Question (Battle Creek, Mich.: Review and Herald, 1897)

Looking Unto Jesus, or Christ in Type and Antitype (Battle Creek, Mich.: Review and Herald, 1897)

Come, Lord Jesus (Battle Creek, Mich.: Review and Herald, 1898)

The Reign of Righteousness (Battle Creek, Mich.: Review and Herald, 1898)

Sunday in the Greek: Is the First Day of the Week Called the Sabbath in the Greek? (Oakland, Calif.: Pacific Press, 1898)

In Memoriam: Mrs. Sarah A. Bourdeau-Geriguere, Born April 8, 1813, Deceased February 9, 1899 (n.p., [1899])

Sabbaton: An Exposition of Matt. 28:1 and Parallel Passages (Battle Creek, Mich.: Review and Herald, [18—?])

A Criticism Answered (n.p., n.d.)

What Was Nailed to the Cross? An Exposition of Colossians 2:14-17 (n.p., n.d.)

Who Changed the Sabbath? (n.p., n.d.)

INDEX

INDEX

195, 215, 224, 243, 244
Smith, Bessie (daughter-in-law), 243
Smith, Charles Stevens (son), 112, 160-162, 199, 243
Smith, Cyrenius, 35
Smith, Harriet Newall (spouse), 35, 46, 47, 61, 68, 84, 112, 113, 137, 158-164, 188-191, 194-201, 207-211, 215, 234-239, 243
Smith, John (brother), 114
Smith, Leon A. (son), 60, 112, 159-161, 164, 189, 190, 211, 233, 235, 243, 245
Smith, Meda (daughter-in-law), 189, 211
Smith, Rebekah Spalding (mother), 18, 22
Smith, S. Parker (son), 112, 161-163, 224, 243, 244
Smith, Samuel (father), 17, 21
Smith, Samuel Wood (brother), 18, 114, 188
Smith, Stephen, 85
Smith, Uriah (grandfather), 17
Smith, Uriah
    against Catholicism, 99-101, 144-146, 150-153, 222, 225, 244, 246
    against immigration, 99, 143, 151, 152, 166, 246
    against labor unions, 94, 96, 144, 150-153, 246
    against non-Seventh-day Adventists, 246
    against slavery, 31, 43-45, 50, 57, 58, 70, 71, 97, 98, 163, 226
    against spiritualism, 55, 94, 100-105, 143, 153-155, 215-220, 244
    against Sunday laws, 143-149
    against Sunday worship, 31
    and "commonsense" philosophy, 29, 41, 42, 86, 168, 171
    and 1888 controversy, 168-186
    and A. T. Jones, 137, 146, 168-184, 218, 219, 225, 229
    and Civil War, 57-59
    and contemporary religion, 99-101
    and doctrine, 101-106, 143-157, 219-224
    and last days, 43-45, 56, 57, 95-99, 220, 246
    and legalism, 39-43, 98, 183, 245, 246
    and malaria, 158, 204-207, 212, 215
    and organization of the church, 50-75
    and prophecy, 142-157
    and Sabbath, 39-41, 54, 101-104, 147, 169, 247
    and unity of truth, 30, 41-43
    artistic, 246
    as author, 244-246
    Battle Creek College conflict, 120-125
    Battle Creek, 1855-1860, 35-49
    Bible the only creed, 42
    churchman, 106-112
    conflict with Battle Creek church, 79-85
    conflict with Ellen G. White, 45-48, 76-79, 172-184
    conflict with the Whites, 45-48, 76-79
    conversion, 22, 23
    death, 237-240
    defending the Whites, 59, 60, 68-73, 125-127
    early days at the *Review*, 26-34
    early life, 17-25
    education, 20-22
    elected member of publishing board, 1896-1899, 240
    Ellen G. White authority, 127, 128, 138
    European trip with Wilton and S. N. Haskell, 188-201
    explains purpose of spiritual gifts, 60
    final apeal to SDA Church, 239
    health issues, 62-66, 80, 157-162, 235-237
    interpreting *Daniel and Revelation*, 85-95
    Michigan Conference president, 52, 106
    ordained (1874), 53, 84
    personal life, 60-62, 112-115, 157-164, 224, 225
    preaching, 66-68
    problems with publishing house, 82, 83
    publications of, 248-251
    Review editor, 33, 38, 53-57, 83, 84, 106, 109, 121, 225-235
    secretary of committee choosing church name, 51
    secretary of General Conference, 52, 106
    senior years, 215-240
    suffers stroke, 234, 237
    vice president of publishing association, 106
    view of Ellen G. White's writings, 245
    visits Rome and Paris, 209-212
    visits Turkey and the Middle East, 202-209
    wood engravings, 22
Smith, Wilton (son), 11, 60, 68, 112, 137, 158-163, 227, 243
    accompanies Uriah on European and Palestine tour, 188-212
Snook, B. F., 53
Snow, Samuel S., 19
Socialism, 153
Spicer, W. A., 157, 233
Spirit of Prophecy Committee, 138